THE WESTERN TRADITION

STUDY GUIDE, SEMESTER I
FIFTH EDITION

JAY BOGGIS

The Annenberg/CPB Project

PRENTICE HALL, Upper Saddle River, New Jersey 07458

NOTE TO THE READER: Every attempt to avoid sexist language has been made. Nevertheless, terms such as "statesman," "clergyman," or the "rights of man" have been retained to draw attention to sexual discrimination in the past or to avoid anachronism. In some cases, the use of neutral language might lead the reader to believe that women were participants in certain activities when, in fact, they were not.

Copyright © 2007, 2004, 2001, 1996, 1989 by WGBH Educational Foundation and The Corporation for Public Broadcasting

PRINTED IN THE UNITED STATES OF AMERICA
10 9 8 7 6 5 4 3 2 1

All rights reserved. No part of this book may be reproduced or transmitted in any form or by any means, electronic or mechanical, including photocopying, recording, or any information storage and retrieval system, without permission in writing from the publisher.

Pearson Education, Inc.
Upper Saddle River, NJ 07458

ISBN 0-13-198527-2

This text has been developed for general use as the Semester I Study Guide for "The Western Tradition" television course. The television course consists of fifty-two half-hour public television programs, this Study Guide for Semester I, a Study Guide for Semester II, a Faculty Guide for each semester, and a choice of existing textbooks. The series was produced by WGBH-TV, Boston, Massachusetts and funded by the Annenberg/CPB Project.

For further information about available television courses, licenses, and off-air taping contact
PBS Adult Learning Service
1320 Braddock Place
Alexandria, VA 22314–1698
1–(800)–ALS–ALS–8

For information about purchasing videocassettes, off-air taping, and print materials contact
Annenberg/CPB Project
P.O. Box 2345
S. Burlington, VT 05407–2345
1–(800)–LEARNER

TABLE OF CONTENTS

Acknowledgments v

Introduction vii

The Telecourse ix

Taking "The Western Tradition" Telecourse xvii

UNIT ONE 1
    Program 1: The Dawn of History
    Program 2: The Ancient Egyptians

UNIT TWO 17
    Program 3: Mesopotamia
    Program 4: From Bronze to Iron

UNIT THREE 33
    Program 5: The Rise of Greek Civilization
    Program 6: Greek Thought

UNIT FOUR 51
    Program 7: Alexander the Great
    Program 8: The Hellenistic Age

UNIT FIVE 69
    Program 9: The Rise of Rome
    Program 10: The Roman Empire

UNIT SIX 87
    Program 11: Early Christianity
    Program 12: The Rise of the Church

UNIT SEVEN 103
    Program 13: The Decline of Rome
    Program 14: The Fall of Rome

UNIT EIGHT 121
    Program 15: The Byzantine Empire
    Program 16: The Fall of Byzantium

UNIT NINE 139
    Program 17: The Dark Ages
    Program 18: The Age of Charlemagne

UNIT TEN 157
     Program 19: The Middle Ages
     Program 20: The Feudal Order

UNIT ELEVEN 175
     Program 21: Common Life in the Middle Ages
     Program 22: Cities and Cathedrals

UNIT TWELVE 191
     Program 23: The Late Middle Ages
     Program 24: The National Monarchies

UNIT THIRTEEN 209
     Program 25: The Renaissance and the Age of Discovery
     Program 26: The Renaissance and the New World

FILM CREDITS 228

ACKNOWLEDGMENTS

We would like to thank the Annenberg/CPB Project, whose support made this telecourse possible. We wish also to acknowledge Dr. Eugen Weber whose lectures were the foundation of the curriculum design for "The Western Tradition," and the invaluable assistance of the members of our advisory committee who directed the development of the print materials:

Eugene Brucker
University of California/Berkeley

Evelyn Edson
Piedmont Virginia Community College

Lon Gault
College of DuPage

Raymond Grew
University of Michigan

Donald Kagan
Yale University

Richard Means
Mountain View College

Theodore Rabb
Princeton University

Dr. Raymond Grew deserves special thanks for the many hours he spent making sure that our work reflected the goals of the course.

A special note of thanks goes to the producers and WGBH staff whose cooperation helped us meet deadlines: Leah Osterman, Jeanne Hartnett, Lisa Mirowitz, Tom Friedman, Fred Barzyk, Art Cohen, Scot Osterweil, Robin Gilbert, Susan Dreier, Lois d'Annunzio, Karen Silverstein, Andy Jablon, and Harlan Reiniger.

Jay Boggis
Author

Ann Strunk
Director of Print Projects

Carol Greenwald
Project Director

WGBH *Educational Foundation*
Boston, MA

INTRODUCTION

"The Western Tradition" is a public television series and a college-level television course based on the presentations of Eugen Weber, Joan Palevsky Professor of History at the University of California at Los Angeles, whose lectures span the range of western history from the ancient world to the present.

Through his writing and lectures, Professor Weber has earned the reputation of one who has successfully synthesized various approaches to the telling of history by focusing on political as well as social events. In fifty-two half-hour lectures Professor Weber integrates such diverse disciplines as religion, demography, government, and economics. He describes the leaders who shaped their worlds, as well as the larger forces that shaped them and their subjects. He relates the story of the unending struggle to create societies that provide order and justice, protection and fulfillment.

Professor Weber explains, in a broad historical sweep, how Europeans shaped and developed their environment to an extent greater than previous civilizations and how, as a consequence, their influence spread beyond Europe's borders. His lectures illustrate (1) the relation between ideas, on the one hand, and conditions and experience, on the other; (2) the link between social order and productive or military structures; (3) the effects of current interests and ideas on arts and architecture; and (4) the profound differences, subsisting into the twentieth century, between the values and living conditions of the elite and popular masses.

"The Western Tradition" is a two-semester telecourse consisting of fifty-two half-hour television programs, two student study guides and two faculty guides (Semesters I and II), and a choice of three currently available textbooks (*The Western Heritage*, Eighth Edition, *The Western Experience*, Eighth Edition; and *Western Civilizations*, Fourteenth Edition). This is the study guide for semester I. A second study guide is available for semester II.

"The Western Tradition" is produced by WGBH-TV, a public television station in Boston, Massachusetts, and is close-captioned for the hearing impaired.

THE TELECOURSE

"The Western Tradition" is a two-semester television course consisting of the following components:

- Fifty-two half-hour television programs

  Semester I—Programs 1-26
  Semester II—Programs 27-52

- Two student study guides (semesters I and II)
- A textbook (assigned by the instructor)
- Two faculty guides (semesters I and II)

THE TELEVISION PROGRAMS

The fifty-two television programs of "The Western Tradition" are grouped into twenty-six units with two programs per unit. Each week students are assigned one unit, or two programs, to view. The twenty-six televised units that make up the series include the following topics of study:

SEMESTER I

UNIT ONE
Program 1: The Dawn of History
Program 2: The Ancient Egyptians

Professor Weber traces the evolution of the human race, describes the origins of agriculture, and concludes with a discussion of one of the earliest civilizations.

UNIT TWO
Program 3: Mesopotamia
Program 4: From Bronze to Iron

Professor Weber describes the Mesopotamian culture and argues that, in many respects, western Europe owes even more to ancient Mesopotamia than to Egypt.

UNIT THREE
Program 5: The Rise of Greek Civilization
Program 6: Greek Thought

This unit examines the growth of Greek civilization and stresses the deep connection between Greek philosophy and Greek political institutions.

UNIT FOUR
    Program 7: Alexander the Great
    Program 8: The Hellenistic Age

Greek culture establishes itself throughout the eastern Mediterranean world as the successors of Alexander the Great establish empires of their own.

UNIT FIVE
    Program 9: The Rise of Rome
    Program 10: The Roman Empire

Rome rises from the obscurity of a small city in Italy to establish an empire that becomes one of the great shaping forces of the Western tradition.

UNIT SIX
    Program 11: Early Christianity
    Program 12: The Rise of the Church

Professor Weber examines the growth of Christianity and the early influence of the church in the midst of a hostile empire.

UNIT SEVEN
    Program 13: The Decline of Rome
    Program 14: The Fall of Rome

The Roman Empire is battered from without by a series of barbarian invasions and from within by moral decay. With the fall of Rome, the church and the barbarian kingdoms become heir to the Western Empire.

UNIT EIGHT
    Program 15: The Byzantine Empire
    Program 16: The Fall of Byzantium

Following the fall of Rome, the Byzantine Empire, based in Constantinople, becomes the stronghold of culture from Egypt, Greece, and Rome. The empire preserves and enriches the heritage of the ancient world throughout the eastern Mediterranean.

UNIT NINE
    Program 17: The Dark Ages
    Program 18: The Age of Charlemagne

A new political and economic order forms in the centuries after the fall of the Western Empire.

UNIT TEN
    Program 19: The Middle Ages
    Program 20: The Feudal Order

By the year 1000 Europe stands firm against outside invaders. Professor Weber describes what society was like in the early Middle Ages and the feudal power structure of the aristocracy, peasants, and clergy.

UNIT ELEVEN
    Program 21: Common Life in the Middle Ages
    Program 22: Cities and Cathedrals

Professor Weber explores the often harsh realities of daily life in the Middle Ages. However, this is also an age when city life revives and European culture blossoms. The period is characterized by the growth of trade and the building of great churches.

UNIT TWELVE
    Program 23: The Late Middle Ages
    Program 24: The National Monarchies

By the late fifteenth century the rulers of many states are centralizing power within their own domains. Professor Weber describes important religious and political thought at the time and the expansion of great states.

UNIT THIRTEEN
    Program 25: The Renaissance and the Age of Discovery
    Program 26: The Renaissance and the New World

Professor Weber argues that the great European explorers shared the Renaissance spirit that appeared in the works of artists, scholars, and writers of the period.

SEMESTER II

UNIT FOURTEEN
    Program 27: The Reformation
    Program 28: The Rise of the Middle Class

The Protestant Reformation arises as many Europeans, particularly in cities, look for new forms of piety and worship.

UNIT FIFTEEN
    Program 29: The Wars of Religion
    Program 30: The Rise of Trading Cities

Trading begins to transform European politics and economics. At the same time much of Europe is devastated by wars between Protestants and Catholics.

UNIT SIXTEEN
    Program 31: The Age of Absolutism
    Program 32: Absolutism and the Social Contract

Some rulers, especially in France, claim they are answerable to no earthly authority. At the same time, in England, some political theorists argue that authority depends on the consent of the governed.

UNIT SEVENTEEN
Program 33: The Enlightened Despots
Program 34: The Enlightenment

In western Europe philosophers argue that the dignity of man can best be raised through practical knowledge and reforms.

UNIT EIGHTEEN
Program 35: The Enlightenment and Society
Program 36: The Modern Philosophers

At this time many writers think of themselves as social reformers, actively working to change society.

UNIT NINETEEN
Program 37: The American Revolution
Program 38: The American Republic

The American Revolution is examined as a test case of Enlightenment ideals.

UNIT TWENTY
Program 39: The Death of the Old Regime
Program 40: The French Revolution

As the kingdom of France collapses, the new revolutionary state becomes an ideal for some Europeans and a terror for others.

UNIT TWENTY-ONE
Program 41: The Industrial Revolution
Program 42: The Industrial World

New sources of power and techniques of production begin the age of industrial expansion.

UNIT TWENTY-TWO
Program 43: Revolution and the Romantics
Program 44: The Age of the Nation-States

By the early nineteenth century many subject peoples in the empires of central and eastern Europe aspire to establish independent countries.

UNIT TWENTY-THREE
Program 45: A New Public
Program 46: Fin de Siècle

By the late nineteenth century the productivity of the Industrial Revolution is raising standards of living throughout Europe and North America. Development of mass communication and culture becomes an important force in modern society.

UNIT TWENTY-FOUR
    Program 47: The First World War and the Rise of Fascism
    Program 48: The Second World War

Wars and revolution arise from the unresolved conflicts of the previous century: class struggle, commercial and colonial rivalries, and struggles for national sovereignty.

UNIT TWENTY-FIVE
    Program 49: The Cold War
    Program 50: Europe and the Third World

The United States and the Soviet Union, the two great victors of the Second World War, now dominate Europe. In the Third World poor countries try to develop in the midst of superpower rivalries and competition from industrialized nations.

UNIT TWENTY-SIX
    Program 51: The Technological Revolution
    Program 52: Toward the Future

The last unit emphasizes the speed with which moden life has changed and considers the future of Western civilization.

STUDENT STUDY GUIDES

The student study guides—Semesters I and II—are designed to help identify and achieve objectives on a weekly basis, to integrate the television programs with textbook reading assignments, and to identify and follow the themes of the course.

The Semester I Study Guide contains the lessons for Units One through Thirteen and make up the first part of the course. The Semester II Study Guide contains the lessons for Units Fourteen through Twenty-six, the remaining units in the course.

Each unit in the study guide corresponds to two, half-hour television programs per week. For example, during the first week of the course students view programs 1 and 2—"The Dawn of History" and "The Ancient Egyptians"—and complete the corresponding activities for Unit One in the Study Guide. The textbook reading assignments for each unit are also given in the study guide. Further, each unit in the study guide contains the following sections:

- **LEARNING OBJECTIVES:** Listed are the essential issues students should understand after finishing the unit. The objectives also synthesize the goals of the textbook readings and television programs.

- **OVERVIEW:** The overview outlines each television program, emphasizing Professor Weber's special lines of argument.

- **KEY TO THE IMAGES:** Additional information about the images that appear in each program is given here.

- **FOCUS QUESTIONS:** The focus questions highlight themes that students should watch for in each television program. They point out issues about which students should take notes.

- **IN CONTEXT:** The in-context section sets each unit in context by raising related issues in earlier or later units.

- **TEXTBOOK ASSIGNMENT:** The student's instructor assigns one of the three textbooks listed in this section. The textbook assignments are an essential part of the course. The exercises in each unit require students to draw information from both the textbook and the programs.

- **ISSUES FOR CLARIFICATION:** Some issues in the programs or readings may require additional explanation. This section amplifies points that might otherwise be misleading or difficult to understand.

- **GLOSSARY:** The glossary provides short explanations of specialized terms in each unit. Students may wish to use the glossaries in conjunction with a dictionary or encyclopedia.

- **TIMELINE:** The timeline exercise asks students to visualize and place events and dates in a chronological manner.

- **MAP EXERCISE:** Each unit contains a map on which students are asked to mark important locations. To prepare for the exercise, students should view the map in each program and refer to the maps in the textbook. In some cases students are asked to search for relevant maps in the textbook or, if necessary, to consult a historical atlas. Answers are provided for only some of the map exercises. There will be no answers for questions requiring nothing more than a location.

- **SELF-TEST:** Part I of the self-test asks questions about important factual issues. Part II tests students' understanding of Professor Weber's interpretations. If students find they disagree with Professor Weber's views, they should be prepared to defend their own interpretations.

- **OPTIONAL ACTIVITIES:** Although these activities are not required unless assigned by the instructor, students are encouraged to read them. The activities contain interesting material on literature, art, and film, some of which students may wish to investigate on their own.

- **REVIEW QUESTIONS:** The review questions require students to interpret important issues discussed in each unit. In some cases, students may disagree with the interpretations of Professor Weber or the textbook; in such instances, students must be prepared to explain how they arrived at their own interpretations.

- **FURTHER READING:** Listed here are additional readings, many of them primary sources, that explore in depth the various issues presented in each unit.

- **FILMS AVAILABLE ON VIDEO:** These films are listed for outside interest, although teachers may wish to make use of them for additional projects.

- **ANSWER KEY:** An answer key to the self-test, timelines, and map exercise appears at the end of each unit.

THE TEXTBOOK

In addition to corresponding directly to the television programs, each study guide unit is cross-referenced to three currently available textbooks:

1. *Western Civilizations,* Fifteenth Edition (Norton, 2005), by Judith G. Coffin and Robert C. Stacey.

2. *The Western Experience,* Eighth Edition (McGraw-Hill, 2003), by Mortimer Chambers, Raymond Grew, David Herlihy, Theodore K. Rabb, and Isser Woloch.

3. *The Western Heritage,* Ninth Edition (Prentice Hall, 2007), by Donald Kagan, Steven Ozment, and Frank M. Turner.

4. *The Western Heritage,* TLC, Fifth Edition (Prentice Hall, 2007), by Donald Kagan, Steven Ozment, and Frank M. Turner.

Students should contact their instructor to find out which textbook is required for the course. The textbook is an essential part of "The Western Tradition" course—students cannot complete the exercises for each unit without it. Further, the textbook helps students to take notes more efficiently. That is, if students generally understand the topics in each assigned chapter, they can avoid unnecessary notetaking as they view the programs and can give full attention to Professor Weber's presentations. The textbook is also an important source of maps and images. After Professor Weber comments on the images that appear in the programs, students can turn to the textbook for similar images and study them more closely.

Finally, the textbook provides interpretations that students can compare with Professor Weber's. Sometimes the program and the assigned reading emphasize different aspects of the same issue; other times, they present the same conclusions, but follow different lines of argument; and, at still other times, they disagree altogether. The most important goal of "The Western Tradition" course may be to teach students to ask an essential question, How do people know what they claim to know?

TAKING "THE WESTERN TRADITION" TELECOURSE

FACULTY GUIDES

Similar to the study guides, the faculty guides have been developed for semesters I and II of "The Western Tradition." The Faculty Guides are for use by instructors only, and are designed to help in teaching the course in the most effective manner. Semester I and II Faculty Guides contain all of the information found in the student study guides, as well as additional classroom activities and reading material.

Following registration in the courses, students must find out

- Which textbook is required.
- If and when an orientation session has been scheduled.
- When "The Western Tradition" will be broadcast.
- When examinations are scheduled for the course and mark the dates on a calendar.
- If any additional on-campus meetings have been scheduled and then plan to attend as many review sessions, seminars, and other meetings as possible.

To learn the most from each unit, students are encouraged to use the various components of the course in the following order:

1. Read the study guide unit that corresponds to the programs to become familiar with the events, people, and vocabulary of the period.
2. View the film, keeping in mind the information and questions in the study guide.
3. Read the textbook chapter that corresponds to the film to gain a better understanding of the events and issues of the time.
4. Reread the study guide unit, attempt to answer the focus questions, and prepare the assignment given by the instructor.

VIEWING THE PROGRAMS

SCHEDULE
If students' viewing areas have more than one public television station, several opportunities to watch the programs may be available. Further, many public television stations repeat the program at least once during the week it is first shown. Schools may also be able to provide videocassettes of the films. Students must determine at what time they will watch each film and adhere to their schedule.

PREPARATION
It is easier for students to follow the films if they first review the study guide sections that correspond directly to the programs. These include the Overview, Key to the Images, and Focus Questions sections. However, it is also recommended that students read the other sections in the study guide in preparation for viewing the films.

BE AN ACTIVE VIEWER
To learn as much as possible from the television programs students must pay careful attention to the films. Watching television for a telecourse requires much more concentration than watching television for entertainment.

NOTETAKING
Some students may find notetaking while viewing the television programs helpful; others may find it distracting and may prefer to make audio- or videotapes of the programs for later review. It is of course helpful to view the programs twice whenever possible.

COURSE ASSIGNMENTS

KEEP UP WITH WEEKLY COURSE ASSIGNMENTS
Each unit of the study guide builds on the knowledge gained from previous units. Therefore, it is imperative that students stay current with the films, readings, and assignments. Some students may find that by entering study activities in a study log, they can better focus on the assignments that require special attention. A study log is also a good place to note questions for the course instructor and to judge the best order of study and review.

KEEP IN TOUCH WITH YOUR INSTRUCTOR
Students should make a note of their instructor's mailing address, telephone number, and call-hours. Students do not need to wait until they have a problem to contact their instructor. Rather, the instructor wants to know how students are doing in the course. Students should contact their instructor whenever a need to discuss the content of the course or to obtain clarification of course content arises.

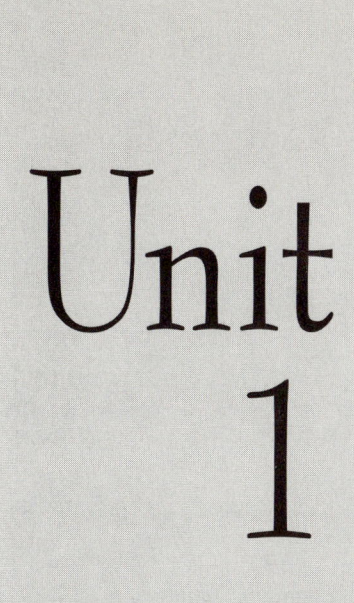

Unit 1

Program 1: The Dawn of History

Program 2: The Ancient Egyptians

LEARNING OBJECTIVES

After completing Unit One students should understand the following issues:

- Influences on the evolution of early anthropoids. Look in your textbook for additional factors that shaped the physical evolution of the human race.

- The relationship between early religions and the development of agriculture. Professor Weber emphasizes the importance of human sacrifice. Draw on your textbook for other important features of early religions.

- The characteristics of the Nile Valley and their influence on Egyptian society.

- The changing position of the pharaoh in Egyptian politics. Use your textbook to trace the times when the pharaoh's power was especially strong and especially weak.

- The ways in which art and architecture reflect issues in Egyptian social or political life.

- The relationships between Egyptian politics and Egyptian religion. Professor Weber emphasizes the ways in which religious beliefs reflected the power of the pharaoh. What other social or political issues were reflected in Egyptian religion?

TV INSTRUCTION

OVERVIEW
PROGRAM 1: THE DAWN OF HISTORY

History is "a trip back to the old country"; a search for our origins. Program 1 traces the origins of the human race from its anthropoid ancestors to the agricultural revolution. Professor Weber argues that many aspects of society and religion arose in response to the terror of living in a violent, precarious world.

I. The evolution of thinking creatures was greatly shaped by the physical characteristics of mankind's ancestors.
   A. They began to walk erect.
      1. The erect posture was especially advantageous to a creature that possessed a large head with a large brain.
      2. The erect posture also freed the hands from walking.
   B. Therefore, the hands could be used for fighting and work.
   C. The evolution of the opposable thumb made it possible to use tools.

II. The ability to use tools affected the physical evolution of the human race.
   A. With tools, our ancestors no longer had to depend solely on their teeth to break or crush objects.
   B. Once our ancestors harnessed fire and could cook meat, an enormous burden was taken off their jaw muscles.
   C. Over time, our ancestors no longer needed massive jaw muscles.
      1. Eventually, the jaw muscles no longer imprisoned the skull.
      2. As the skull expanded, a larger brain evolved.

III. The earliest human beings were probably nomads who lived in small clans, following the animals on which they preyed.
   A. Most early cave paintings are the work of hunting societies.
      1. The paintings portray great numbers of animals, many of them belonging to species now extinct.
      2. The paintings may well have been involved with rituals supposed to ensure a plentiful supply of game.
   B. Early societies probably practiced an important division of labor between the sexes.
      1. The men were hunters.
      2. The women were gatherers, and at a later time were probably the guardians of the first crops.

IV. Ten to twelve thousand years ago, certain peoples cultivated the beginnings of the agricultural revolution.
   A. They learned to domesticate animals.
   B. They learned to plant crops.
   C. In response, people developed a sense of property.
      1. Naturally, they claimed ownership of the fruits of their labor.
      2. Eventually, land and water would be claimed as property.
      3. Systems of inheritance passed on property to future generations.

V. To summarize, the above developments took place over millions of years.
   A. The first stone tools date back to two and a half million years ago.
   B. The first flaked flints appeared only a million years later.
   C. The first burials are believed to have been performed about 70,000 B.C.

VI. About 10,000 B.C. came the beginnings of the Neolithic or New Stone Age, the beginnings of civilization.
   A. Neolithic societies depended on security and on the fertility of the soil.
   B. Unfortunately, danger and its attendant terrors were never far away.

VII. Professor Weber argues that Neolithic peoples developed rituals and religions to guard against such dangers.
   A. Many early religions practiced human sacrifice.
      1. To ensure success in fighting and hunting.
      2. To ensure fertility and plentiful crops.
      3. To send emissaries into the next world as
         a. messengers to the gods.
         b. servants for powerful people who had recently died.
   B. In some cases the victim, such as the Corn King of the ancient Britons, was thought to incarnate the forces of nature.
   C. Such victims could even be powerful rulers, until they were sacrificed.
   D. Eventually, some prospective victims were able to persuade their people to substitute another person or an animal for the sacrifice.
      1. Human sacrifice became less common.
      2. Figures such as the Corn King now became long-term rulers.

VIII. In many early societies women were worshipped as the creators of life.
   A. Because the first crops were probably tended by women, the early stages of the agricultural revolution may have created matriarchies in which women were rulers.
   B. Some historians have argued that around 3000 B.C. men reasserted their power with the invention of the ox-plow, which was too heavy for most women to manage.

IX. With the agricultural revolution, societies developed a class structure, as certain people devoted all their efforts to specialized tasks.
   A. Priests were among the first of these specialists, because their magic rites were supposed to:
      1. heal the sick.
      2. ensure fertility.
      3. preserve the community from danger.
   B. Professor Weber argues that priests were the first economic class not directly involved in producing its own food.
   C. Eventually other specialized classes developed:
      1. potters.
      2 miners.
      3. tradesmen.
   D. Economic specialization led to social divisions between rich and poor.

X. Professor Weber argues that societies evolved in this general manner all over the world, but that the most rapid social development took place in areas of relatively high population density where people struggled for land. Such areas included:
   A. Egypt.
   B. Mesopotamia.

KEY TO THE IMAGES

Bones as evidence:
The bones of human beings and animals are among the most valuable evidence for the prehistory of the human race. For instance, if a site contains human or humanoid bones mixed in with those of other animals, scientists can speculate about the kind of prey that early peoples hunted and about the kind of hunting life they may have lived.

Some scientists have noticed that bones from certain parts of the body, such as the jaw, seem to appear in bone piles with especially great frequency. They have speculated that a high frequency of jawbones in a site may be evidence that the place was once inhabited by the ancestors of human beings. The theory is that even before hominids could fashion tools themselves, they made a practice of saving certain bones, especially jaws, to use as a sort of ready-made tool.

Although this theory is tantalizing, it presents many problems. The fact is that certain bones, especially teeth and jaws, are harder than the bones in other parts of the body. It is not surprising that they should survive more frequently than other bones.

Fertility statues:
Much of the evidence for Professor Weber's discussion of early religion comes from the statues of fertility goddesses, such as the pieces that are now called "The Venus of Willendorf," "The Seated Goddess," and "The Venus of Laussel."

Such statues appear in a variety of styles and were fashioned in many different times and places. Most of them, however, exaggerate the breasts, hips, and buttocks of the figure. Such statues reveal a great deal about early religious practices but archeologists have to be wary of circular reasoning. They have to be careful not to call a statue a fertility goddess simply because it portrays a plump woman.

Flints and pottery:
Because flints and pottery are durable, they are the early human artifacts that survive in greatest numbers. As well as providing evidence about material life, flints and pottery provide important information about dating. The terms *Old Stone Age*, *Middle Stone Age*, and *New Stone Age* refer to the different styles and methods with which stone, especially flint, was worked.

Pottery provides archeologists with especially valuable clues, because styles of pottery can vary widely over time and from one place to another.

FOCUS QUESTIONS

1. What physical characteristics did early anthropoids possess that are not commonly found among other mammals?
2. How did the physical characteristics of our anthropoid ancestors affect the evolution of thinking creatures?
3. Why did social evolution develop so rapidly after the discovery of agriculture?
4. How did the problems of survival affect the religious beliefs of early peoples, especially after the development of agriculture?
5. How did the changing roles of women in agriculture affect the religious beliefs of early peoples?

OVERVIEW
PROGRAM 2: THE ANCIENT EGYPTIANS

One of the first civilizations to arise in the world, Egypt preserved many of the essential forms of its culture for nearly three thousand years. Program 2 shows some of the ways in which Egyptian life was shaped by the special problems and opportunities of life in the Nile Valley.

I. A number of early civilizations grew up in the area of Asia and Africa known as the Fertile Crescent, which includes Egypt, Syria, and Mesopotamia.
   A. Oddly enough, much of the area is arid.
      1. Three great river systems, however, bring water through parts of the region:
         a. the Tigris.
         b. the Euphrates.
         c. the Nile.
      2. Areas that received sufficient water were fertile and could produce several crops a year, even though the desert began only a few miles away.
      3. It was in these fertile areas that the first civilizations arose.
   B. Professor Weber argues that societies in the Fertile Crescent had to be tightly organized because large-scale cooperation was necessary for irrigation and flood control.
      1. Governments had to be able to control great numbers of people to carry out these projects.
      2. Governments also had strong powers of coercion because they could destroy rebels or malcontents by cutting them off from water.

II. In addition to these issues, the Egyptians enjoyed several other blessings of geography.
   A. Although the Nile Valley was very long, it was only seven miles wide. Because troops could move easily up and down the river, rulers were usually able to hold the country together.
   B. Because Egypt was surrounded by deserts, it was protected from invading armies throughout long stretches of its history.

III. The Nile created and shaped Egyptian life into the form it was to retain for nearly three thousand years.
   A. Around 10,000 years ago the people in the marshes and swamps of the Nile Valley began to sow crops, in addition to their hunting and fishing.
      1. They cleared land for crops.
      2. They learned to build waterworks to retain the waters of the flooding Nile.
   B. By 3000 B.C. the Egyptians had made a number of crucial discoveries to help in their struggle to control the river:
      1. astronomical charts were made to:
         a. trace seasonal regularities for crops.
         b. predict the flooding of the Nile.
      2. A writing system was developed.
         a. It recorded and coordinated projects.
         b. It made extensive use of hieroglyphics in which the symbol for a word was an image resembling the concept or thing it represented.

IV. Important aspects of Egyptian religion reflected the interplay of the two great forces in Egyptian life: the sun and the river.
   A. Ra (or Re) was the Sun God who had created all life and order, both human and divine.
   B. Osiris was the earth, the god of fertilizing water and vegetation.
      1. Osiris was also the god of death.
      2. Osiris was the god of resurrection as well.

C. Osiris had a wicked brother, Set, the god of all arid, wicked, unpleasant things. Set was the god of:
   1. the desert.
   2. the night.
   3. the foreigner.
   4. Warfare.
D. In many of their most important myths the Egyptians portrayed the struggle between Osiris and Set as the root of the cosmic cycle of life, death, and resurrection.

V. About 3000 B.C. a warrior prince united Egypt and took the title pharaoh. From this date until the death of Cleopatra in 31 B.C. pharaohs ruled Egypt for nearly three thousand years.
   A. The Egyptians believed the pharaoh was the embodiment of a god. They believed that:
      1. he ensured the sun would rise each day after its journey through the night.
      2. he guaranteed the harvest with his ceremonial hoe.
      3. each year he cast a written order into the Nile, commanding it to flood.
   B. The pharaoh was the embodiment of the state.
      1. All officials acted in his name.
      2. All officials held their positions at his pleasure.
      3. Law was simply the pharaoh's word.
         a. At first this law was not written down.
         b. Written laws might acquire an authority of their own that could conflict with the authority of the pharaoh.
   C. Only the pharaoh could express the ultimate truth and justice, the goodness and cosmic force, which the Egyptians called Ma'at.

VI. The pharaoh was so powerful that he was believed to control access to the next world.
   A. In the early stages of Egyptian religion only the pharaoh could be assured of entering the afterlife.
   B. For his family and followers, the only hope of eternal life was to be taken along to serve him in the next world.

VII. The pyramids reflect the pharaoh's power in political and religious life.
   A. Around the pyramid at Sakkara, built in the Third Dynasty, can be seen the smaller tomb of a nobleman, who must have believed that he had improved his chances of entering the next world by building his tomb so close to the pharaoh's.
   B. Noblemen would also try to have their effigies placed in the royal tombs.
   C. The climax of this obsession with building came around 2600 B.C., during the Fourth Dynasty.
      1. The Great Pyramid of Cheops was built at Giza, the greatest of all the pyramids.
      2. The nearby sphinx was carved out of living rock.
      3. The Egyptians also built the great obelisks, which were imitated throughout much of the world.

VIII. Many of these projects were constructed during the flooding of the Nile when peasants were not working the land and when the river could be used for transportation. The pharaohs soon found, however, that they could not build on this scale forever.
   A. Between 2500 and 2300 B.C. the kings of the Fifth and Sixth dynasties built much smaller pyramids.
   B. Smaller scale building was a sign that the pharaohs were losing some of their power to:
      1. priests.
      2. nobility.

IX. To some extent the pharaohs lost power as a result of their successes.
   A. As the state became powerful and effective the pharaoh needed greater numbers of servants.
      1. Some of these servants were sent to rule distant parts of the kingdom.
      2. If successful, the servants might be rewarded with gifts of land.
      3. They might be able to pass their offices down to their descendants.
      4. Eventually, a class of noblemen arose who ruled in the pharaoh's name but, in fact, enjoyed a considerable degree of independence.
      5. In earlier days nobles tried to build their tombs close to the pharaoh's but eventually began to build them in their own territories, as though they no longer felt the need for the pharaoh's patronage in the next world.
      6. They even believed that they could interpret Ma'at, which had once been the sole province of the pharaoh.
   B. Among the great tombs and temples of the pharaohs there grew a powerful caste of priests who in many cases were able to oppose the pharaoh's will.

X. About 2300 B.C. the Sixth Dynasty came to an end in fragmentation and anarchy.
   A. Under the Middle Kingdom a new dynasty of pharaohs restored order.
   B. The pharaohs, however, never regained their old prestige and power.
      1. The pharaoh's word was no longer law.
      2. Laws were now written down.
      3. Pharaohs were increasingly dependent on the nobility.

XI. Between 1700 and 1500 B.C. another period of anarchy broke out.
   A. For the first time Egypt was conquered by a foreign people, the Hyksos.
      1. Their horses and chariots made them more mobile than the Egyptians.
      2. With their bows they were better armed.
   B. Although the foreigners were eventually cast out, Egyptians never regained their earlier security.

XII. Under the New Kingdom, from 1500–1000 B.C., Egypt again knew times of strength and prosperity.
   A. With the threat of invasion a powerful class of administrators and professional soldiers came to power, alongside the omnipresent priests.
   B. Although the façade of older forms and rituals remained, Professor Weber argues that the New Kingdom was very different in spirit from the older Egypt.
      1. The New Kingdom was a stiff, formal bureaucracy, based on rules and laws rather than on tradition.
      2. Egyptians had also lost the confidence that came with security from attack.
   C. Professor Weber argues that the Egyptians were not good soldiers.
      1. Military service was unpopular.
      2. Armaments were consistently backward.
      3. When the Egyptians faced strong armies they generally lost.

XIII. Nevertheless, for nearly three thousand years the image of the pharaoh remained much the same.
   A. The political realities had been completely transformed.
   B. But Egyptian forms and styles had endured longer than anything else in the Western tradition.

KEY TO THE IMAGES

Foreigners:
Although Egypt was a remarkably self-contained society, the Egyptians were curious about other peoples. Many paintings and wall carvings depict foreigners. Some of the drawings are so accurate that modern anthropologists have been able to speculate about the origins of the people shown. For instance, Egyptian art shows a number of African peoples who closely resemble tribes now living in the modern Sudan.

Artistic evidence often shows what most impressed the Egyptians. The Hyksos, for instance, conquered Egypt in the seventeenth century B.C. and ruled the country for more than a century. The Hyksos kings are often shown riding in chariots and hunting or fighting with great bows. In fact we know that the chariot and bow were two of the weapons that gave the Hyksos crucial military advantages.

Pharaoh:
Professor Weber notes that the pharaoh was held responsible for the fertility of the soil and the flooding of the Nile River. Images of the pharaoh continually refer to these beliefs. For instance, he often appears holding an agricultural implement such as a flail, a crook, or a sickle. These tools do not suggest that the pharaoh worked the soil himself but rather that he was responsible for its fertility. If you look closely at the image, you will also see him holding a cross with a loop at the top. This is the ankh, a symbol of life.

Changes in the depiction of the pharaoh reflect changes in Egyptian society. In the New Kingdom a number of pharaohs were great warriors. Their images often show them hunting or fighting wars from chariots.

Tombs:
Much of our knowledge of Egyptian society comes from tombs. When you look at the pyramids and the smaller tombs, keep in mind how closely historians and archeologists have had to examine this evidence. In several images of the great pyramid you can see a great number of smaller tombs clustered near the base. These are the tombs of noblemen who wanted the pharaoh to protect them in the afterlife. Similarly, many of the inscriptions inside the nobles' tombs are lists of titles granted by the pharaoh or accounts of the good service the nobleman had done his master.

In some cases noblemen were actually able to get their portraits placed inside their masters' tombs so as to remind the pharaoh to protect his servants when they entered the next world. In later periods, however, noblemen seem to have worried less about the pharaoh's protection in the afterlife. They now built tombs far away from the pharaoh, as though his protection was no longer as important as it had once been.

FOCUS QUESTIONS

1. What discoveries helped the Egyptians adapt to the problems of living in the Nile Valley?
2. The Egyptian pharaoh was supposed to be an omnipotent ruler but in practice his subjects were sometimes able to oppose him. Who were some of the classes of people who were able to resist his will?
3. In what ways did beliefs about Egyptian gods reflect the realities of life in Egypt?
4. How did changing beliefs about immortality reflect changes in the pharaoh's political power?
5. On the surface, Egyptian society changed little in three thousand years. In fact, however, the country went through many profound changes. Look for examples to explain how these changes came about.

The Western Tradition: Unit One

ASSIGNMENTS & ACTIVITIES

IN CONTEXT

Themes and issues that set Unit One in context with later units include the following:

- Professor Weber argues that many features of early religion grew out of an attempt to create stability and order in a dangerous world. This concept reappears in later units. Look for ways in which Egyptian religion reflects the problems of living in the Nile Valley. In the following units pay special attention to the religions of Mesopotamia and Greece. How do they reflect the problems of their areas?

- Much of Egyptian political life centered around the control and irrigation of arable land. In Unit Two we learn that Mesopotamian kingdoms faced similar problems along the Tigris and Euphrates. In Unit One we concentrate on the problems peculiar to Egypt. When you read of similar problems in later units, remember the features that made Egypt different from societies similar in many other ways.

- As the pharaohs grew in strength, their power often became diluted because they were forced to give great responsibility to distant officials, over whom they often had little control. In later units look for examples of other kingdoms or empires that overextended themselves. In Unit Two Professor Weber mentions the problems of the Persian Empire. In later units watch for problems of overextension in the Hellenistic and Roman empires.

- Professor Weber emphasizes that priests, noblemen, and soldiers all gained power at the pharaoh's expense. In later units look for the ebb and flow of power among important classes in other cultures. In Unit Two, for instance, we learn that secular rulers in Mesopotamia gradually gained power at the expense of the temples.

TEXTBOOK ASSIGNMENT

Read the following pages in your assigned textbook:

    Text: *Western Civilizations*, Fifteenth Edition (Norton, 2005)
    Read: From Chapter 1, "The Origins of Western Civilizations," pp. 7-17, 31-46; and Chapter 2, "Gods and Empires in the Ancient Near East, 1700-500 B.C.E," pp. 51-62, 79-85.

    Text: *The Western Experience*, Eighth Edition (McGraw–Hill, 2003)
    Read: From Chapter 1, "The First Civilization," pp. 4-7, 13-35.

    Text: *The Western Heritage*, Ninth Edition (Prentice Hall, 2007)
    Read: From Chapter 1, "The Birth of Civilization," pp. 4-26.

    Text: *The Western Heritage*, TLC, Fifth Edition (Prentice Hall, 2007)
    Read: From Chapter 1, "The Birth of Civilization," pp. 4-31.

ISSUES FOR CLARIFICATION

Polytheism

The Egyptians worshipped so many gods that it is often difficult to understand their religious beliefs. Here are two observations that may be helpful:

1. The Egyptians often thought of related forces in terms of kinship. They believed, for instance, in a struggle between the god, Osiris, and his wicked brother, Set. This struggle was the cause of the opposition between life and death, day and night, fertile land and desert, Egyptian and foreigner.
2. Changes in beliefs about the gods could reflect important changes in society as a whole. Osiris, for instance, had always been important as the god of vegetation and of fertilizing water. As god of resurrection, however, his cult grew even more prominent as Egyptians came to believe immortality was not the monopoly of the pharaoh.

Survivals

Long after a practice dies away it may still leave traces that we can detect if we look carefully. Professor Weber mentions the stories of Agamemnon's sacrifice of his daughter Iphigenia and Abraham's preparations to sacrifice Isaac. Neither the Israelites of the Old Testament nor the Greeks of classical times practiced human sacrifice themselves, but these stories may reflect memories, or "survivals," of even earlier times.

GLOSSARY

Ma'at: Truth, justice, or goodness. The Egyptians thought of *Ma'at* as a cosmic force of harmony, order, stability, and security, which gave form to the proper relationship of people and things in this world and eternity. The Egyptians believed that the pharaoh alone expressed *Ma'at*.

Osiris: God of the earth, of vegetation, and of fertilizing water. Because he was also a god of resurrection, Osiris's cult became even more important once the Egyptians came to believe that the pharaoh did not exercise a monopoly over the afterlife.

Ra (or Re): Sun god; creator of the universe and the other gods. Ra was thought to have created all order, both human and divine.

Set: God of the desert, night, and wickedness. Set was locked in a struggle with his brother, Osiris.

The Western Tradition: Unit One 11

TIMELINE

Place each of the following events on the timeline. In some cases you may have to specify a roughly defined period of time rather than a precise date.

1. First stone tools
2. First burials
3. Appearance of Homo sapiens
4. Ox–plow
5. First Egyptian Dynasty
6. Great pyramid
7. New Kingdom
8. Alexander's Conquest

|—— 2,000,000 B.C. ———————————————————————— 1 B.C. —|

|——— 100,000 B.C. ————————————————————————— 1 B.C. —|

|————— 3,000 B.C. ————————————————————————— 1 B.C. —|

MAP EXERCISE

Find the following locations on the map. You may need to do extensive cross-referencing in your textbook. If you do not find all these places on the maps associated with Unit One, look at the maps in later units.

1. Mesopotamia
2. The Nile Valley
3. Thebes
4. The Sudan
5. Inhabited part of ancient Egypt
6. Modern Israel
7. Libya
8. The first cataract

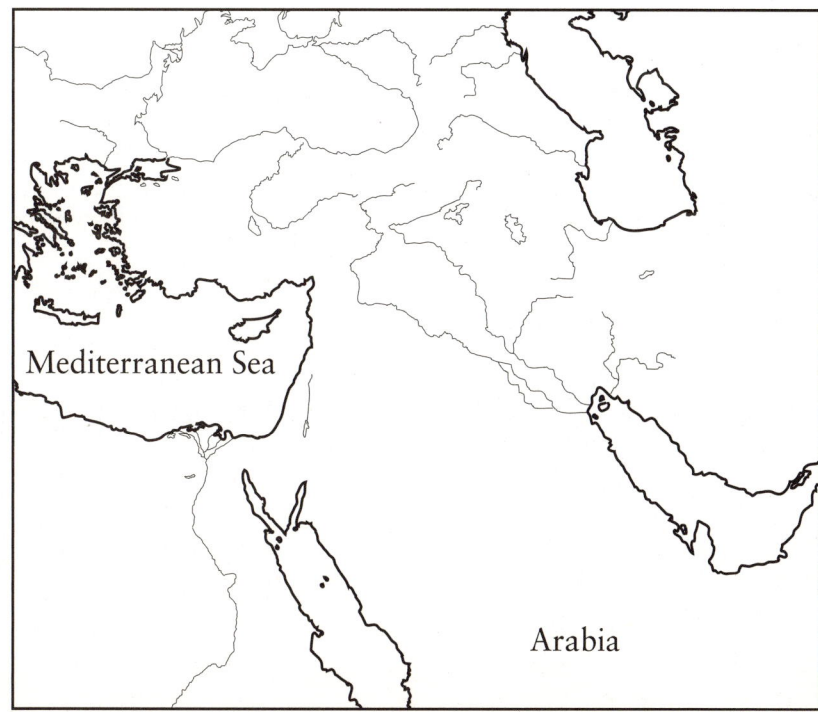

SELF-TEST

Part I of the self-test asks about important factual material. Part II is interpretive. The answers in Part II are keyed to Professor Weber's interpretations. If you disagree with an answer, be prepared to defend your own understanding of the material. Check your answers at the end of Unit One.

Part I

1. Mark the false choice. The development of tools and the use of fire
    a. had no discernible effect on human evolution.
    b. began well before the development of agriculture.
    c. were spaced out over enormous periods of time.
    d. took place while the ancestors of humankind were living by hunting and gathering.

2. List three crucial developments made by the Egyptians as direct responses to the problems of living in the Nile valley:

3. _____ was the Egyptian god of the earth, vegetation, and fertilizing water.
    a. Ra
    b. Osiris
    c. Set
    d. Isis

4. The fertile, inhabited part of ancient Egypt was approximately
    a. half the size of modem Egypt.
    b. the size of the state of Texas.
    c. the size of the state of Maryland.
    d. the size of England.

5. Which of the following peoples did *not* conquer Egypt at some time during the period we are studying?
    a. Hyksos
    b. Israelites
    c. Greeks
    d. Romans

Part II

1. Which of the following physical characteristics did *not* play an important role in the development of intelligence in the ancestors of humankind?
    a. The ability to walk erect
    b. Exceptional speed and agility
    c. The opposable thumb
    d. An exceptionally large brain

2. Mark the false choice. In the early stages of agriculture
   a. men naturally played the dominant role because they have always been stronger than women.
   b. the invention of the ox-plow may have given men a more important role.
   c. growing crops may at first have been only a supplement to hunting and gathering.
   d. the division of labor between the sexes was often reflected in religious beliefs.

3. Mark the false choice. Agriculture was a necessary condition for the development of civilization
   a. because it allowed people to live in much denser settlements.
   b. because groups of people could live in relatively permanent settlements.
   c. because it discouraged such destructive customs as human sacrifice.
   d. because it encouraged more complex forms of social organization.

4. Mark the false choice. The enormous tombs of the pharaohs
   a. were built by conscripted peasants.
   b. often reflect the religious and political power of the pharaoh.
   c. were built on an increasingly grand scale throughout Egyptian history.
   d. were copied on a smaller scale by the nobility.

5. Mark the false choice. The Egyptians were *not* among the great warrior peoples of the ancient world but
   a. their technical skill gave them weapons at least as good as those of their enemies.
   b. their geographical position protected them for long periods of time.
   c. they did enjoy military successes under the New Kingdom.
   d. Egypt's very compactness made it easy to defend.

OPTIONAL ACTIVITIES

Although the following activities are not required for the course unless assigned by the instructor, students are encouraged to read them as sources of interesting material for further study.

Herodotus

Herodotus was a Greek historian and traveler of the fifth century B.C. Because he actually visited Egypt, many of his observations were firsthand observations. At the same time, Herodotus also recorded a great number of legends. Although he was skeptical about many of these stories, he was not always sure of what to accept and what to question.

Read the relevant sections of Herodotus's *Histories* (Book II contains the most concentrated section about Egypt). The Penguin Classics edition, edited by Aubrey de Selincourt, is readily available.

As you read Herodotus, remember that one of the historian's most important tasks is to compare different sources. In many cases you will find Herodotus making claims that other sources do not support.

Write a paper of 3-5 pages in which you discuss at least one of the following issues:

- Is anything to be learned from his accounts, even when they seem most clearly wrong?
- Why do you suppose that he made such errors?
- What do these mistakes tell you about Herodotus's own culture?

Compare Herodotus's account of the Egyptians to what we know from other sources.

The Egyptians and the Bible
Read different parts of the Bible to see the changing relations between the Jews and Egyptians. In Genesis 37–50 their relations are often friendly. Exodus 1–14 tells a different story. Reconstruct the events of the Bible from the point of view of the Egyptians.

Pay particular attention to the story of Joseph in Genesis. Write a paper of 3–5 pages in which you discuss at least one of the following issues:

- How did the Israelites come to Egypt in the first place?
- What was their position in the country after Joseph invited his family to settle there?
- How can you account for the different picture you find in Exodus?

REVIEW QUESTIONS

The following questions are designed to help you think critically and to construct explanations from factual knowledge. Remember that whenever you learn a new piece of information you should always ask yourself "so what?" In one sense or another these are all "so what?" questions.

Keep in mind that historians continually disagree on emphases, interpretations, and even on simple matters of fact. Many of the following questions emphasize Professor Weber's particular point of view and ask you to compare it to what you find in your textbook. When you find important disagreements, you should remember that historians are always struggling with each other; this struggle is one that you can enter yourself.

1. In his discussion of our primitive ancestors Professor Weber claims that technical discoveries affected the social and, in some cases, even the physical evolution of mankind. Evaluate this assertion and provide examples to support your conclusions.

2. In exploring the development of agriculture Professor Weber lays out a complex set of relationships among agriculture, religion, and the role of the sexes. Which of these factors most influenced the others? Are you convinced by the way Professor Weber draws relationships among these factors? What other relationships are possible?

3. Professor Weber claims that a society dependent on a complex system of irrigation must be authoritarian and tightly knit. Explain. How does control of irrigation help a ruler to maintain control over his opponents? What other social conditions would you expect to find in a society that depended so heavily on irrigation?

4. Egyptian beliefs about immortality changed over time. How did these changes in belief reflect changes in the political power of the pharaoh? As part of your answer, draw on your knowledge of art and architecture. What, for instance, can you learn from the size and location of the tombs of the nobility?

5. The Egyptians believed that their pharaoh was the incarnation of a god but at times they were quite capable of opposing his will. Explain this apparent contradiction. How could the Egyptians dare to oppose the will of a god?

6. The Egyptian New Kingdom was harsher and more authoritarian than most of the earlier regimes. What reflections of this change can you find in Egyptian art? What, for instance, were some of the typical ways of depicting the pharaoh in earlier times? How did artists portray the pharaoh in the New Kingdom?

FURTHER READING

Aldred, Cyril. *The Egyptians.*

Binford, Lewis. *In Pursuit of the Past: Decoding the Archeological Record* (1983). A good discussion of the scientific analysis that helps archeologists draw conclusions about social behavior.

Butzer, Karl W. and Leslie G. Freeman, eds. *Early Hydraulic Civilization in Egypt* (1976). A good treatment of the ecology of the Nile Valley

Gardiner, Alan. *Egypt of the Pharaohs* (1984). The Aldred and Gardiner texts concentrate on Egypt throughout the major periods of its history.

Hallo, W. W. and Simpson, W. K. *The Ancient Near East* (1971). The text sets Egypt in context with other civilizations of the ancient Near East. It is especially helpful in linking the themes of the first three lectures.

Pfeiffer, John. *The Emergence of Humankind* (1985). A review of the field of paleoanthropology.

Simpson, W. K. *Literature of Ancient Egypt* (1972). A collection of essays by one of the authorities in the field.

Smith, W. S. *The Art and Architecture of Ancient Egypt* (1981). An especially important book because so much of our knowledge of ancient Egypt comes from art and architecture. A good reference to follow up Professor Weber's comments on the images.

Wilson, John A. *The Burden of Egypt* (1951). An excellent one-volume survey.

FILMS AVAILABLE ON VIDEO

The Bible (1966). John Huston's treatment of five stories from the Bible.

King Tut: The Face of Tutankhamun (1992). A four-part series that examines the artifacts from one of the best-known archeological discoveries of this century.

Moses (1975). Originally a TV miniseries, starring Burt Lancaster.

The Ten Commandments (1956). One of the best of the Hollywood biblical epics.

ANSWER KEY

Timeline

1. ca. 2,500,000 B.C.
2. ca. 70,000 B.C.
3. ca. 80,000 B.C.
4. ca. 3000 B.C.
5. ca. 3000 B.C.
6. ca. 2600 B.C.
7. ca. 1500 B.C.
8. 330 B.C.

Self-Test

Part I
1. (a) had no discernible effect on human evolution.
2. Irrigation, writing, astronomy, and the calendar are all good answers
3. (b) Osiris
4. (c) the size of the state of Maryland
5. (b) Israelites

Part II
1. (b) Exceptional speed and agility
2. (a) men naturally played the dominant role because they have always been stronger than women.
3. (c) because it discouraged such destructive customs as human sacrifice.
4. (c) were built on an increasingly grand scale throughout Egyptian history
5. (a) their technical skill gave them weapons at least as good as those of their enemies

Unit 2

Program 3: Mesopotamia

Program 4: From Bronze to Iron

LEARNING OBJECTIVES

After completing Unit Two students should understand the following issues:

- Ways in which the civilizations of Mesopotamia were shaped by the dangers to which they were exposed.

- Ways in which Professor Weber and your textbook analyze the major technological and intellectual contributions made by the civilizations of this area.

- The role of the great empires in spreading culture and technology. How does your textbook supplement or dispute Professor Weber's interpretations?

- The ways in which peoples on the edge of the empires learned to resist more powerful states. How does your textbook supplement Professor Weber's description of the peoples who lived on the borders of the Mesopotamian empires?

- The ways in which trade and economic issues in general led to important social and intellectual achievements.

- The impact of literacy on the spread and development of civilization.

- The continual mixing of peoples and cultures throughout the empires and their peripheries. Use your textbook to supplement Professor Weber's analysis.

TV INSTRUCTION

OVERVIEW
PROGRAM 3: MESOPOTAMIA

Many of the most important developments of Mesopotamian civilization came about in response to the pressures of geography. Because they occupied a precarious position in the midst of their enemies or competitors, the Mesopotamians were forced to develop skills and forms of social organization that would help them to survive. As Mesopotamians spread, however, their very successes often undermined the foundations of social life.

I. Many of the differences between the civilizations of Egypt and Mesopotamia resulted from their different geographical settings.
   A. The Nile flooded in predictable patterns and could be more easily controlled.
      1. The Tigris and Euphrates valleys, on the other hand, were subject to hurricanes, floods, and torrential downpours.
      2. Therefore, flood-control and irrigation had to be more elaborate in Mesopotamia than in Egypt.
   B. Egypt was protected by deserts on three sides whereas the Mesopotamian rivers were major avenues of travel.
      1. Egypt could develop its culture in isolation for long periods of time.
      2. Mesopotamian life was constantly affected by trade, migration, and the movement of armies.

II. Therefore, security was a constant preoccupation that had crucial effects on Mesopotamian civilization.
   A. Professor Weber suggests that this insecurity led the Mesopotamians to imagine their gods as cruel and capricious.
   B. Insecurity also led the Mesopotamians to be highly inventive.
      1. The wheel (first used for pottery) was probably invented in this area.
      2. Wheels with spokes were invented around 2000 B.C.
      3. Axles gave added strength to vehicles.
      4. Chariots became a great weapon in war.
   C. Priests had especially important roles.
      1. By 3000 B.C., when the first written records appear, priests dominated Mesopotamian society.
      2. Priests directed the building of temples, cities, and irrigation projects.
      3. Writing was invented to serve the needs of the priests.
         a. Inventories
         b. Accounts
         c. Building plans

III. Geography and the insecurity that followed from it shaped Mesopotamian culture, especially its inventiveness and its religious organization.
   A. Professor Weber suggests that the Mesopotamians possessed a special talent for abstract thinking.
      1. Evidence of their writing system
      2. Talent for mathematics
      3. Their tendency to portray their gods as being different from human beings
   B. As a result of geography the Mesopotamians were constantly involved in war and trade to obtain necessities they could not find in their own region.
      1. Timber

2. Stone
3. Metals
4. Precious stones

IV. As these civilizations flourished their contact with a wider world increased and spread their influence.
   A. Effects on population
      1. Influx of slaves
      2. Traders from foreign parts
   B. Cultural effects
      1. Cities were exposed to foreign customs and inventions.
      2. Mesopotamian inventions spread.
         a. Socket-ax
         b. Pottery
         c. Glass (invented in Mesopotamia ca. 2500 B.C., spread to Egypt ca. 1500 B.C.)
         d. Copper (fourth millennium)
         e. Bronze (third millennium)
         f. Iron (second millennium)

V. In Professor Weber's view these developments created new pressures for change and undermined the social order even further.
   A. Professor Weber suggests that, because wealth was concentrated in a small number of hands, the Mesopotamian cities always needed new lands to support the expanding rural economy. These needs led to
      1. reclamation projects.
         a. irrigating desert.
         b. draining swamps.
      2. warfare.
   B. Professor Weber argues that the mixture of peoples in Mesopotamian cities undermined the blood principle on which religion had previously been based.
   C. The temples, which claimed to rule in the name of the gods, began to lose power.
   D. Secular rulers gained strength.
      1. Written law codes appeared (Hammurabi, 1800 B.C.).
      2. The law began to acquire a life of its own.
      3. In theory rulers were themselves subject to the law.

VI. Professor Weber argues that economic requirements forced Mesopotamian societies to expand, whether through peace or through war.
   A. Around 2400 B.C. a series of empires tried to dominate the region.
      1. Ur
      2. Lagash
      3. Akkad
      4. Babylon
   B. Professor Weber argues that the demands of trade and empire led the Mesopotamians to develop standardized practices.
      1. A standardized writing system
      2. A day that was divided into twelve double-hours
      3. The week
      4. Money
         a. Barley was first used as money.
         b. Silver and copper was used by 1800–1700 B.C.
         c. Assyrian kings stamped silver bars (eighth century B.C.).
         d. Lydian kings issued the first coins in the seventh century.

KEY TO THE IMAGES

Building materials:
Because building stone was often in short supply in Mesopotamia, many buildings that appear in this program were built from brick. Brick architecture was common throughout this part of the world and many of the most widely copied forms, such as the ziggurat or step temple, were developed by the Mesopotamians.

Reliefs:
Among the greatest of the Mesopotamian works of art were low reliefs, both in stone and brick. Among the most common themes were the victories of rulers on the battlefield or on the hunt. Many reliefs depict rulers receiving tribute, often from distant lands. In one relief the Israelite King Jehu is seen prostrating himself before the Assyrians.

As another way of demonstrating their power, Mesopotamian rulers were often depicted hunting from chariots, often in pursuit of lions. These hunting scenes display a seeming paradox in Mesopotamian art. In many cases the human figures appear rigid and awkward, whereas the action of the animals is strong and dynamic. When Mesopotamian art appears stiff, be careful not to assume that artists were simply too unskilled to depict motion. The Mesopotamians were interested in motion only when portraying certain subjects. What looks like stiffness in other subjects is often a sign of power or authority.

Statues:
Professor Weber notes that many Mesopotamian statues, especially those of the gods, stand perfectly upright with great, staring eyes. He argues that this style emphasized the differences between the world of the gods and the world of human beings. Keep this point in mind in later units on the Greeks. In Greek art, heroes, gods, and athletes are often portrayed in similar forms.

FOCUS QUESTIONS

1. How did the geography of the Fertile Crescent shape the civilizations that developed there?
2. What were some of the achievements of these civilizations in science, mathematics, and language?
3. How did trade and warfare influence the technology of Mesopotamia?
4. What were the stages in the transition from religious to secular authority?
5. How did the great empires of Mesopotamia contribute to the codification of law, to the standardization of weights and measures, to the measurement of time, and to the development of money?

The Western Tradition: Unit Two

OVERVIEW
PROGRAM 4: FROM BRONZE TO IRON

Professor Weber demonstrates some of the ways in which warfare created social and economic changes throughout the Near East. The great empires of this region created a cosmopolitan culture by subjugating a great diversity of peoples. On the borders of the empires peoples such as the Phoenicians, Greeks, and Etruscans spread culture and technology throughout the Mediterranean world.

I. Great plundering wars spread wealth and broke up many older institutions in the Near Eastern world.
   A. The greatest of these wars were conducted by the leaders of the great empires, such as the kings of
      1. Akkad.
      2. Babylon.
      3. Nineveh.
   B. Rulers sent out armed expeditions to secure jewels, ores, or other raw materials.
      1. The Egyptians, for instance, sent armed expeditions to extract copper ore in the Sinai Peninsula.
      2. The Sumerians and later the Semitic kings of Akkad and Babylon sent expeditions to the north and west in search of
         a. metals.
         b. stone.
         c. timber.
   C. In addition to slaughtering great numbers of victims these wars transformed the economy of the empires.
      1. The great quantities of loot could create a glut on the market.
      2. Prisoners of war swelled the number of slaves, many of them with valuable skills.
   D. A new social class arose as merchants contracted to dispose of the plunder.
      1. When merchants made a profit some of the wealth was passed on to those who worked for them.
      2. A new middle class arose between the poor masses on the one hand and the warriors and priests on the other.
   E. War also spread culture and technology abroad.
      1. The Akkadians, for instance, depended on bronze weapons.
      2. Foreign peoples who wanted to resist them were forced to learn Akkadian techniques.
         a. Smiths had to be found or trained.
         b. Raw materials had to be supplied.
         c. Therefore, trade had to be organized.

II. All these factors were at work in the early Bronze Age (ca. 2400 B.C.). They were still at work six to seven hundred years later, as one barbarian dynasty destroyed another in Babylon.
   A. Professor Weber argues that in these times of danger and uncertainty people wanted to put their wealth in a form that was mobile and incorruptible. "It was easier to safeguard a bag full of silver than a field full of barley."
   B. Therefore, money began to play a greater role in economic life.
      1. Businesspersons speculated by importing cargoes to be sold on the market.
      2. Producers began to manufacture goods for the market instead of depending on commissions from the ruler or priests. These developments affected even relatively humble people such as
         a. craftsmen.
         b. peasants.

C. In part as a result of this economic activity, there arose a class of literate officials:
   1. clerks to keep records.
   2. judges to
      a. collect fines.
      b. levy taxes.
      c. render judgment in an increasingly complex society.

III. Professor Weber argues that, because peasants and craftsmen could find a market for their goods, even the masses of the population could now benefit from technological innovations.
   A. Bronze was expensive because it was made from two ores that were often difficult to obtain:
      1. copper.
      2. tin.
   B. The great change came with the widespread use of iron.
      1. Around 1700 B.C. iron had been so rare that it was twice as valuable as gold.
      2. By 1300 B.C., however, when craftsmen learned to harden it by carburation, iron began to spread.
   C. Iron democratized agriculture, industry, and warfare. By 900 or 800 B.C.
      1. peasants could afford iron axes and plowshares.
      2. artisans could afford iron tools.
      3. impoverished barbarians could now challenge the armies of the great states that had once depended on their monopoly of bronze weapons.

IV. The Bronze Age collapsed at the end of the second millennium. After several centuries of anarchy the world of the Near East and Mediterranean was transformed.
   A. One after the other, great military empires unified much of the Middle East.
      1. Assyrian Empire
      2. Neo-Babylonian Empire
      3. Persian Empire
   B. Partly as a result of these empires the zone of literate, urban culture expanded enormously between 1000 and 500 B.C.
      1. Through political unification the empires created travel and trade over huge areas.
      2. Because many different peoples needed to communicate with one another, a need arose for a *lingua franca*, a common language that would be understood over a wide area.
         a. This language was Aramaic, a Syrian language spoken around Damascus.
         b. It was spread by the Chaldeans who ruled in Babylon.
         c. Later it became the official language of the Persian Empire around the seventh century.
         d. It replaced Hebrew as the language of some of the Old Testament texts.
         e. Jesus and His disciples probably spoke Aramaic.
         f. Aramaic was written in an alphabet of twenty-two letters, representing the consonants. The alphabet served as a model for many other languages when they were first put in written form.
   C. The great empires were also responsible for bringing different peoples into contact with one another.
      1. The Assyrians and Persians were great road builders and made trade and travel possible throughout their empires.
      2. The Assyrians and Neo-Babylonians also transported whole communities across their empires.
      3. Many different peoples served in the imperial armies. In the sixth and fifth centuries B.C. the Persians employed:
         a. archers from Central Asia.
         b. Indian chariot troops.
         c. Syrian levies.
         d. Greek mercenaries.

V. The largest of these empires was established in the sixth century B.C. when Cyrus the Great of Persia allied himself with the Babylonians and overthrew the Medes.
   A. Eventually the Persian Empire spread from India to the Aegean Sea.
   B. The Persian Empire suffered many of the problems of overexpansion.
      1. Although the Persian kings did not claim to be divine, they ruled over many disparate peoples, some of whom were used to worshipping their rulers as gods.
      2. Only the subject peoples had to pay tribute.
      3. As conquerors the Medes and Persians only owed military service.
      4. Because there were not enough Modes and Persians to govern a huge empire, the kings were forced to arm subject peoples, whose loyalty was often doubtful.

VI. Culture and technology were also spread by peoples who lived just outside the great empires.
   A. After the ninth century B.C. the Phoenicians founded new cities around the Mediterranean.
      1. They founded Carthage in North Africa.
      2. From there, they spread out to colonize:
         a. western Sicily.
         b. Sardinia.
         c. the coast of Spain.
   B. After the eighth century B.C. the Greeks established colonies:
      1. around the Black Sea.
      2. in eastern Sicily.
      3. in southern Italy.
      4. at Marseilles.
   C. The Etruscans, who may have originated in Asia Minor and served in the armies of the great empires, established themselves as a ruling class in central Italy.
      1. Some of their subjects were eventually able to expel the Etruscans.
      2. The Romans were the most notable of the peoples who won their freedom from the Etruscans.

VII. The cities established by the Greeks and Phoenicians were not simply provincial garrisons. They were meant to provide new homes for colonists from the home country.
   A. The Phoenicians and Greeks brought a simplified system of writing, the alphabet.
      1. The Phoenician alphabet contained only twenty-two letters, representing the consonants.
      2. The Greeks adapted this alphabet and added letters to represent the vowels.
   B. These alphabetic scripts were much easier to learn than older systems of writing.
   C. Literacy was no longer the preserve of a specialized caste of priests and scribes. It was not uncommon to find people from other classes who were now literate, such as:
      1. merchants.
      2. engineers.
      3. medical men.
      4. soldiers.
   D. Literacy was still uncommon but it was much more widely spread.
   E. Further, the colonizing peoples spread the alphabet to people with whom they came in contact.
      1. The Etruscans probably learned from the Greek colonists in Italy.
      2. The Romans learned from the Etruscans and Greeks.
   F. Even though literacy was still confined to a relatively small number of people, it had a profound effect on the growth of culture.
      1. It facilitated communication.
      2. It preserved learning and allowed it to accumulate.

KEY TO THE IMAGES

Scenes of labor:
A number of reliefs show huge gangs of laborers at work on construction sites. Notice that instead of having animals pull heavy loads it was common to have great teams of men pulling sledges. None of the civilizations of the ancient world had developed harnesses that could yoke animals one behind the other. This deficiency meant animals could be used only for comparatively small loads, to which they could be harnessed three or four abreast. Even when there was an abundant supply of draft animals, the Mesopotamians still needed human labor.

Chariots:
The chariot was one of the great tools of war in the ancient world. Because the saddle had not yet been invented, horses could be most efficiently used in warfare when they were yoked to chariots. Armies now became more mobile than before and chariots could be used in a number of ways, such as for head-on attacks or assaults on the flanks and rear of an enemy army.

Seals:
Most Mesopotamian sites contain great numbers of cylinder seals, which were the size and shape of a spool of thread. Most documents were incised in soft clay and the seals were then pressed and rolled across the tablet to produce a signature.

FOCUS QUESTIONS

1. How did trade, culture, and technology affect one another in the wars of the great Mesopotamian empires?
2. How did the development of different sorts of metals affect warfare and agriculture?
3. How did the expanding economies of the Mesopotamian states affect the lives of their rural populations?
4. What are some of the reasons for the great spread of literacy between 1000 B.C. and 500 B.C.?
5. What were some of the inherent weaknesses of the great empires, particularly of the Persian Empire?
6. What peoples on the outskirts of the great empires were also involved in conquest or colonization?

The Western Tradition: Unit Two 25

ASSIGNMENTS & ACTIVITIES

IN CONTEXT

Themes and issues that set Unit Two in context with earlier and later units include the following:

- Professor Weber emphasizes the different geographical problems faced by Egyptians and Mesopotamians. In the programs that follow look for ways in which the geography of Greece promoted or hindered cooperation among Greek cities. The problem of border warfare, as discussed in Unit Two, also plagued the Hellenistic and Roman empires.

- The Mesopotamian empires created a continual mixing of peoples, religions, technologies, and ideas. In the units that follow look for ways in which this continual mixing of peoples affected the life of the Hellenistic and Roman empires. In what parts of these empires did change develop most rapidly? Which parts resisted change most strongly?

- Professor Weber emphasizes that literacy is a skill that transforms a social order. In later units we learn that the Greeks and Romans, as well as the Christian and Islamic religions, were responsible for the spread of literacy and learning throughout their spheres of influence. Look for ways in which the spread of culture goes hand in hand with political or religious domination.

- In his discussions of Egyptian and Mesopotamian societies Professor Weber discusses ways in which religion reveals a people's social, intellectual, and moral qualities. In later units look for ways in which traditional Greek religion reflected the life of the classical city-states. How did the developing religious life of the Hellenistic and Roman empires reflect the problems and achievements of these great states?

- As the Mesopotamian empires grew, so too did trade and the money economy. Look for corresponding developments in Egypt. In later units, note that the state of trade and economic life in general often reflects more general developments in the Hellenistic and Mesopotamian empires.

TEXTBOOK ASSIGNMENT

Read the following pages in your assigned textbook:

Text: *Western Civilizations*, Fifteenth Edition (Norton, 2005)
Read: Chapter 1, "The Origins of Western Civilizations," pp. 9-27, 31-47; Chapter 2, "Gods and Empires in the Ancient Near East, 1700–500 B.C.E.," pp. 74-95; and from Chapter 3, "The Greek Experiment," pp. 100-135.

Text: *The Western Experience*, Eighth Edition (McGraw-Hill, 2003)
Read: Chapter 1, "The First Civilization," pp. 4-13, and review pp. 23-35.

Text: *The Western Heritage*, Ninth Edition (Prentice Hall, 2007)
Read: Review from Chapter 1, "The Birth of Civilization," pp. 4-26.

Text: *The Western Heritage*, TLC, Fifth Edition (Prentice Hall, 2007)
Read: Review from Chapter 1, "The Birth of Civilization," pp. 4-31.

GLOSSARY

Akkadians: An ancient Mesopotamian people who reached the height of their power around 2400–2200 B.C.

Aramaic: A Syrian language originally spoken in the area around Damascus. Bureaucracies of the great empires made Aramaic a universal language throughout the ancient Middle East. A number of passages in the Old Testament were written in Aramaic and it is likely that Jesus and His first disciples spoke a dialect of the language.

Assyrians: A people of the ancient Middle East. At the height of their power, between 911 and 609 B.C., they ruled an empire more extensive than the region had ever seen before.

Etruscans: A people who may have originated in Asia Minor. Like the Phoenicians and Greeks, they moved west across the Mediterranean. For a time they dominated north-central Italy until their power was destroyed by the Romans.

Israel: The collective name of the twelve Hebrew tribes. Also the name of the monarchy ruled by Saul, David, and Solomon. After the death of Solomon the monarchy split into two separate kingdoms: Israel in the north and Judah in the south. Israel was conquered by the Assyrians in 722 B.C.

Judah: A Hebrew kingdom in southern Palestine founded after the death of King Solomon in 922 B.C. and conquered by the Babylonians in 586 B.C.

Lingua franca: A language used for communication among peoples who speak different native languages.

Mesopotamia: The region of the Middle East bounded by the Tigris and Euphrates Rivers.

Persia: The greatest empire in the Middle East between 550 B.C. and the conquests of Alexander the Great in 330 B.C.

Phoenicians: A people who built cities along the eastern coast of the Mediterranean during the first millennium B.C. They also established colonies along other parts of the Mediterranean coast, most notably at Carthage in North Africa.

Smelting: The process of melting or fusing ore to extract pure metal.

Sumerians: An ancient people who by 3000 B.C. had founded a civilization in what is now southern Iraq, on the plain between the Tigris and Euphrates rivers.

Ziggurat: A kind of temple, often consisting of many stories, arranged in terraces, each of which is smaller than the one below.

TIMELINE

Place each of the following events on the timeline. In some cases you may have to specify a roughly defined period of time rather than a precise date.

1. The conquest of Israel by the Assyrians
2. When did the first written records appear in Mesopotamia?
3. When did the Sumerians learn to smelt the following metals?
    a. copper   b. iron   c. bronze
4. The first appearance of coins
5. Beginning of Greek colonies around the Mediterranean basin
6. Establishment of the Persian Empire
7. Appearance of the first Sumerian cities
8. When did iron become cheap enough to be used for weapons and tools?
9. When does the first great empire attempt to unify Mesopotamia?
10. The date of the first Babylonian law code

|4,000 B.C.   1 B.C.|

MAP EXERCISE

Find the following locations on the map. You may need to do extensive cross-referencing in your textbook. If you do not find all these places on the maps associated with Unit Two, look at the maps in earlier or later units.

1. first Sumerian cities
2. Babylon
3. Tigris River
4. Kingdom of Israel
5. Ur
6. Nineveh
7. Judah
8. Syria
9. Homeland of Phoenicians
10. Persia

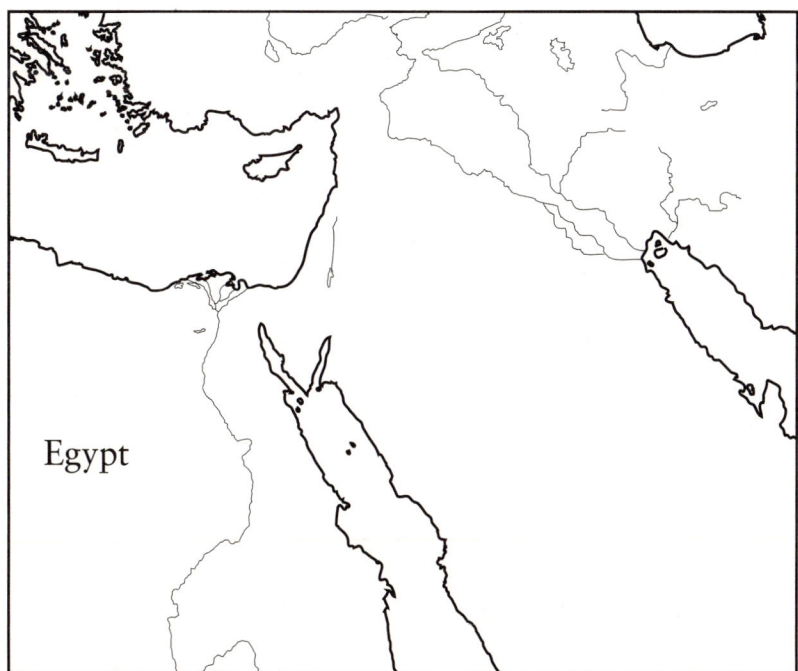

SELF-TEST

Part I of the self-test asks about important factual material. Part II is interpretive. The answers in Part II are keyed to Professor Weber's interpretations. If you disagree with an answer, be prepared to defend your own understanding of the material. Check your answers at the end of Unit Two.

Part I

1. Who proclaimed the great Babylonian law code in approximately 1800 B.C.?
   a. Cyrus the Great
   b. Nebuchadnezzar II
   c. Hammurabi
   d. Assurbanipal

2. Mesopotamians were responsible for the invention of all but one of the following:
   a. saddle.
   b. wheel.
   c. glass.
   d. socket ax.

3. All but one of the following peoples had established far-flung colonies by the sixth century B.C.:
   a. Phoenicians.
   b. Romans.
   c. Etruscans.
   d. Greeks.

4. Which of the following peoples was not responsible for developing or spreading an alphabetic script?
   a. Greeks
   b. Phoenicians
   c. Sumerians
   d. Jews

5. _____was a *lingua franca* throughout much of the Persian Empire. Some passages of the Old Testament are written in this language.

Part II

1. Which of the following metals in Professor Weber's words "democratized" agriculture, warfare, and industry?
   a. copper
   b. bronze
   c. iron
   d. steel

2. The founders of the first Mesopotamian civilization were
   a. the Persians.
   b. the Babylonians.
   c. the Sumerians.
   d. the Chaldeans.

The Western Tradition: Unit Two

3. Mark the false choice. The Assyrians and Persians
   a. built extensive roads throughout their empires.
   b. incorporated subject peoples on the periphery of their empires.
   c. used a *lingua franca* throughout most of their empires.
   d. tried to impose a uniform religion.

4. Outline the zone of literate, urban societies around the year 500 B.C. in one or two sentences.

5. Mark the false choice. The Nile, the Tigris, and the Euphrates all
   a. created bands of extremely fertile land.
   b. were the seats of highly competitive urban states.
   c. necessitated extensive waterworks.
   d. gave rise to civilizations dominated, at least for a time, by religious figures.

OPTIONAL ACTIVITIES

Although the following activities are not required for the course unless assigned by the instructor, students are encouraged to read them as sources of interesting material for further study.

The Bible
The Bible is one of the most important sources for the ancient history of the Middle East. The Old Testament contains hundreds of references, many of them quite lengthy, to societies studied in Unit Two. For a systematic study of the Old Testament you need a biblical concordance, which is an expanded index to the Bible.

This exercise, however, only asks you to look at two important books.

Daniel
The book of Daniel describes the conquest of the Neo-Babylonian Empire by the Persians. Write a short paper of 3–5 pages in which you discuss the following issues:
- How did the Jews of the Old Testament explain the political turmoil of this time?
- In what ways did they see God's will at work in history?

Because the book of Daniel is known to be unhistorical in some places, you should also read the articles on Daniel in a biblical commentary such as *Harpers Bible Dictionary*, edited by Paul J. Achtemeier.

Esther
The book of Esther describes the situation of the Jews under Persian domination. As well as examining the main points of the story, you should try to look behind the scenes of the book.

Write a short paper of 3–5 pages in which you discuss the following issues:
- The Jews were a subject people at this time but a number of Jews held important offices within the conquering empires. How can you explain this apparent contradiction?
- How does this paradox tie in with what Professor Weber says about the strengths and weaknesses of the great empires?

REVIEW QUESTIONS

The following questions are designed to help you think critically and to construct explanations from factual knowledge. Remember that whenever you learn new information you should ask yourself "so what?" In one sense or another these are all "so what?" questions.

Keep in mind that historians continually disagree on emphases, interpretations, and even on simple matters of fact. Many of the following questions emphasize Professor Weber's particular point of view and ask you to compare it to what you find in your textbook. When you find important disagreements, you should remember that historians are always struggling with each other; this struggle is one that you can enter yourself.

1. In several instances Professor Weber claims that Egypt was a relatively static society whereas the civilizations of Mesopotamia were much more fluid. First of all, do you agree with this comparison? Were the Egyptians really so static? Were the Mesopotamians really so innovative? Whatever your conclusion, how do you explain the differences between Egypt and Mesopotamia?

2. For approximately 2000 years writing was practiced only by small, exclusive castes of scribes. Around 1000 B.C., however, with the development of alphabetic scripts, writing became much easier and more widespread. What were some of the effects of the new literacy in law, religion, administration, and literature?

3. In discussing the use of new metals in warfare Professor Weber argues that the Mesopotamians created a technological arms race. Other peoples were forced to learn Mesopotamian techniques or be conquered themselves. Do your other sources support this claim? Was warfare really such a great instrument of social change?

4. By the end of this period money had developed as a medium of exchange. Why could the economies of the Middle East no longer rely on simple barter? How do the following issues relate to the development of money: the growth of great empires; the insecurity of conquest and civil war; the growth of long-distance trade; and overseas colonization?

5. Throughout this period different cultures and nations continually confronted and mixed with one another. What were some of the most important of these contacts between different peoples? How did the effects of conquest differ from those of colonization?

6. At first sight many of the Mesopotamian reliefs, especially those of the Assyrian Empire, seem to combine great skill in some respects with extreme awkwardness in others. For instance, in the lion-hunting scenes the animals are done with great clarity and power. The carvers portrayed motion beautifully. But in other scenes human figures seem stiff and awkward, and out of proportion with one another. How can you explain this disparity? Were artistic skills so unevenly developed? Were the carvers aiming at something different from what we would consider realistic depiction? What do you think these artists were trying to do?

FURTHER READING

Ancient Sources

The Epic of Gilgamesh (1972). One of the oldest pieces of literature from any culture. Most of the poems in the epic had been written down by 2500 B.C. and had probably been told as tales for centuries before then. The narrative contains an account of a great flood, similar in some respects to the story of Noah in the Old Testament. The hero Gilgamesh also descends to the underworld in an attempt to bring back a dead friend.

Pritchard, James B., Id. *Ancient Near Eastern Texts Relating to the Old Testament* (1969). The Bible is one of the most important sources for Near Eastern history. This collection of documents in translation systematically compares accounts in the Old Testament with those found in other sources from the area.

Modern Histories

Contenau, G. *Everyday Life in Babylonia and Assyria* (1954). Based on archeological sources and useful when used together with ancient texts. Well illustrated.

Frankfort, H. *The Art and Architecture of the Ancient Orient,* rev. ed. (1971). Especially important because art and architecture are such important sources for this period.

Frye, R. N. *The Heritage of Persia* (1963). Because it traces Persian history from the earliest times to the coming of Islam in the seventh century A.D., this book is a good source not only for this unit but for many later units.

Hallo, W. W. and Simpson, W. K. *The Ancient Near East: A History* (1971). Especially good on tracing the development and relationships of the different civilizations of the area. One of the best surveys.

Hermann, Siegfried. *A History of Israel in Old Testament Times* (1975). An iconoclastic survey.

Lloyd, Seton. *The Archeology of Mesopotamia* (1984). A good technical account.

Redman, Charles L. *The Rise of Civilization* (1978). Uses the methods of anthropology, archeology, and the natural sciences to trace the development of early urban civilizations. Especially useful for its comparative focus.

Saggs, H. W. F. *The Encounter with the Divine in Mesopotamia and Israel* (1982). Good comparative study.

ANSWER KEY

Timeline

1. 722 B.C.
2. 3000 B.C.
3. a. fourth millennium B.C.
   b. second millennium B.C.
   c. third millennium B.C.
4. seventh century B.C.
5. after the eighth century B.C.
6. sixth century B.C.
7. fourth millennium B.C.
8. ca. 900–800 B.C.
9. 2400 B.C.
10. 1800 B.C.

Self-Test

Part I
1. (c) Hammurabi
2. (a) the saddle
3. (b) the Romans
4. (c) the Sumerians
5. Aramaic

Part II
1. (c) iron
2. (c) the Sumerians.
3. (d) tried to impose a uniform religion.
4. It extended from Spain in the west to the Ganges River in the east and from southern Arabia to the Black Sea. Note that there were literate societies in India and China outside the cultural sphere of the civilizations studied in this unit.
5. (b) were the seats of highly competitive urban states.

Unit 3

Program 5: The Rise of Greek Civilization

Program 6: Greek Thought

LEARNING OBJECTIVES

After completing Unit Three students should understand the following issues:

- The contrast between the values of the Greek heroic age and those of the classical period. How do Professor Weber and your textbook explain the transition from one period to another?

- Some of the factors that united the Greeks, despite the many problems that kept them apart. Use your textbook to supplement Professor Weber's interpretation.

- The problems that led to destructive rivalries among Greek cities. Use your textbook to look at the ways in which the rivalries took different forms in different cities.

- The most important questions addressed by Greek thinkers.

- The relationship of Greek art to Greek history, politics, and society.

TV INSTRUCTION

OVERVIEW
PROGRAM 5: THE RISE OF GREEK CIVILIZATION

Greek civilization was built on competition. The warrior or athlete tried to win glory for himself and for his city. Classical Greece consisted of city-states, many of them quite small, often in competition or at war with one another. At the same time, however, a notion of a common Greek civilization was arising, a notion that was greatly strengthened when most of the Greek cities united to resist a series of invasions by Persia.

I. Around 1200 B.C. a series of wars and invasions shook the ancient world from Anatolia to Egypt.
    A. Much of what historians surmise about the period from 1200–800 B.C. comes from Homer's two epic poems:
        1. *The Iliad*, which describes the destruction of the city of Troy at the hands of a Greek army.
        2. *The Odyssey*, which describes the journey home from Troy, traveled by Odysseus, one of the Greek leaders.
    B. Homer's poems describe a society of warriors and petty chieftains, continually in competition for honor and riches. The poems also describe an ideal of heroic behavior that was to endure for thousands of years.
        1. The hero sails, hunts, and fights.
        2. He does not buy and sell.
        3. He exchanges gifts but does not produce himself.
        4. In addition to these privileges, however, he feels an obligation to achieve great deeds at the risk of his life if necessary.
    C. By the eighth century B.C. the Greeks had ritualized their quest for glory in a series of competitive games, the best known of which are the games established, according to tradition, in 776 B.C. at Olympia.
        1. The Greek word for the games was *agon*, the source of our word agony.
        2. The honor of winning was so great that athletes were ready to suffer any amount of agony to win. This ideal of heroic suffering would endure for ages to come among the
            a. early Christians.
            b. Protestants of the sixteenth century.
            c. nineteenth-century Victorians.
        3. The athletes did not compete for honor alone.
            a. Prizes were generally great.
            b. A winner might be clothed and fed for the rest of his life.
            c. He might be exempted from taxation.
    D. The Greeks expected their heroes to be brave but they were also supposed to be clever.
        1. Odysseus, for instance, was preeminently a clever man, a master of "deceit and artful tales."
        2. The goddess Athena praised him for his cleverness and said that she herself was "celebrated among all the gods for craft and speech."

II. For the most part the gods took human form and even shared human passions. According to Professor Weber this humanization of the gods was one of the most important features of Greek culture.
    A. During the classical period only the gods were worshipped.
        1. The Greek historian Xenophon explained that unlike other peoples the Greeks worshipped no man as master.

            2. Further, the gods were not worshipped with human sacrifice, which the Greeks considered unworthy of civilized people.
        B. In the fifth century B.C. the Greek philosopher Protagoras declared that man was "the measure of all things."

III. These ideals of glory and competitiveness were essential parts of political life in the Greek "polis" or city-state.
    A. The city-states spread from the Black Sea to the western Mediterranean. The greatest concentrations of Greek cities, however, were
        1. on the Greek mainland.
        2. on the Greek islands.
        3. in Ionia, on the western coast of Asia Minor.
            a. In the seventh and sixth centuries B.C. the cities of Ionia were especially prosperous.
            b. They were closest to the trade and culture of the Middle Eastern Empires.
    B. The scale of the polis was usually small
        1. partly for reasons of geography.
            a. Greece and Ionia are checkerboards of small valleys and plains separated by mountains.
            b. Both on the islands and on the mainland, water was often the best means of communication.
        2. The Greeks also believed that political life could flourish only in a fairly small city.
            a. Plato believed that the ideal city should have five thousand citizens. Because women, foreigners, and slaves were not citizens, such a city would have had a population of roughly twenty thousand.
            b. Aristotle believed that a polis of one hundred thousand would be ungovernable because it would be impossible for all the citizens to know one another by sight.
        3. In fact, during the fifth century B.C., only Athens and two other Greek cities had more than twenty thousand citizens.

IV. Although the Greek cities were always in competition with one another and often at war, they shared a common pride in being Hellenes, as they generally referred to themselves.
    A. Part of this sense of community was traditional. The Homeric myths claimed that Greeks were all descended from a common ancestor, a hero called Helen or Helenus.
    B. The story of the Trojan War was itself a powerful story of Greeks acting against a common enemy.
    C. Perhaps the greatest example of Greek unity, however, was the alliance of most Greek cities against the Persians.

V. Between the middle of the sixth century B.C. and the beginning of the fifth century, the Greeks withstood several attacks by the Persian Empire.
    A. The Greeks defeated the Persians:
        1. at Marathon in 490 B.C.
        2. at Salamis in 480 B.C.
        3. at Platea in 479 B.C.
    B. Marathon and Platea were victories for the Greek Hoplites, heavily armed infantry fighting in close formation. Hoplites would be the basis of many Greek victories over the next two hundred years.
    C. Even more, the Persian wars demonstrated that Greeks could unite on at least some occasions.

VI. Although Greek city-states were often at war with one another in the years after the victory over Persia, they shared an enormous cultural and political heritage.
    A. Although several dialects of Greek were spoken at this time, the language itself created a sense of cultural unity.
        1. The Greek version of the alphabet had spread literacy throughout the Greek world.
        2. When Greeks called someone a barbarian they meant that he could not speak Greek.

B. Greek art, although it had borrowed from many sources in the ancient world, had now achieved a distinct style of its own.
   1. The Greeks did not invent pottery but they became great masters of it.
      a. Objects of great beauty came into daily use.
      b. By the sixth century B.C. potters and other artists were signing their work, a practice that proclaimed the artist as an individual.
   2. The Greeks copied the freestanding statue from the Egyptians but they liberated and humanized its form.
   3. They invented the nude as an art form. Professor Weber argues that by celebrating the beauty of the body they were proclaiming their confidence in humanity.

VII. In the fifth and fourth centuries B.C. Greek art reached one of its peaks.
   A. The Persians had burned Athens in 480 B.C. but thirty years later Pericles, the leader of the city, decided to rebuild the Acropolis, the great hill around which the city was built.
      1. Perhaps the greatest of the new buildings was the Parthenon, the temple of Athena, the patron goddess of the city.
         a. The temple included a frieze by the sculptor Phidias.
         b. Phidias was considered one of the greatest artists of antiquity and was widely imitated in ancient times.
      2. The restraint, nobility, and harmony of Phidias's style made it a model for classical art.
   B. Praxiteles, one of the other great sculptors of antiquity, worked in the mid-fourth century B.C., one hundred years after Phidias.
      1. One of his greatest works is the Aphrodite of Cnossos.
      2. Praxiteles liberated some of the classical shapes, which had a tendency to stiffness, and gave them warmth.

VIII. By the end of the end of the sixth century B.C. most of the Greek city-states had cast off the rule of kings or princes and were experimenting with a variety of governments.
   A. A tyranny was a kind of constitutional dictatorship, not necessarily unpopular.
   B. Aristocracy was "rule of the best," or best-born.
   C. Oligarchy was rule of the few.
   D. Democracy was rule of the "demos," the people or crowd.
   E. Many city-states were ruled by a mixture of these forms:
      1. as in the Athens of Pericles in the mid-fifth century B.C.,
         a. all citizens had equal rights.
         b. men of distinction were more highly honored.
      2. These political categories were ideals rather than literal descriptions.
         a. An aristocracy, for instance, usually was not the rule of the best but rather the rule of the old, wealthy families.
         b. Nevertheless, in a city like Athens even a poor man like Demosthenes could become an important politician.

IX. Professor Weber argues that, because methods of government were apt to change in a city-state, the Greeks were keenly aware of the changes in all political life, and this sense of change created a sense of history.
   A. Other peoples, of course, possessed a historical sense but they understood history differently from the Greeks.
      1. The Egyptians, for instance, were less impressed by change than by long historical continuity.
      2. The Mesopotamians were sensitive to change but they tended to think in terms of catastrophes caused by supernatural powers.

The Western Tradition: Unit Three

    B. Thucydides, who lived in the fifth century B.C., was the greatest Greek historian.
       1. His experiences in the Peloponnesian War made him sensitive to change.
       2. But he did not look for supernatural causes. Instead:
          a. He looked for discernible human motives.
          b. He explained decisions, actions, and outcomes to objective factors such as culture and economics.

X. Although the Greeks fought one another bitterly in the years after the Persian wars, Professor Weber argues that they were developing a sense of having a common civilization.
    A. The wars taught them that it could make sense to fight not only for one's own home but also for the homes of others.
    B. A number of great men appeared who were important not only to their own cities but to all of Greece:
       1. Themistocles, the Athenian commander who defeated the Persians in 480 B.C. at the naval battle of Salamis.
       2. Aristides the Just, a contemporary of Themistocles, was famous for managing the finances of Athens and all of Greece.
       3. Miltiades, the hero of Marathon.
       4. Hecateus of Miletus, a historian who made a great picture of the world.
       5. Pythagoras, a philosopher and mathematician.
    C. These men were not simply bigger, stronger, richer, or better born than others. They possessed two virtues especially prized by the Greeks:
       1. *sophia*, or wisdom.
       2. *arete*, virtue or courage.
    D. According to Professor Weber some Greeks were beginning to believe that anyone could learn, that anyone could acquire these virtues, even a peasant.

KEY TO THE IMAGES

Athletics:
Professor Weber emphasizes the close connection in the Greek mind between glory in war and glory in athletics. As you would expect, athletes are an important theme in Greek art. As you look at the images, however, keep in mind that in some cases athletics were not so different from war. In some of the wrestling scenes the athletes are fighting almost without rules. In certain fights everything was permitted except biting and eye-gouging.

Humanization of the gods:
As you look at Greek statues you may sometimes find it difficult to tell the difference between a statue of a god and one of an athlete or a warrior. This is a concrete example of Professor Weber's claim that the Greeks believed the gods shared the same passions and forms of thought as human beings. As time passed, Greek statues became warmer, more human, and more fluid. Strangely enough, these changes did not apply only to statues of human beings; the new statues of the gods also changed in just these ways. In Program 5 pay special attention to the Aphrodite of Cnossos and to Praxiteles's statue of Hermes.

Images of warfare:
As you view various images of warfare, especially on Greek vases, pay special attention to the formations in which men are fighting. On the older vases, especially those that depict stories from legend or myth, the warriors are usually fighting individually or in a confused melee. In some of the later vases and carvings, however, you can see tightly-knit units of soldiers. These men are fighting in the phalanx formation that made the Greeks so successful during the Persian wars and afterward.

Vases:
Many of the strongest images in Programs come from vases. In some cases these works are among the finest in Greek art. Keep in mind, however, that the vases or urns were practical objects in constant use and the images would be seen in daily life not simply in temples or collections of the wealthy. In the Middle Ages many people who were illiterate could nevertheless study Bible stories in the stained-glass windows of great churches. Vases played a similar role in Greek antiquity. Many of the vases tell stories from mythology or from the *Iliad* and *Odyssey*. In Program 5, for instance, vases depict two of the adventures of Odysseus. In one scene he is blinding the Cyclops, whereas in another he has lashed himself to the mast of his ship as he sails past the sirens.

FOCUS QUESTIONS

1. What were some of the heroic values expressed in *The Iliad* and *The Odyssey*? What sort of society do these poems describe?
2. In what ways do the Greek gods share some of the characteristics of human beings? Why is this an important issue for the history of religion?
3. What was distinctive about the politics of the "polis," the Greek city-state?
4. What factors promoted unity among the Greek cities? What factors worked against it?
5. What special contributions did the Greeks make to art, culture, and science?
6. What are some of the special characteristics of Greek art as seen in Program 5?

OVERVIEW
PROGRAM 6: GREEK THOUGHT

Greek philosophy was not a kind of abstract game, cut off from the concerns of everyday life. On the contrary, Greek philosophy was deeply engaged with the political and social lives of cities. Program 6 traces the interplay between politics and philosophy during the one hundred and fifty years after the Persian wars.

I. At the end of the fifth century B.C. there appeared a group of philosophers called Sophists.
   A. For the most part they made their living as itinerant teachers and lecturers.
   B. Some of these "teachers of wisdom" simply taught clever arguments that were useful in:
      1. law courts.
      2. political debates.
   C. Some of the Sophists were considered subversive because they were often prepared to carry an argument to dangerous lengths.
      1. Thrasymachus, for instance, argued that governments make laws simply for their own advantage and that justice is simply the best interest of the stronger.
      2. Callicles argued that institutions and moral precepts had not been established by the gods but rather for the convenience of powerful men.
   D. Some of the Sophists, however, may in reality have been less subversive than they appear. Much of what we know about them comes from Plato who strongly disapproved of them.

II. Plato (427–347 B.C.) founded a school of philosophy, known as the Academy, which was the first real university.
   A. Plato was especially disturbed by those Sophists who claimed that man was the measure of all things and that there was no certain way of knowing whether the gods existed.
   B. Nevertheless, Professor Weber argues that Plato and his teacher Socrates were also subversive thinkers, simply because they taught men to think for themselves.

III. In a sense Socrates had been the greatest of all the sophists, although he did not want to be considered one and never taught for money.
 A. He was not an enemy of tradition as such, but his favorite pastime was to argue with his fellow Athenians and to force them to examine the real basis of their accepted ideas.
 B. Many Athenians were disturbed by his teachings, especially by his ideas about the gods.
  1. Greek mythology, such as in *The Iliad* and *The Odyssey*, often portrayed the gods as being very much like human beings:
   a. telling lies.
   b. committing adultery.
   c. even committing murder.
  2. Socrates argued that a sinful god was a contradiction in terms and that many of the Greek's most treasured legends and poems were obviously lies.
 C. He argued that the voice of conscience and critical reason was a better guide than unthinking belief.

IV. Socrates's attacks on traditional ways of thinking were especially unwelcome in the midst of the political disasters suffered by the Athenians at the end of the fifth century.
 A. By the middle of the fifth century Athens had become an empire, with client states circling the Aegean Sea.
  1. This expansion led to constant tension with other Greek states.
  2. Especially with the states of the Peloponnesus, led by Sparta.
  3. These tensions led to a series of wars, collectively known as the Peloponnesian War.
 B. The two major wars (431–421 B.C. and 414–404 B.C.) extended for nearly thirty years.
  1. In 422 B.C. Athens was attacked by Sparta and achieved a standoff.
  2. Instead of stopping at that point, however, the Athenians pursued a policy of aggressive expansion.
  3. In 413 B.C. Athens and her allies suffered a catastrophic defeat in Sicily.
  4. Finally, in 404 B.C. Athens surrendered unconditionally to Sparta and her city walls were torn down as a symbol of total defeat.

V. After such disasters Socrates's arguments were less popular than ever.
 A. In 399 B.C., after a close vote, he was found guilty of
  1. atheism.
  2. corrupting the young.
  3. Professor Weber argues that his real offense was asking uncomfortable questions in a time of crisis.
 B. Socrates could have gone into exile but he preferred to be executed by taking poison.
 C. Three hundred years later the Roman philosopher Cicero wrote that Socrates had brought philosophy down from the heavens. Professor Weber argues that in bringing philosophy down to earth Socrates also created a crisis in Greek religion.

VI. Professor Weber argues that this crisis resulted from the widespread questioning of civic religion.
 A. Each city-state had its own laws and its own patron gods.
 B. To be a good citizen a man had to
  1. obey the laws.
  2. worship his city's god.
 C. Religion and politics were not really separate from one another.
 D. Unfortunately, civic religion was badly equipped to answer the questions asked by Socrates or the sophists, such questions as:
  1. What is the true basis of justice and morality?
  2. What is the nature and fate of the soul?
  3. Is one's first duty to the civic law or to one's conscience?
  4. Which is more important, the individual or the state?

VII. Because none of these questions has an obvious answer, a bewildering variety of answers appeared.
   A. Some sophists argued that because the traditional gods and goddesses, such as Athena, are linked to individual cities, then the gods themselves must vary from city to city. Therefore:
      1. the gods were only relative.
      2. the laws were only relative.
   B. The philosopher Xenophanes argued that different peoples simply imagined the gods in their own image. If horses could draw, they would portray the gods as horses.
   C. Nor could any religious teacher explain why the good should suffer and the wicked prosper.
      1. According to Professor Weber, some myths, such as that of Oedipus, even suggested that the gods enjoyed testing and tormenting human beings.
      2. How could anyone worship such wicked gods?

VIII. Another set of bewildering questions arose as philosophers tried to explain the physical nature of the universe.
   A. The philosopher Anaximander had a conception of evolution that claimed that human beings were descended from fish.
   B. Xenophanes, who died in 475 B.C., had studied fossils and had some shrewd ideas about what they really were.
   C. In medicine Hippocrates attacked older medical practice as superstitious.
   D. In mathematics Thales and others learned much from the Babylonians and Egyptians and went on to make important discoveries of their own. They found that mathematics could:
      1. aid navigation.
      2. locate heavenly bodies.
      3. make sundials more accurate.
   E. Thales himself:
      1. predicted the eclipse of 585 B.C.
      2. accompanied King Croesus of Lydia as a military engineer.
      3. diverted a river.
   F. In the sixth century B.C. engineers at Samos used geometry to bore a hole to convey water one-third of a mile through a mountain.

IX. Although Greek mathematics had many practical applications, philosophers also hoped that mathematics would reveal the true nature of the universe.
   A. Everyday life seemed fleeting and changing but mathematics seemed to be a model of an eternal, unchanging order.
   B. Plato, in fact, suggested that the truths of geometry were really memories of the eternal truths.
   C. Plato argued further that the real world consisted of eternal forms, or ideas, and that our daily life was only a debased reflection or imitation of that world.

X. Greek physicists were also trying to understand the origin of the universe.
   A. Thales believed that water was the original element, from which all others were derived.
   B. Anaximander argued that the universe began with a spiritual force, or nous, whose action on matter produced movement and order.
   C. These ideas were similar to that of the "first principle" or "prime mover": a cosmic god who had created all things and maintained them in their order, and who was the ultimate source of truth, justice, beauty, and goodness.
   D. Such a god was abstract and hard to imagine, different from the older gods with their wars and love affairs.
   E. In this world the order of the heavenly bodies, in what seemed to be their timeless regularity, was the best model of this abstract notion of divinity.

XI. The old civic religions were suffering from political as well as philosophical weaknesses.
   A. The cities themselves were less important than they had once been.
      1. The city-states had been weakened during and after the Peloponnesian War.
      2. Many of them lost their independence as they were absorbed into larger states.
   B. As the cities lost political power, Professor Weber argues that civic religion lost its hold on the imagination of the elites.
   C. The Platonic notion of a perfect, abstract, remote god became more and more attractive to philosophers.
      1. In his dialogue *The Timaeus*, Plato suggested that the human soul was akin to the stars and would return to the stars after death.
   D. Professor Weber argues that in earlier times the ideal man had lived a socially active life.
      1. Once the cities lost their real independence, however, philosophers tended to remove themselves from the turmoil of daily politics.
      2. Thinkers now preferred to meditate on eternal things.

KEY TO THE IMAGES

Images of the gods:
Professor Weber shows that Greek art portrays gods and human beings in much the same ways. Although these resemblances would endure throughout the ancient world, by the time of Socrates the precise relationship between gods and people was troubling many philosophers. Socrates, for instance, objected that much art and literature portrayed the gods committing sins that were all too obviously human. The gods were shown lying, cheating, fornicating, and even committing murder. Socrates argued that these fables or works of art slandered the gods.

Motion in statuary:
Mesopotamian and Egyptian sculptors had usually not been very interested in depicting motion. In free-standing sculptures the figure was often portrayed sitting or standing stiffly upright. To indicate motion an upright statue might be shown with one foot advanced before another. In its earliest period Greek sculpture was similarly static. As the classical age developed form loosened up and became more varied. The great age of dynamic movement in sculpture would come somewhat later during the Hellenistic Age.

Portrait busts:
Programs 5 and 6 have shown a great number of portrait busts of Greek soldiers and statesmen. In this period most of the busts that survive are of men who were prominent in their cities, but a few centuries later, during the Hellenistic period, even private individuals might have portraits carved of themselves. Some of these portraits appear idealized, to create an image of the ideal soldier or statesman. In later periods, however, especially under the Romans, portrait busts became increasingly realistic, displaying a keen psychological insight. Roman portraits, in particular, were among their most original works of art.

FOCUS QUESTIONS

1. What were some of the different currents of early Greek thought?
2. What were some of Socrates's special contributions to philosophy?
3. How did war and civil disturbance weaken the Greek cities during the period covered by Program 6?
4. What were some of the Greek theories about the nature of the physical world?
5. What were some of the reasons for the decline of the city gods?

ASSIGNMENTS & ACTIVITIES

IN CONTEXT

Themes and issues that set Unit Three in context with earlier or later units include the following:

- Professor Weber emphasizes that in classical times the armies of the Greek cities were staffed in large part by their own citizens. Contrast these armies to those of the Egyptians and Mesopotamians. In the following units we learn that the Roman armies originally consisted of citizen-soldiers. Pay special attention to the changing composition of the army as the Roman Empire grew.

- As you watch the programs you will see that Greek statues, especially in earlier times, were heavily influenced by Egyptian art. Look for ways in which the Greeks introduced greater movement into their statuary. It has sometimes been claimed that the Romans simply copied Greek art and made few contributions of their own. As you view Programs 5 and 6 for Unit Three keep this claim in mind. In later units be prepared to determine if the Romans made important developments of their own.

- In earlier units Professor Weber argues that the Semites' gift for abstraction can be seen in the portrayal of their gods. How do the portrayals of gods in Greek art supplement Professor Weber's discussion of Greek social and intellectual life?

- Professor Weber argues that Greek civic religion was closely tied to the political life of the city-states. In the later units you learn how the once independent cities were later absorbed into great empires. Look for ways in which changes in religious life reflect changes in political life.

TEXTBOOK ASSIGNMENT

Read the following pages in your assigned textbook:

Text: *Western Civilizations*, Fifteenth Edition (Norton, 2005)
Read: Chapter 3, "The Greek Experiment," pp. 101-135; and Chapter 4, "The Expansion of Greece," pp. 136-163.

Text: *The Western Experience*, Eighth Edition (McGraw-Hill, 2003)
Read: Chapter 2, "The Forming of Greek Civilization," pp. 38-71; and Chapter 3, "Classical and Hellenistic Greece," pp. 74-101.

Text: *The Western Heritage*, Ninth Edition (Prentice Hall, 2007)
Read: Chapter 2, "The Rise of Greek Civilization," pp. 38-67; and Chapter 3, "Classical and Hellenistic Greece," pp. 68-107.

Text: *The Western Heritage*, TLC, Fifth Edition (Prentice Hall, 2007)
Read: Chapter 2, "The Rise of Greek Civilization," pp. 32-55; and Chapter 3, "Classical and Hellenistic Greece," pp. 58-85.

ISSUES FOR CLARIFICATION

Civic Religion

The Greeks worshipped a large number of gods and goddesses, but each polis, or city-state, had its own divine protector who was accorded special reverence in temples maintained by the city. Although other gods were also worshipped in the city, citizens usually felt most attached to their patron god or goddess. Religion and patriotism were difficult to tell apart.

The Crisis in Belief

Socrates himself was a pious man who scrupulously observed his local duties. He did not wish to undermine the old cults as such but many Athenians felt that his relentless questioning of all beliefs would eventually destroy reverence for the old gods. Greek religion at this time was a collection of rituals, legends, and traditions that had come down from much more ancient times. Although this religion could bring great strength to a city, it could do little to answer questions about such matters as the nature of goodness or the origins of the cosmos.

GLOSSARY

Academy: School of philosophy founded by Plato.

Acropolis: Hilltop citadel of Athens. When the city was rebuilt after the Persian wars, many of the greatest Greek buildings were erected here.

Anaximander: Greek thinker who died in 547 B.C. He argued that the human race had begun in the water and had evolved through several stages, of which the fish were one.

Arete: Greek word for virtue or courage. *Arete* and *sophia* were the prime qualities of a good man.

Aristocracy: Literally, "the rule of the best," in effect the rule of the best born. Athena: Greek goddess of wisdom. She was the patron goddess of Athens. In *The Odyssey* she is the special protector of Odysseus.

Callicles: Sophist who argued that law and morality were not established by the gods but were set up by men simply as a matter of convenience.

Democracy: Rule of the people or crowd. Even in a democracy, however, foreigners, women, and slaves had no political rights.

Homer: Poet traditionally considered to be the author of *The Iliad* and *The Odyssey*.

Hoplites: Heavily armed Greek infantrymen who fought in close formation. They were the key to Greek military successes for over two hundred years.

The Iliad: Homer's epic poem that describes the destruction of Troy, a city in western Asia Minor, by a coalition of Greeks.

The Odyssey: Homer's second epic poem, which describes the journey home of Odysseus, the cleverest of the Greek leaders in the Trojan War.

Oligarchy:	Rule of the few.
Parthenon:	Great temple to Athena built on the Acropolis in the middle of the fifth century B.C. The construction was directed by Phidias, one of the greatest sculptors of antiquity.
Pericles:	Leader of Athens during the fifth century B.C. He was famous for his speeches in praise of democratic government.
Phidias:	One of the greatest sculptors of antiquity, he directed construction of the Parthenon. Although much of his work has not survived, many copies of his work were made in antiquity.
Plato:	One of the greatest of the Greek philosophers (427–347 B.C.). His dialogues not only teach his doctrines but also demonstrate the forms of reasoning and discussion he wished to promote.
Polis:	Greek term for city-state.
Praxiteles:	Along with Phidias, he was one of the most widely admired sculptors of antiquity. Working a hundred years after Phidias, Praxiteles gave warmth and movement to some of the rather stiff classical forms.
Protagoras:	Greek philosopher of the fifth century B.C. who stated that "man is the measure of all things."
Socrates:	Teacher of Plato. Socrates left no writing of his own. Perhaps his greatest contribution to philosophy was his example as a relentless analyst of other men's arguments. He died in 399 B.C.
Sophia:	Greek word for wisdom. Along with *arete*, *sophia* was one of the prime characteristics of a good man.
Sophists:	Group of teachers and philosophers who appeared at the end of the fifth century B.C. Some of them were considerable thinkers; others seemed to concentrate on clever debating tricks.
Thales:	Greek astronomer, mathematician, and engineer.
Themistocles:	Athenian commander at the naval battle of Salamis in 480 B.C. He gave credit to all Greeks for the victory, not just to the Athenians.
Thrasymachus:	Sophist who, according to Plato, argued that justice is simply the best interest of the strongest.
Thucydides:	One of the greatest Greek historians and author of The Peloponnesian War. He is famous for demanding a careful examination of evidence and for refusing to explain events simply by invoking fate or the supernatural.
Tyranny:	Kind of constitutional dictatorship. Tyrants were not necessarily unjust or unpopular.
Xenophanes:	Greek thinker who died in 475 B.C. He noticed fossils and had a fairly accurate understanding of what they were.
Xenophon:	Greek historian of the fifth and fourth centuries B.C. who claimed that, unlike the Persians, the Greeks did not worship men, only gods.

TIMELINE

Place each of the following events or developments on the timeline. In some cases you may have to specify a roughly defined period of time rather than a precise date.

1. The year of Aristotle's death
2. The century during which Pericles lived in Athens
3. Approximate dates for the wars with Persia
4. The date of the Spartan attack on Athens
5. Approximate dates for the Greek Dark Ages
6. The date of the Athenian defeat in Sicily
7. The date of Athens's unconditional surrender to Sparta
8. The year in which the Persians burned Athens
9. The year of Socrates's death
10. Traditional date for the first Olympic games

|1,300 B.C.   1 B.C.|

MAP EXERCISE

Find the following locations on the map.

1. Athens
2. The Peloponessus
3. Troy
4. Aegean Sea
5. Ionia
6. Macedonia
7. Marathon
8. Sicily
9. Sparta
10. Salamis

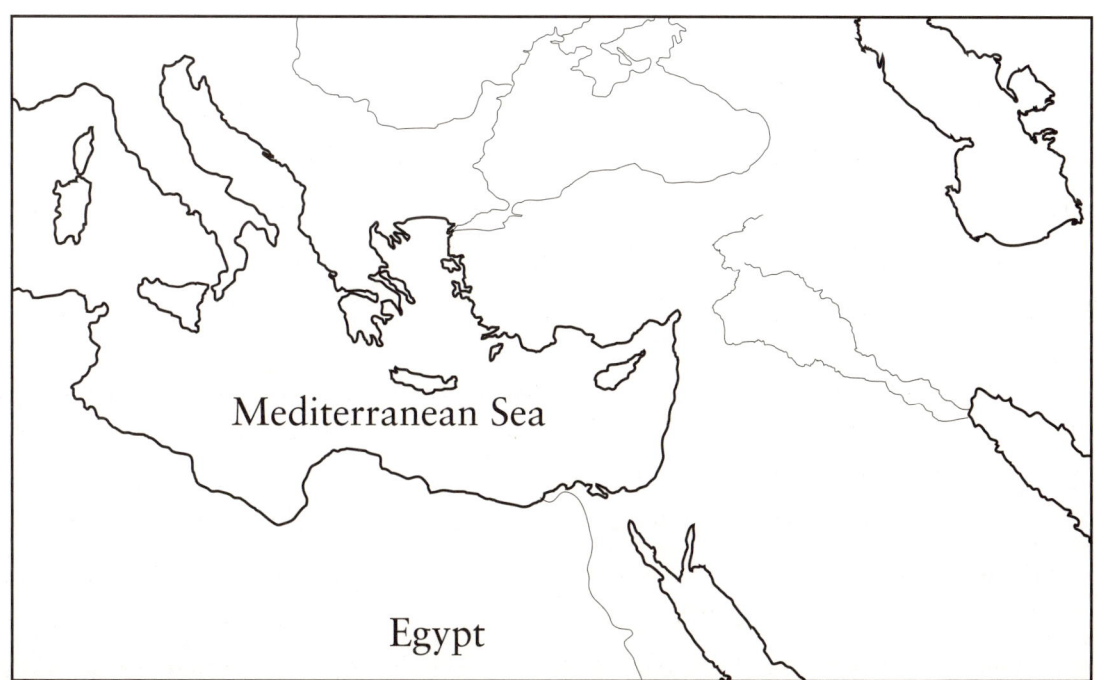

SELF-TEST

Part I of the self-test asks about important factual material. Part II is interpretive. The answers in Part II are keyed to Professor Weber's interpretations. If you disagree with an answer, be prepared to defend your own understanding of the material. Check your answers at the end of Unit Three.

Part I

1. *The Iliad* and _____, attributed to the Greek poet _____, are two important sources for the epic poems _____ of the Greek Dark Ages.

2. The goddess _____ was the patron goddess of Athens and the protector of the hero Odysseus.

3. Marathon, Salamis, and Platea were Greek victories in the wars against the empire of _____.

4. Name the Athenian commander at the naval battle of Salamis:
   a. Pericles.
   b. Miltiades.
   c. Themistocles.
   d. Thucydides.

5. The artistic director of the Parthenon was:
   a. Phidias.
   b. Praxiteles.
   c. Pythagoras.
   d. Aristides.

Part II

1. Although Socrates left no writings of his own, he is the most prominent figure in the dialogues of his disciple:
   a. Pythagoras.
   b. Anaxagoras.
   c. Plato.
   d. Aristotle.

2. By the last quarter of the fourth century B.C., _____ and his son Alexander had destroyed the independence of the Greek cities.

3. The _____ War ended with the total surrender of Athens in 404 B.C.

4. All but one of the following were Greek philosophers who tried to explain the origins of the physical world:
   a. Anaximander.
   b. Thales.
   c. Plato.
   d. Thucydides.

5. All but one of the following were important factors contributing to a sense of unity among the Greek cities:
   a. geography of Greece.
   b. Greek language.
   c. myth of their cooperation in the Trojan War.
   d. victory over the Persian Empire.

OPTIONAL ACTIVITIES

Although the following activities are not required for the course unless assigned by the instructor, students are encouraged to read them as sources of interesting material for further study.

Art History
Kenneth Clark's *The Nude* traces the representation of the human figure throughout western art. Because the book covers almost the precise stretch of time studied in this course, it ties together observations on art that appear throughout the programs.

For Unit Three, study the chapters on Egyptian and Greek nudes in Clark's text. Write a paper of 3–5 pages in which you discuss the following issues:

• What does Clark see as the most important developments made by the Greeks?
• Do the developments correspond to the historical trends discussed by Professor Weber?

REVIEW QUESTIONS

The following questions are designed to help you think critically and to construct explanations from factual knowledge. Remember that whenever you learn new information you should ask yourself "so what?" In one sense or another, these are all "so what?" questions.

Keep in mind that historians continually disagree on emphases, interpretations, and even on simple matters of fact. Many of the following questions emphasize Professor Weber's particular point of view and ask you to compare it to what you find in your textbook. When you find important disagreements, you should remember that historians are always struggling with each other; this struggle is one that you can enter yourself.

1. Professor Weber emphasizes the rationalism of the Greeks, their constantly questioning minds. In earlier programs he describes the Mesopotamians as innovators and inventors. What then makes the Greeks different from the Mesopotamians? What was new or special about Greek rationalism?

2. Compare your impressions of Greek art to examples of Egyptian and Mesopotamian art. How do these different civilizations portray their gods? How do they portray human beings? Professor Weber claims that Greek art, particularly its portrayal of nudes, reveals a new valuation of human beings. Do you agree or disagree? State your reasons.

3. In Program 6 Professor Weber claims that in the fourth century B.C. philosophers formulated a new conception of the ideal life. Earlier times had conceived of the wise man as one who was actively involved in the affairs of his city. As more and more cities lost their independence, however, philosophers came to believe that a wise man should try to escape the business of this world as much as possible; he should devote himself to contemplation of an ideal world. Because this is a controversial claim, look at the ways your textbook treats these issues. Do you make the connection between politics and philosophy in quite this way? Explain.

4. Although Athens and Sparta built powerful empires, no one state ruled the whole of Greece until the end of this period. Nevertheless, the Greeks thought of themselves as one people, living in one culture. What were some of the factors that created a single culture out of so many competing, often warring cities?
5. Competition in war, athletics, trade, and even philosophy was at the heart of Greek life. Why do you think the Greeks made competition for honor, glory, or riches such an important part of their civilization? What were some of the benefits of such a highly competitive life? What were some of the drawbacks?

FURTHER READING

Austin, M. and P. Vidal-Naquet. *The Economic and Social History of Ancient Greece* (1977).
Burkert, Walter. *Greek Religion* (1985). Very thorough, an excellent reference.
Finley, M. I. *The Ancient Greeks: An Introduction to Their Life and Thought* (1963). A brief but expert introduction.
Finley, M. I. *The World of Odysseus* (1978). A fascinating attempt to use the poems of Homer as sources for Greece in the Dark Ages. Particularly good on the tendencies of some scholars to read too much into their evidence.
Herodotus, *The Histories* (1954). A wonderful mixture of legend, myth, and close observation. Herodotus was also a traveler and describes much of the ancient world apart from Greece. There are long chapters on Egypt and Mesopotamia. Available in paperback.
Homer, *The Iliad. The Odyssey* These translations, by Robert Fitzgerald, are the best made.
Kagan, Donald. *Pericles of Athens and the Birth of Democracy* (1991).
Pollitt, J. J. *Art and Experience in Classical Greece* (1972). An excellent follow-up to Professor Weber's observations on the relationship of art and history. Good illustrations.
Renault, Mary. *The Bull from the Sea* (1962).
The Last of the Wine (1956). Excellent novels on ancient Greece and especially good on Greece in the time of legends.
The Praise Singer (1978). A good text about the poet Simonides.
Thucydides, *The Peloponnesian War* (1954). Thucydides was the father of modern history. An exact study of sources and motivations.

FILMS AVAILABLE ON VIDEO

Oedipus Rex (1957). Good version of Sophocles's tragedy, directed by Tyrone Guthrie.
The Trojan Women (1972). An antiwar film about the grief-stricken survivors of the Trojan War.

ANSWER KEY

Timeline

Part I
1. 322 B.C.
2. Fifth century B.C.
3. Middle of the sixth to the first part of the fifth century B.C.
4. 432 B.C.
5. 1200–800 B.C.

Part II
1. 413. B.C.
2. 404 BC.
3. 480 B.C.
4. 399 B.C.
5. 776 B.C.

Self-Test

Part I
1. *The Odyssey*, Homer
2. Athena
3. Persia.
4. (c) Themistocles.
5. (a) Phidias.

Part II
1. (c) Plato.
2. Philip of Macedon
3. Peloponnesian
4. (d) Thucydides.
5. (a) geography of Greece.

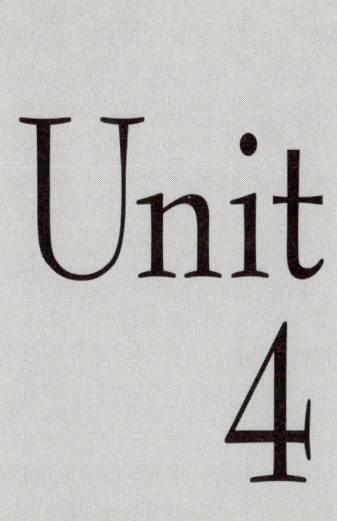

Unit 4

Program 7: Alexander the Great

Program 8: The Hellenistic Age

LEARNING OBJECTIVES

After completing Unit Four students should understand the following issues:

- The reasons why the various Greek states finally supported Alexander's campaigns in the east. Use your textbook to supplement Professor Weber's explanation of this issue. How did the support of the Greek states vary from one city to another?

- The motives that led Alexander and his successors to demand to be worshipped as gods in some parts of their realms.

- Some of the causes that made Hellenistic art different from classical art. Professor Weber emphasizes political and social causes. How does your textbook supplement his interpretation?

- The ways in which Greek culture affected or failed to affect conquered peoples.

- The principal features of the philosophical movements in the Hellenistic period.

- The similarities and differences among the various mystery religions.

TV INSTRUCTION

OVERVIEW
PROGRAM 7: ALEXANDER THE GREAT

After the conquests of Philip and Alexander of Macedon, political power in the Hellenistic world no longer lay with the city-states but with the empires of Alexander and his successors. Alexander had quadrupled the size of the world known to the Greeks, and the Hellenistic empires that followed him created a mixing of peoples and cultures, even greater than that of the great Middle Eastern empires.

I. Long before the conquests of Alexander, the Greeks discovered great opportunities for conquest in the east.
   A. In 401 B.C. a Persian prince raised a force of twelve thousand Greek mercenaries to fight his older brother for the throne.
      1. Although the Greeks defeated a huge Persian army, the prince was killed in the first major battle.
      2. Trapped in the middle of the Persian Empire, the mercenaries were forced to march fifteen hundred miles through hostile territory until they reached Byzantium.
   B. The expedition, as recounted in Xenophon's Anabasis, demonstrated to the world that Greek armies were much more powerful than those of the east.
      1. The phalanx formation, as used by the Hoplites, seemed invincible.
      2. Greek soldiers also reasoned that if the phalanx were supported by cavalry it would be able to overcome any army on earth.

II. Two generations after the expedition, the kingdom of Macedonia took advantage of Greek military power.
    A. The Macedonians were Greek themselves, although the rest of Greece often looked down on them.
       1. The country was still wild, controlled by various tribes and clans.
       2. A hereditary king, with religious and military powers, ruled over them in theory.
       3. The royal court and nobility had absorbed the culture of the rest of Greece but Macedonia remained a backwater until the mid-fourth century B.C.
    B. At that time King Philip tamed the local warlords.
       1. He subjected all free men to conscription.
       2. He made soldiers serve as royal troops under his own officers.
       3. He adopted the Greek phalanx but strengthened it with methods of his own.
          a. He combined it with light infantry.
          b. More importantly, he added heavy cavalry.
    C. Philip first conquered the rest of Greece. He was successful for several reasons.
       1. He had a superior army completely loyal and obedient to him.
       2. The Greek city-states were even more divided than usual:
          a. partly for traditional reasons.
          b. and partly because the Persians had been trying to keep them from uniting and invading Persia.

III. After Philip conquered Greece he decided to invade the Persian Empire.
     A. The Macedonians realized that they needed more than passive submission from the Greek cities. To win the active support of other Greeks, Philip and his son Alexander
        1. Appealed to myths and legends of conquest in the east, such as:
           a. the story of Hercules.
           b. the Iliad.

The Western Tradition: Unit Four 53

      2. They cherished pride in the Greek victories in the Persian War.
      3. They called for vengeance against the Persians, who still controlled Greek cities in Asia Minor.
      4. They promised that enormous wealth could be won in the east.
   B. The other Greeks had additional reasons for joining the Macedonians:
      1. A war of conquest in the east would defuse internal violence.
      2. A war in the east would open new areas for expansion and colonization.
         a. The power of Carthage prevented further expansion in the west.
         b. Greek colonies in Italy were meeting resistance from local forces.
      3. In fact the Greek colonial world had not expanded since the seventh and sixth centuries, even though expansion was vitally important because
         a. constant warfare had weakened the Greek economy.
         b. the economy could not support even a stagnant population.
   C. Even so, the Macedonians did not persuade all Greeks.
      1. Some Greeks hated the Macedonians even more than the Persians.
      2. Especially because the Persians were far away whereas the Macedonians were much closer to home.
   D. Nevertheless, the Macedonians successfully proclaimed themselves the champions of Hellenism.
      1. The Greek cities that did not support the Macedonians at least remained neutral.
      2. The Macedonians also neutralized the Greek mercenaries, many of whom worked for the Persians.
         a. Any Greek who fought for the Persians was declared a traitor.
         b. If captured, such Greeks would be massacred or sent to the mines as slaves.
      3. Thus, the Persians lost many of their best soldiers.

IV. Although King Philip was assassinated in 336 B.C., his son Alexander launched the invasion in 334 B.C.
   A. Although he was only twenty at the time, Alexander had long been preparing himself for the task.
      1. He was a pupil of the philosopher Aristotle.
      2. He had studied Xenophon's *Anabasis*.
      3. He modeled himself on the heroes of the *Iliad*.
   B. In the next ten years, before his death in Babylon in 323 B.C., Alexander quadrupled the world known to the Greeks.
      1. He overthrew the Persian Empire.
      2. He made conquests from Libya to Afghanistan.
      3. He created an empire that moved Greeks and Greek culture throughout the east.
   C. Although he was a military genius, Alexander was also a man of megalomaniac ambitions.
      1. He was capable of great brutality when thwarted.
      2. He insisted on being worshipped as a god.
         a. In the east such claims were readily accepted, especially where there was a tradition of worshipping rulers as gods.
         b. Many Greeks, however, felt it beneath their dignity to accord divine honors to a human being.
      3. He created a leadership cult that would be imitated for millennia to come by men such as:
         a. Julius Caesar.
         b. Napoleon.
   D. Alexander did everything on a grand scale.
      1. He tried to be the sort of philosopher-king described in Plato's dialogues.
      2. As a pupil of Aristotle, he took scientists on his expeditions.
      3. He burned the royal palace at Persepolis as revenge for the burning of Athens a century and a half before.
      4. He then conducted a mass marriage between Persian maidens and Greek nobles as part of his plan to create a unified empire.

V. Alexander's generals fought over the empire as soon as he died.
   A. By the second century B.C. a number of smaller empires had taken its place.
      1. They were a mixture of Greek and Asian customs and institutions.
      2. Because they were not wholly Greek, they are referred to as the Hellenistic Empire.
   B. Professor Weber finds a number of similarities between the Hellenistic era and our own times.
      1. Antirationalist trends, such as:
         a. preoccupation with the self.
         b. exotic fads such as astrology, magic, eroticism.
         c. depersonalization.
         d. a retreat from political involvement.
      2. A preoccupation with size that led to:
         a. rigid bureaucracies ruling great expanses of territory.
         b. detachment from local roots.
         c. a vague feeling that the whole world was one's home.
         d. wars of resistance to the great empires.

VI. The empires created a new kind of social and political life.
   A. Several empires followed similar patterns of development, such as the empires of the:
      1. Ptolemies in Egypt.
      2. Seleucids in Babylon.
   B. In structure these empires were:
      1. traditional monarchies.
      2. highly regulated.
      3. bureaucratic.
   C. Important elements of the empires were mostly Greek.
      1. Cities
      2. Royal courts
      3. Army
      4. Higher officials
   D. The Greek influence was widespread but superficial.
      1. In the countryside people retained their own traditions.
      2. Although many Greeks objected to the ruler's divine pretensions, in the countryside the king was often worshipped as a god quite readily.
   E. Thus, there was no cultural synthesis during this period. Many different elements were brought in contact with one another but they did not readily combine to form something new.

VII. Nevertheless, Greek learning and institutions spread over an enormous area.
   A. Greek cities were founded as far away as northern Afghanistan.
   B. The Hellenistic rulers encouraged trade and were great merchant-princes themselves.
      1. They built networks of roads, which were largely used by soldiers and administrators but which also aided in overland trade.
      2. Trade became increasingly important because the economy was becoming increasingly interdependent.
   C. There were many trade wars during this period, such as those between
      1. the Ptolemies of Egypt and
      2. the Seleucids of Asia
      3. as they fought for the ports of Syria.
   D. Trade expeditions were sent to:
      1. Africa.
      2. Arabia.
      3. India.

The Western Tradition: Unit Four   55

      E. These expeditions were seeking:
         1. elephants.
         2. incense.
         3. spices.
         4. slaves.

VIII. A new international world was developing.
    A. A Greek dialect called the koine was being used as a *lingua franca* from Gibraltar to the Caspian Sea.
    B. Intellectuals had contacts and could feel at home in cities throughout this region.
    C. Numerous professions had international organizations, such as of:
      1. actors.
      2. athletes.
    D. Some gods had temples throughout the Hellenistic world.

KEY TO THE IMAGES

Portrayals of Alexander the Great:
Professor Weber notes that Alexander demanded to be worshipped as a god. Although many Greeks resented or were skeptical about such demands, in many parts of his empire people were accustomed to worshipping their rulers with divine honors. Much of the art shown in Program 7 portrays Alexander the Great in various guises of divinity. He is shown with the horns of the god Pan and with the sun-god Helios.

Even works that do not explicitly identify him with a god often emphasize his miraculous or nearly miraculous deeds. One statue shows him taming his horse Bucephalus, a magnificent animal that only he could ride.

Alexander remained a popular subject for art long after his empire fell. The House of the Faun in the Roman city of Pompeii, which was enveloped by volcanic ash in the first century A.D., contains a magnificent painting of Alexander's victory at the battle of Issus.

Art and work:
In his lectures Professor Weber argues that the Greeks accorded relatively little respect to manual labor. Nevertheless, a certain amount of their art is devoted to scenes of work. Metalworking seems to have fascinated some artists. One black-figure vase shows workers at a shaft furnace, although it is not clear whether the metal was to be cast or forged. A red-figure vase shows workers at a forge, beating the metal in turn.

FOCUS QUESTIONS

1. What were some of the reasons that led the Greeks to consider making conquests in the east, even before the reign of Alexander the Great?
2. What were some of the military advantages the Greeks had over other peoples?
3. Why was Hellenism, a unified Greek culture, an important factor in the conquests of Alexander?
4. What were Alexander's greatest achievements during his ten years of conquest?
5. Why did Alexander and so many of his successors demand to be worshipped as gods?
6. What comparisons does Professor Weber make between the Hellenistic Age and our own times?
7. How far did Greek culture spread? How deep did it penetrate?

OVERVIEW
PROGRAM 8: THE HELLENISTIC AGE

From the last part of the fourth century onward, the Greek city-states were absorbed by the Hellenistic empires. These political changes affected every sphere of life, including art, religion, literature, and philosophy. Although some historians have considered the Hellenistic period as an age of decline, others have seen it as a time that opened up new possibilities.

I. Classical and Hellenistic art reflected the most profound characteristics of their societies.
   A. The artists of Classical Greece had created artistic forms that were timeless and ideal. These forms are:
      1. Calm.
      2. Fixed in their perfection.
   B. The art, especially the statues, of the Hellenistic period appears to move like human beings. It:
      1. Expresses human emotions.
      2. Strives for greater realism.
      3. Is often highly sensual.
   C. Hellenistic art lacks the moderation of the Classical period.
      1. It often shows off technical virtuosity, purely for its own sake, as in the statue of Laocoon and his sons being killed by a gigantic snake.
      2. It can be grotesque.
      3. Or sickly sweet.
   D. Nevertheless, Hellenistic art has virtues of its own. It is:
      1. natural.
      2. dramatic.
      3. dynamic.
   E. The Hellenistic era also had a keen sense of history.
      1. Works of art and literature often contain references to works of earlier periods.
      2. This was an age of museums, collections, and libraries.

II. The art of the Classical period centered on the polis; Hellenistic art was concerned with the individual.
   A. In architecture the design of private houses changed.
      1. A growing number people could afford comfort and privacy.
      2. They could not afford palaces.
      3. But they could appreciate beauty and good proportions.
   B. Painting also reflected the importance of private life.
      1. Lifelike portraits became common, which were not simply idealizations of heroes or statesmen.
      2. Landscapes and still-lifes appeared, which would have seemed trivial in earlier times when art was only concerned with the city and the gods.
   C. Alexandria was now the center of artistic and intellectual life. The city was famous for works of:
      1. Psychological investigation.
      2. Biography.
      3. Autobiography.
   D. The theater still produced the old Greek tragedies but also created a new sort of comedy and melodrama. Plays often centered about such matters as:
      1. thwarted lovers.
      2. wills and dowries.
      3. stolen letters.
   E. A taste developed for melodramatic recreations of everyday life.

III. Political and social life no longer centered on a native city with which people were intimately familiar.
   A. To play an active role in politics, a man had to enter the service of one of the great kings in
      1. Macedonia.
      2. Egypt.
      3. Syria.
   B. The kings ruled so many different peoples that their pretensions to be gods were probably necessary to hold their kingdoms together.
   C. The idea that a living man could claim to be a god violated the older Greek virtue of moderation.
      1. It violated the dignity of free men who were subject only to the laws of their city.
      2. The Greeks of the Classical period believed that such pretensions were sure to be punished by the gods.
   D. These ideals, however, were no longer practicable now that the cities had lost their independence.

IV. Philosophers asked how a free man could live in such a world.
   A. In the Classical period the answer to such a question had been easier: a free man was one who lived in accordance with the laws and gods of his city.
   B. Now that the cities had lost their independence the answers became various and complex.
   C. Whatever their disagreements, the new Greek philosophies all argued that freedom had to be found within the individual. A wise man could be free, even if he was a slave.
      1. The Cynics believed that freedom came from dropping out of society and abandoning all family and property.
      2. Epicurus (341–270 B.C.) taught that a wise man spent his life seeking pleasure and avoiding pain.
         a. These pleasures were not those of the body, however.
         b. They were the pleasures of a cultivated mind, at rest from the cares of the world.
   D. People who drop out of society have a necessarily limited effect on it. The Stoic philosopher Zeno (335–263 B.C.), however, taught a doctrine that had considerably greater social impact.
      1. The Stoics taught that freedom came from being in tune with the cosmic order.
      2. Like other philosophers, the Stoics had a harsh view of the dangers of life in this world.
         a. But because this world was a reflection of the cosmic order, it could not simply be ignored.
         b. The Stoics believed that once a wise man understood the cosmic order he could even improve the world around him.
   E. The various philosophies had different social consequences.
      1. The Cynics were anarchists.
      2. The Epicureans were passive contemplatives.
      3. The Stoics became conservative social activists.
   F. Stoicism affected political and religious life for centuries to come.
      1. The belief in a moral law of nature that governed all people was translated into Roman legal terms and became one of the justifications for large-scale government.
      2. The Stoic idea that the world, however imperfect, was god's creation, made an important contribution to Christianity.

V. The popular mystery religions were another side of Hellenistic beliefs.
   A. Because the religions were mystery religions, only a limited number of initiates were permitted to learn the secrets of the cults.
      1. Initiates might undergo rituals of purification.
      2. They might acquire sacred learning.
   B. The mystery religions had a variety of sources.
      1. Some of them were old earth religions:
         a. The Eleusinian cult.
         b. The Dionysiac cult.

2. Several came from Egypt:
   a. The cult of Serapis.
   b. The cult of Isis.
3. The cult of Mithras, one of the most widespread, came from Persia.
C. Whatever their origins, they shared a number of features:
   1. They were the business of the individual, not of the polis.
   2. They were not concerned with political responsibility.
   3. They created communities of worshipers who were quite separate from the state religion.
D. The mystery religions were based on an ideal of personal salvation.
   1. They often feature a redeemer figure.
   2. In some cults there was a fertility goddess who was the wife, sister, or mother of the redeemer.
E. The heavenly bodies were thought to influence or even govern life in this world.
   1. The planets were thought to occupy seven spheres surrounding the earth, each sphere with its own guiding spirit.
   2. Their ordered movement was thought to create an eternal harmony.
   3. This movement reflected the will of providence.
F. These heavenly bodies governed earthly life.
   1. The initiate of a mystery cult, however, received help from his redeemer.
   2. An initiate could move beyond the influence of the planets, even to ultimate union with god.
G. To receive this aid, the initiate:
   1. Went through sacred rituals.
   2. Learned the gnosis theou, the knowledge of god.
H. Many religions, not all of them mystery cults, worshipped redeemers:
   1. Attis or Adonis in Asia Minor.
   2. Osiris in Egypt.
   3. Dionysios in Greece.
   4. the Messiah expected by the Jews.

VI. Some of the cults influenced the early Christians, but whatever their teaching, the cults were exclusive.
   A. Unlike Christianity they never intended to spread their message to the entire world.
   B. Salvation was restricted to a limited band of initiates.

KEY TO THE IMAGES

Hellenistic art:
Hellenistic artists loved drama and motion. When you look at the art of the immediately preceding period, you notice that many figures are shown in poses that they could hold for all eternity.

Classical artists appeared to be more interested in timelessness than in the immediate moment. The great exceptions to this generalization are the statues of athletes and the painting on vases, which are often highly dramatic.

In the Hellenistic Age artists carried this love for drama even further. The statue of Laocoon and his sons enwrapped in great reptilian folds captures an instant of highly dramatic, or melodramatic, agony.

The feeling for drama and pathos was often combined with careful observation. The sculptor of "The Dying Gaul" must have observed Gauls quite carefully. The face conforms to the Gauls' ethnic features and the dying warrior is wearing a Gaulish torque around his neck.

Hellenistic religions:
Professor Weber argues that as the Greek city-states lost their independence the old civic cults lost prestige. Many people joined mystery religions or other cults, many of them imported from other cultures.

In Program 8 you see images of the gods Isis, Apis, and Mithras. These gods, along with many others, would be worshipped into Roman times.

Some of the representations of the gods affected religious art for centuries to come. In the mystery religions it was common to represent the redeemer as a good shepherd watching over his flock. After the birth of Christianity some of the first representations of Christ would be of just such a good shepherd.

FOCUS QUESTIONS

1. In what ways did Hellenistic art differ from the art of the Classical period?
2. How did the growth of great Hellenistic states affect the ways in which people thought about themselves and their societies?
3. What were the principal teachings of Cynicism, Stoicism, and Epicureanism?
4. What were the beliefs of the old earth religions such as the Eleusian, Orphic, or Dionysiac cults?
5. What were some of the common features of the cults of Isis, Serapis, and Mithras?
6. In which religions or philosophies was the idea of a redeemer prominent?

ASSIGNMENTS & ACTIVITIES

IN CONTEXT

Themes and issues that set Unit Four in context with earlier or later units include the following:

- Professor Weber argues that mystery religions grew out of the fears and anxieties of people living in the Hellenistic empires. In the following units trace the continuing popularity of mystery cults under the Roman Empire.

- Most mystery cults centered on the figure of a redeemer who would bring salvation in the afterlife. In later units, look for similarities and differences between these cults and early forms of Christianity.

- Alexander the Great conquered most of the territories that had once belonged to the great Middle Eastern empires. When his empire broke up, one important section, the one ruled by the descendants of his general Ptolemy, corresponded closely to the kingdom of ancient Egypt. The Seleucids ruled much of the area once controlled by the Mesopotamian kingdoms. Use your textbook to consider reasons why Alexander's empire should have broken up along these lines. In the following units look for the administrative problems that Romans faced as they tried to hold their own empire together.

- The various Hellenistic states preserved much of the art and literature of Classical Greece. In later units remember that the Romans gained much of their knowledge of the ancient world through Hellenistic intermediaries. How would these intermediaries influence Roman understanding of the Classical world?

- Professor Weber emphasizes the mixing of peoples and cultures in the Hellenistic world. Remember that in earlier lectures he claims that the Mesopotamian world owed much of its vitality and many of its innovations to a similar mixing of peoples. In later units consider this same issue as a source of strength or weakness in the Roman Empire.

TEXTBOOK ASSIGNMENT

Text: *Western Civilizations*, Fifteenth Edition (Norton, 2005)
Read: Chapter 4, "The Expansion of Greece," pp. 136-163.

Text: *The Western Experience*, Eighth Edition (McGraw-Hill, 2003)
Read: Review from Chapter 3, "Classical and Hellenistic Greece," pp. 74-101.

Text: *The Western Heritage*, Ninth Edition (Prentice Hall, 2007)
Read: Chapter 3, "Classical and Hellenistic Greece," pp. 68-107.

Text: *The Western Heritage*, TLC, Fifth Edition (Prentice Hall, 2007)
Read: Chapter 3, "Classical and Hellenistic Greece," pp. 58-85.

ISSUES FOR CLARIFICATION

Heavenly Bodies

Many Hellenistic religions—Professor Weber discusses Mithraism as one prominent example—believed that the heavenly bodies influenced or in some cases almost totally governed life in this world. Each of the planets possessed its own god or guiding spirit, the *Kosmokratores*, and the harmony of the heavens reflected the will of providence. Several important consequences followed from these beliefs. Astrologers, for instance, claimed that study of the heavens allowed them to make accurate predictions of the future. These beliefs could lead to profound fatalism. If the heavens governed all our actions, what was the use of trying to lead our own lives? In many religions the salvation figure such as Mithras was supposed to guide his follower through the heavens to the realm of freedom or union with god.

Mystery Religions

Professor Weber points out a number of similarities between mystery religions and early Christianity. In particular the idea of a savior who redeemed his followers can be found both in Christianity and in many mystery religions. Be careful to remember that mystery religions were precisely that: mysteries. Their doctrines and rites were kept secret and their followers never attempted to save or redeem great numbers of people. Most of these cults assumed that only a small number of people would achieve salvation. Christians, on the other hand, spread their teachings as widely as possible.

GLOSSARY

Alexander the Great: He succeeded his father as king of Macedonia in 336. In 334 he began a cam-
(356–323 B.C.) paign of conquest that ultimately reached India. Although his empire did not survive his death, he brought great areas of the world under Greek control.

Cynics: Hellenistic philosophers who advocated severing all social bonds and responsibilities as a way of avoiding the pain of the world. Diogenes, a contemporary of Alexander, was the best known Cynic.

Epicureanism: Named for Epicurus (341–270 B.C.), a doctrine that advocated the pursuit of pleasure as a way of escaping the troubles of the world. This pleasure, however, was calmness of spirit rather than sensual enjoyment.

Hoplites: Heavily armed infantrymen who fought in a close formation known as a phalanx.

Koine: Greek dialect that served as a *lingua franca* from Gibraltar to the Caspian Sea.

Kosmokratores:	Rulers or guiding spirits associated with various heavenly bodies. They were thought to have great influence over the fate of people in this world. In Mithraism various rites and formulas were used to allow a worshiper of Mithras to escape the power of the *Kosmotratores*.
Mithras:	Unconquered sun; central figure in one of the most widespread mystery religions.
Museion:	Great museum and research center planned by Alexander when he founded Alexandria.
Mystery religions:	Diverse collection of cults, most of which believed in a savior who would deliver his followers from the troubles of existence. In some cases salvation came from divine wisdom, the *gnosis theou* or knowledge of god; in others followers had to undergo a series of rites.
Philip of Macedonia:	King who subdued his warlords and created a powerful army with which he conquered most of Greece. He was assassinated in 336 B.C.
Ptolemies:	Descendants of one of Alexander's generals, the Ptolemies ruled Egypt after his empire broke up.
Seleucids:	Descendants of one of Alexander's generals, they ruled much of the Middle East after his empire broke up. Their capital was Babylon.
Stoicism:	Ancient philosophy founded by Zeno (335–263 B.C.). Although the picture of the world found in Stoicism is often as harsh as that of in Epicureanism or Cynicism, the Stoics did not advocate withdrawal from the world. Inner peace was to be found by living in harmony with the cosmos.
Xenophon:	Greek historian whose *Anabasis* tells the story of the Greek mercenaries who fought their way across Asia at the end of the fifth century B.C. The book was an inspiration to Alexander the Great.
Zeno: (335–263 B.C.)	Founder of Stoicism.

TIMELINE

Place each of the following events on the timeline. In some cases you may need to specify a roughly defined period of time rather than a precise date.

1. Lifetime of Epictetus
2. Death of Alexander the Great
3. Alexander crosses into Asia
4. Classical period of Greek art

5. Date of expedition described by Xenophon
6. Lifetime of Epicurus
7. Lifetime of Zeno
8. Assassination of Philip of Macedonia

800 B.C.	1 B.C.

MAP EXERCISE

Find the following locations on the map.

1. Gibraltar
2. Alexandria
3. Macedonia
4. The Hellespont
5. Afghanistan
6. Babylon
7. Byzantium
8. Carthage
9. Libya
10. Persepolis

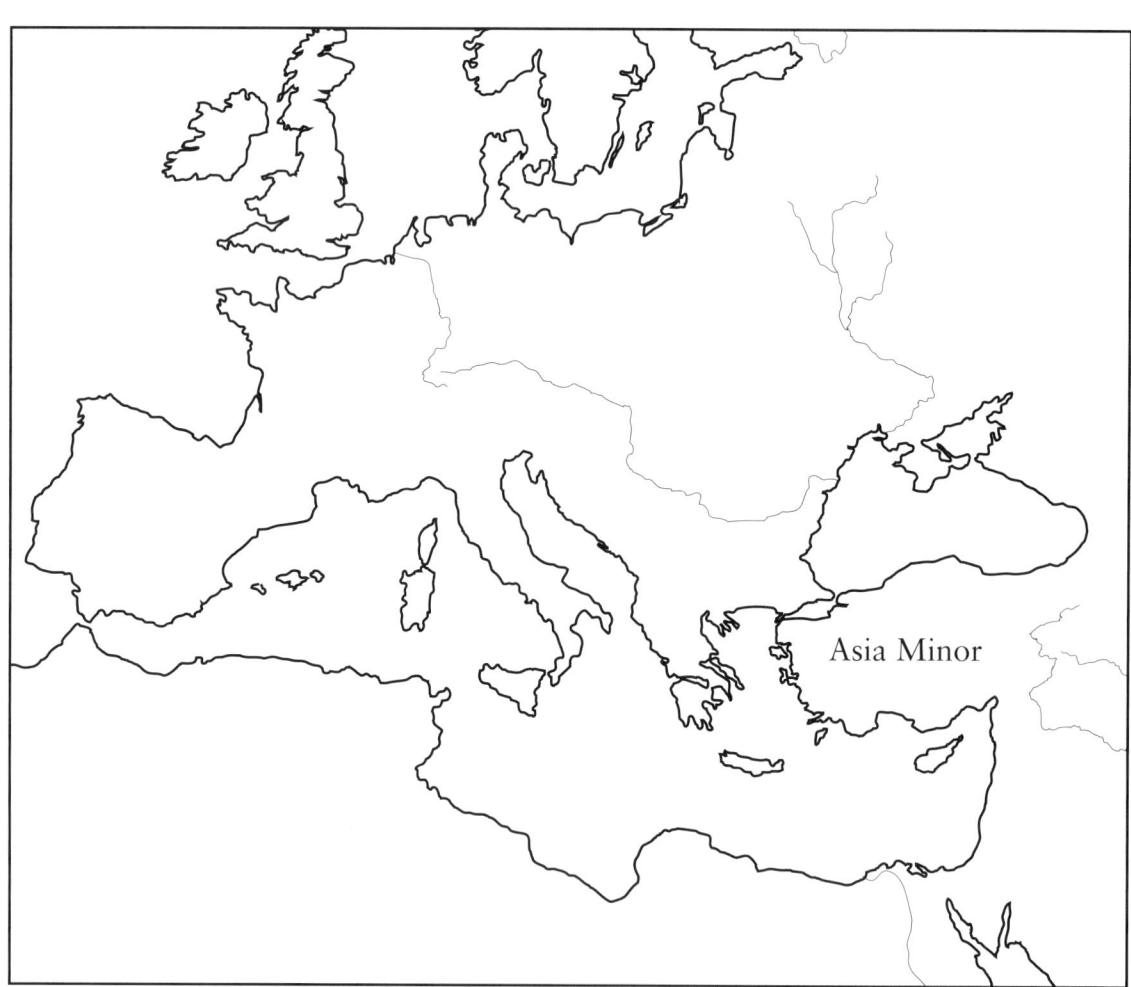

SELF-TEST

Part I of the self-test asks about important factual material. Part II is interpretive. The answers in Part II are keyed to Professor Weber's interpretations. If you disagree with an answer, be prepared to defend your own understanding of the material. Check your answers at the end of Unit Four.

Part I

1. Which of the following was an important mystery religion with similarities to religions of the Middle East?
   a. Mithraism
   b. Cynicism
   c. Epicureanism
   d. Stoicism

2. Which of the following states finally united Greece by conquest?
   a. Athens
   b. Sparta
   c. Thebes
   d. Macedonia

3. A Greek dialect called _____ became a *lingua franca* spoken from Gibraltar to the Caspian Sea. The New Testament is written in this language.

4. The phalanx, the military formation to which the Greeks owed so much of their success, consisted of:
   a. charioteers supported by bowmen.
   b. heavily armed infantrymen in close formation.
   c. mounted archers.
   d. cavalrymen who could land from ships.

5. In the year 334 B.C., which of the following began his conquests in the east?
   a. Themistocles
   b. Philip of Macedon
   c. Alexander the Great
   d. Miltiades

Part II

1. The center of literary life throughout the Hellenistic world was:
   a. Athens.
   b. Antioch.
   c. Alexandria.
   d. Thebes.

2. Which of the following was *not* an important motive for the Greek conquests in the east?
   a. The desire to recapture the wealth of Greek cities still held by the Persians.
   b. The need to expand and found colonies.
   c. A religious mission to destroy the false beliefs of the Persians.
   d. The precedents of myth and legend.

3. Which of the following gods or goddesses was important as an example of the center of a civic cult?
   a. Isis
   b. Serapis
   c. Athena
   d. Mithras

4. Which of the following was *not* worshipped as a redeemer or Messiah?
   a. Jesus Christ
   b. Attis
   c. Osiris
   d. Zeno

5. Mark the false choice. Although Macedonia was considered backward by most of the Greek world,
   a. Alexander always presented himself as the champion of Hellenism.
   b. Alexander was in touch with some of the most important Greek philosophy of the time.
   c. all Greek cities quickly supported Philip and Alexander.
   d. Macedonians made important contributions to Greek military tactics.

OPTIONAL ACTIVITIES

Although the following activity is not required for the course unless assigned by the instructor, students are encouraged to read it as a source of interesting material for further study.

Mystery Religions

Because the followers of mystery religions took great care to keep their rites and doctrines secret, much of what we know about them is speculative or based on the testimony of their enemies. Apuleius, however, who belonged to the cult of Isis, wrote a short novel usually translated as *The Golden Ass*. Although the book itself takes place in Roman rather than Hellenistic times, the novel is a good description of fears and superstitions that ran throughout the two periods.

At the beginning of *The Golden Ass* a witch transforms the hero, Apuleius, into an ass. Because he is forced to wander through the world in the form of an animal, the hero is able to see much that people ordinarily hide from each other. In the end he regains his human shape, thanks to the mercy of the goddess Isis.

Write a paper of 3–5 pages in which you discuss at least one of the following issues:

- What were the most important beliefs of this particular cult?

- How well does Professor Weber's discussion of mystery religions describe the cult of Isis? How would you supplement or modify his interpretation?

- *The Golden Ass* also makes references to a wide range of other religions, especially early Christianity. What can you learn about the great mixture of religions in Hellenistic and Roman times?

REVIEW QUESTIONS

The following questions are designed to help you think critically and to construct explanations from factual knowledge. Remember that whenever you learn new information you should ask yourself "so what"? In one sense or another these are all "so what?" questions. Keep in mind that historians continually disagree on emphases, interpretations, and even on simple matters of fact. Many of the following questions emphasize Professor Weber's particular point of view and ask you to compare it to what you find in your textbook. When you find important disagreements, you should remember that historians are always struggling with each other; this struggle is one that you can enter yourself.

1. What connections does Professor Weber make between art and politics? Describe some of the features of art under the independent city-states. How did Greeks in the Classical period conceive of the function of art? How did artistic standards change in the Hellenistic Age? What new functions did art assume?

2. It has been claimed that, although the Greeks won on the battlefield, Asia finally conquered in the throne room, for the kingdoms of Alexander and his successors resembled an oriental despotism much more than the traditional Greek city-state. State your reasons for agreeing or disagreeing. Also explain how in some ways the Greeks were victims of their own success.

3. The philosopher Alfred North Whitehead notes that when trying to understand the different philosophies of any period in the past, one should first look not at their differences but at the assumptions they all shared. Despite their divergence on other points, the Stoics, Cynics, and Epicureans agreed that the world was a place of suffering. What explanations can you find for deep pessimism on the part of three different philosophies? What, if any, were their solutions to the desperate problems of living in this world? State your reasons for agreeing or disagreeing with Professor Weber's interpretation of this issue.

4. The mystery religions also considered this world a place of suffering but their solutions were different from those of the philosophers. Explain. The redeemer figure found in many of the mystery cults shared some features with the Jewish Messiah and with Jesus Christ. In your interpretation how do the redeemers of the mystery cults resemble or differ from Christ and the Jewish Messiah? State your reasons for agreeing or disagreeing with the interpretations of Professor Weber and in your textbook.

5. Professor Weber claims that the mystery religions and the Hellenistic philosophies made people more self-conscious, more aware of themselves. In a sense people were developing a new kind of soul. What other reasons can you find for this increasing self-awareness, both in the individual and in the culture as a whole?

6. The Hellenistic Age saw a great mixing of cultures in art, politics, and religion. People were also quite aware that classical art and literature had been different from their own. How did these factors lead to a greater historical sense? How did this sense of history affect political and intellectual life?

FURTHER READINGS

Arrian. *Life of Alexander the Great* (1958). One of the best ancient lives of Alexander.

Engels, Donald W. *Alexander the Great and the Logistics of the Macedonian Army.* (1978). A study of Alexander's campaigns.

Ferguson, J. *The Heritage of Hellenism* (1973). A general study of the period.

Fox, J. R. Lane. *Alexander the Great* (1973). A biography that has especially good sections on Persia. Useful for making connections to earlier units of the course.

Grant, Michael. *From Alexander to Cleopatra: The Hellenistic World* (1982). A good basic introduction.

Green, Peter. *Alexander to Actium: The Historical Evolution of the Hellenistic Age* (1990). A many-faceted, sweeping account.

Havelock, C. M. *Hellenistic Art* (1971). A good source for evidence to test Professor Weber's ideas about the relationship of art to social and political life.

Renault, Mary. *Fire from Heaven* (1977). *The Persian Boy* (1972). Some of the best historical novels on the ancient world.

FILMS AVAILABLE ON VIDEO

Alexander the Great (1956). Hollywood epic with a good cast, including Richard Burton and Fredric March.

ANSWER KEY

Timeline

1. 120–60 B.C.
2. 323 B.C.
3. 334 B.C.
4. Fifth and sixth centuries B.C.
5. 401 B.C.
6. 341–270 B.C.
7. 335–263 B.C.
8. 336 B.C.

Self-Test

Part I

1. (a) Mithraism
2. (d) Macedonia
3. the Koine
4. (b) heavily armed infantrymen in close formation.
5. (c) Alexander the Great

Part II

1. (c) Alexandria.
2. (c) A religious mission to destroy the false beliefs of the Persians.
3. (c) Athena
4. (d) Zeno
5. (c) all Greek cities quickly supported Philip and Alexander.

Unit 5

Program 9: The Rise of Rome

Program 10: The Roman Empire

LEARNING OBJECTIVES

After completing Unit Five students should understand the following issues:

- The cultural and economic strengths of the early Roman republic.

- The ways in which Rome changed its policies toward conquered nations.

- The effects of overseas victories on the economy and politics of Rome. Use your textbook to supplement Professor Weber's discussion of imperialism under the republic.

- The failures and successes of the Roman state in adapting to new social conditions. Compare Professor Weber's interpretations to those in your textbook.

- The ways in which social forces shaped the Roman army. Does your textbook give as much weight to this issue as Professor Weber does? State your reasons for agreeing or disagreeing with each interpretation.

- The ways in which the army affected Roman politics.

- The principal differences between the Roman republic and the new state established by Augustus.

TV INSTRUCTION

OVERVIEW
PROGRAM 9: THE RISE OF ROME

The Roman army, which was the best disciplined in the ancient world, originally consisted of citizens fighting to defend their country. As Roman power expanded, however, the army came to consist of long-term soldiers who enlisted in hopes of winning booty. When the Roman Empire expanded beyond Italy, the Romans abandoned the liberal policy they adopted toward their conquests on the peninsula.

I. Up until the present day, ambitious rulers have invoked the tradition of Rome.
 A. In 800 A.D., Charlemagne was crowned "Roman Emperor," centuries after the original Roman Empire had fallen in the west.
 B. In 1804, Napoleon had himself crowned in the same tradition and called his heir "the King of Rome."
 C. The Russian title "Tsar" is a form of "Caesar" and the Russians referred to Moscow as "the Third Rome."
 D. In the twentieth century the Italian dictator Mussolini called his movement "fascism" after the "fasces" that were the symbols of power of Roman magistrates.

II. In the early days Rome was simply a modest city in a fortunate location.
 A. It lay on a fertile plain that could support a dense population.
 B. It also straddled the Tiber River, only fifteen miles from the sea, where boats could still come upriver.
 C. The main north-south road crossed the river here.

III. The virtues admired by the early Romans called for discipline and self-discipline.
 A. *Pietas* was respect for established authority and tradition.
 B. *Fides* was faithfulness to responsibilities.
 C. *Religio* was the collective name for the common beliefs that bind people together.
 D. *Graritas* was sober seriousness.
 E. *Virtus*, or virtue, meant manliness or courage.
 F. This was a sober, serious society.
  1. The word *luxus*, from which luxury derives, meant the weeds that choke a crop.
  2. Anyone who abandoned himself to luxury and idleness was a threat to society.

IV. Early Roman society was strictly patriarchal.
 A. A father had enormous control over his family, in some cases even the power of life and death.
 B. The status of women was low.

V. The Romans were careful to divide political power, to prevent any one man from becoming too powerful.
 A. Each year, the patricians, who monopolized most public office, chose two consuls to be the chief executive officers.
 B. The consuls enjoyed broad powers but because there were two of them neither could monopolize power.
 C. And because their terms were short it was difficult to build a broad base of supporters or conspirators.
 D. Further, after leaving office the consuls became members of the senate, the main legislative body. Because senators held office for life, most consuls avoided offending their future colleagues needlessly.

VI. The army reflected some of the deepest aspects of Roman social structure.
   A. Every soldier had to own a farm or some other source of income to pay for:
      1. body armor.
      2. a sword.
      3. a spear.
      4. a pack.
   B. Therefore, without sufficient income the landless poor did not
      1. serve in the army.
      2. pay taxes.
      3. have a say in the government of the city.
   C. For two centuries, the patricians, who held most public offices, struggled for power against the claims of the more prosperous commoners. Military service gave the commoners their greatest bargaining power.
   D. One of the most powerful attractions for serving in the army was the possibility of sharing the spoils of war.

VII. In 295 B.C. war with the Samnites, a people who lived in the mountains southeast of Rome, began a series of changes that transformed the Roman army.
   A. At the beginning of the war the Romans fought in phalanxes, much like those used by Greek armies.
      1. These formations were solid.
      2. But hard to maneuver.
   B. The Romans switched to smaller units, called *maniples*, consisting of 120 men.
      1. Three maniples made a cohort of 360 men.
      2. Ten cohorts made a legion of 3,600 men.
   C. The smaller units operated in a checkerboard pattern that was much more flexible. But
      1. the new tactics made greater demands on the individual soldier.
      2. the new maneuvers required strict training and discipline.
      3. the Roman infantry was nearly always better trained than its enemies.

VIII. By the middle of the third century B.C. Rome controlled nearly all of Italy
   A. At this time the Romans made one of their wisest political decisions.
      1. Instead of slaughtering or enslaving their defeated enemies, the Romans made them allies.
         a. The Romans confiscated some lands for Roman colonists.
         b. The Romans granted their conquests various sets of terms so that the vanquished would find it difficult to act together.
      2. In general, however, the Romans granted quite generous terms.
         a. Rome controlled foreign policy,
         b. and demanded military aid in war,
         c. but in other respects, the conquered cities were allowed to control most of their own affairs.
   B. Eventually, the Romans granted citizenship throughout Italy.
   C. Public works built by the Romans helped tie the continent together.
      1. First-class roads
      2. Sewers
      3. Aqueducts
      4. Lighthouses

IX. By about 270 B.C. the Romans had defeated their last enemies in Italy, the Greek cities of the south, but were now drawn into conflict with another great power, Carthage.
   A. The First Punic (Carthaginian) War began in 264 B.C.
      1. The Carthaginians had become involved in a local war in Sicily.
      2. The Romans intervened to protect the cities of southern Italy.
   B. Because Carthage was a naval power, the Romans had to build a fleet.

C. When the war ended twenty-four years later, Rome had made Sicily a province. Soon it added:
  1. Corsica.
  2. Sardinia.
  3. parts of Spain.

X. Now that the Romans were a successful naval power, they were drawn into conflicts throughout the Mediterranean world. After defeating Carthage, Rome conquered:
  A. the Macedonians.
  B. the Greeks.
  C. the Asian heirs of Alexander the Great.
  D. the Egyptians.

XI. In the Second Punic War (218–201 B.C.), however, Rome came close to defeat.
  A. Because Rome controlled the sea, the Carthaginian general Hannibal went overland:
    1. beginning in Spain,
    2. he crossed the Pyrenees
    3. and the Alps
    4. into Italy.
  B. In 216 B.C., after inflicting a series of crushing defeats on the Romans, Hannibal camped under the walls of Rome.
  C. At this point Hannibal was close to victory.
    1. He called on the other cities of Italy to rise against Rome.
      a. The cities, however, were mindful of the generous treatment they had received from Rome.
      b. They refused to turn against Rome.
  D. The Romans still controlled the seas.
    1. They cut off Hannibal's supplies.
    2. The Romans landed troops
      a. in Spain
      b. and then near Carthage itself.
  E. Rome was saved as Hannibal was forced to return home to defend his own city.
  F. In 149 B.C. the Carthaginians went to war again. They were completely defeated and the city was destroyed in 146 B.C.

XII. This series of wars transformed Roman society.
  A. The army had once consisted of annual levies of soldiers. Now soldiers:
    1. signed up for long terms of duty.
    2. were paid by the state or by successful generals who shared their booty.
  B. Rome had once fought to defend itself against the Carthaginians and other enemies.
  C. War was now becoming a quest for loot.
  D. Conquest enriched
    1. victorious soldiers.
    2. patricians who went out to govern Rome's new acquisitions.
  E. Rome abandoned its generous policies toward conquered peoples. Romans looked on their new conquests as a source of wealth.

XIII. Roman culture changed as well.
  A. Professor Weber argues that as Romans came in contact with more sophisticated peoples, the old virtues of austerity and self-discipline began to diminish.
  B. In the second and first centuries B.C. wealthy Romans began to show off their wealth in various ways, including:
    1. expensive homes.
    2. enormous banquets.

The Western Tradition: Unit Five

XIV. Lavish display became an element of politics.
  A. Politicians such as Julius Caesar paid for lavish public games.
  B. After the suppression of a slave rebellion in the first century B.C., six thousand rebels were crucified along the Appian Way.

XV. Art became a form of propaganda to display Rome's power.
  A. Honorific statues
  B. Portraits
  C. Historical paintings
  D. Public architecture was a proclamation of greatness.
    1. Temples
    2. Palaces
    3. Triumphal arches
    4. Columns

KEY TO THE IMAGES

Villas:
In the countryside prosperous Romans lived in villas. The villas ranged from the seats of country gentlemen to great palaces that dominated the life of the countryside for miles around.

The architecture of villas is a good clue to the general security of Roman life. In times of relative tranquillity villas were often sprawling collections of buildings that covered a good deal of ground. As times became dangerous, however, such as at the end of the Western Empire, villas became compact so they could be more easily defended.

Public works:
The Romans were probably the greatest civil engineers of the ancient world. Program 9 and many of those that follow have many images of Roman aqueducts, roads, bridges, and sewers, some of which continued to be used long after the fall of Rome.

The projects were more than luxuries; they were vital to the Roman Empire. Without the aqueducts and sewers, the Romans could not have maintained their great cities. Without the roads and bridges, the Roman army could never have mobilized to defend such a sprawling empire.

Portrait busts:
In Program 9 and in the following programs on Rome (Programs 10, 13–14), many portrait busts of prominent Romans appear. Roman artists are sometimes accused of copying Greek models, an accusation that is false in the area of portraiture.

Although the busts of relatively modest people survive, keep in mind that most of the men and women you see were among the most important people of their times. Even so, Roman artists often presented them in quite unidealized busts. Scipio Africanus was the great Roman hero of the Punic Wars, but his bust makes him look like a nervous middle-aged man.

FOCUS QUESTIONS

1. What were the geographical advantages of early Rome?
2. What were the virtues most admired in early Roman society?
3. What was Rome's policy toward its conquests in Italy?
4. What were some of the reasons that Rome finally was able to triumph over the Carthaginians?
5. How did Rome's conquests affect the Roman army?
6. How did the conquests affect society as a whole?

OVERVIEW
PROGRAM 10: THE ROMAN EMPIRE

By the middle of the second century B.C. Rome suffered the consequences of its own victories. Cheap grain and produce, imported from newly conquered provinces, destroyed many of the small farmers who had once formed the core of the Roman infantry. At the same time, the Roman generals became increasingly independent and the country suffered generations of civil war as various factions of the army fought for power. The wars came to an end only after Augustus defeated his rivals and laid the foundations for the long Roman peace.

I. Rome's victories ironically destroyed the small farmers who had once formed the backbone of the Roman infantry.
   A. Cheap grain from conquered provinces sent prices so low that many small farmers could no longer survive.
   B. In many cases their land was actually better suited to other uses, such as:
      1. cattle.
      2. grapes.
      3. olives.
   C. Most crops, however, could be grown most cheaply on large spreads worked by slaves.
      1. Slaves were especially cheap after the long run of Roman victories.
      2. Many family farms went out of business and became parts of large estates.
   D. Agriculture could be quite profitable, but only for large estate owners with a good deal of capital.
   E. Many small farmers lost their property and migrated to the city, where they were manipulated by politicians.

II. By the late second century B.C. Rome was torn between poor citizens, who had often lost their property, and the rich, who were becoming even richer from the booty of Rome's conquests.
   A. These problems were aggravated because the senate did little to help the poor.
      1. The senate was a glorified municipal council not well suited to govern an empire.
         a. It could deal with foreign affairs by dispatching an army,
         b. but it had no grasp of economic problems.
   B. Further, most senators were rich men with little concern for the problems of the poor.
   C. In 133 B.C., however, Tiberius Gracchus, the grandson of the general who defeated Hannibal, tried to help the poor by:
      1. limiting the size of large estates.
      2. providing land for the landless.
   D. Gracchus was murdered by a group of conservative senators.
   E. Gracchus's brother, Caius, who tried to carry on his work, was also murdered.

III. Nevertheless, Tiberius and Caius Gracchus had permanently changed the shape of Roman politics.
    A. For the first time a popular party had grown to challenge the power of the senate.
        1. However, the popular party did not create democracy.
        2. On the contrary, it provided opportunities for ambitious politicians to manipulate class hatred.
            a. Some claimed to defend the people.
            b. Others fought for the rich.
    B. The most powerful of these politicians were the army commanders who used their troops to further their ambitions:
        1. Marius.
        2. Sulla.
        3. Pompey.
        4. Julius Caesar.
    C. Army commanders became enormously powerful after 107 B.C. when Marius dropped the property requirement for military service.
        1. The landless poor enlisted to be equipped and paid by the state.
        2. Because army pay was low, even for the landless, soldiers hoped to make money from the spoils of war.
        3. Because booty was controlled by the victorious general, soldiers became more loyal to their commanders than to the state.
    D. The first century B.C. was a time of civil war as army commanders fought to control the state.
        1. With their armies behind them they could easily force the senate to grant them extraordinary powers,
        2. Until they were supplanted by their rivals.

IV. By the middle of the first century B.C. the Roman republic controlled a vast expanse of territory, but expansion brought the Romans in contact with powerful enemies along the borders.
    A. The Parthian Empire that had replaced the Persians in the east
    B. The Germanic peoples in the north
    C. The Arabs, raiding into Asia
    D. The Numidians in Africa

V. Nor had the Romans devised an efficient system of provincial administration.
    A. Provincial governors, appointed in Rome, changed each year.
    B. Because a permanent civil service did not exist, the governor's performance depended on his personal character.
    C. Taxes were collected inefficiently.
        1. Joint-stock companies paid the government a lump sum for the right to collect taxes in a given area.
        2. To increase their profit the companies taxed the area as heavily as possible.
        3. However, relatively little of the money went to Rome.

VI. Many people saw the system of government in Rome and the provinces needed to be changed.
    A. But change was unlikely to come from the conservative senate, which had already lost much of its power.
    B. Most of the radical reformers were actually demagogues, more interested in increasing their power than in reforming the state.

VII. By 46 B.C. Julius Caesar had defeated his rivals.
    A. The senate loaded him with honors:
        1. he was voted consul and first dictator for life.
        2. he took the title *imperator*.
        3. the month of his birth was renamed "July."
    B. In 44 B.C. Caesar was assassinated by men who did not want the republic to die.

VIII. Civil war broke out again, until 31 B.C., when Caesar's grandnephew Octavian defeated the last of his serious enemies.
   A. At the battle of Actium in 31 B.C. Octavian defeated Marc Antony, who had allied himself with Cleopatra, the last Ptolemaic queen of Egypt.
   B. Within a few years Octavian's powers had become even greater than those of Julius Caesar.
      1. He assumed the semireligious title of Emperor Augustus.
      2. He too had a month named in his honor: August.

IX. During the forty years of his reign, Augustus laid the foundations of the *Pax Romana*, or Roman Peace.
   A. He created an imperial civil service,
      1. which was nominally under senate scrutiny,
      2. but which was actually answerable to him.
   B. These administrators were drawn from the general body of citizens and not only from the aristocracy.
      1. Opportunities for social advancement appeared.
      2. Some administrators were even freedmen or ex-slaves.
   C. Augustus also tried to reawaken the old Roman virtues:
      1. through the writing of historians, such as Livy.
      2. through works of literature, such as Virgil's *Aeneid*.
   D. Among his most important measures was the reform of the army.
      1. Generals now depended on the emperor and not on the senate or the people.
      2. Generals were no longer entrepreneurs on the lookout for booty and power.
      3. As employees of the state, generals could be transferred from unit to unit as in most modern armies.
   E. With the exception of the Praetorian Guard (the emperor's household troops), most of the army was stationed along the frontier.

X. According to Professor Weber, the old Roman aggressiveness was disappearing, in part because
   A. the Roman world was sick of fighting.
   B. there were few enemies along the Roman borders who were wealthy enough to be worth conquering.
   C. from now on the greatest threat came from poor, hungry barbarians trying to raid the riches of the empire.
   D. army camps became outposts of Roman civilization. Many European cities were originally Roman outposts:
      1. Vienna.
      2. Budapest.
      3. York.
      4. Lisbon.
      5. Bordeaux.
      6. Cologne.

XI. These centuries of security, protected by the Roman army, allowed Greco-Roman culture to take such deep root that not even the barbarian invasions were able to destroy it.
   A. Education in Latin became common throughout the Roman Empire.
      1. It was a key to social advancement.
      2. It instilled Roman values.
   B. Roman art and architecture created a common vocabulary of styles and forms throughout the Roman Empire.
      1. The Romans invented domes and large-scale vaulting, to open up vast interior spaces.
      2. The Romans also enlarged many Greek designs through advances in engineering.
      3. Romans also brought a new realism to Greek models.

The Western Tradition: Unit Five 77

XII. Professor Weber argues that Augustus and the Pax Romana preserved the Greco-Roman tradition.
    A. Without Augustus, Romans might have lost their conquests one by one.
    B. The barbarians of the north and east would have invaded centuries earlier than they did.
    C. A parochial Rome would have been destroyed by civil war.
    D. The legacy of Greece would have been destroyed rather than preserved by Roman students.
    E. When Christianity appeared, the forms of the Roman Empire profoundly shaped the organization and thinking of the church.

KEY TO THE IMAGES

Triumphal monuments:
Some of the best sources for Roman art are the monuments erected to victorious generals or emperors: Trajan's Column, the Arch of Septimius Severus, and the Arch of Constantine. It is not surprising that so many images of warfare appear.

The monuments also provide evidence about the people with whom the Romans went to war, people who sometimes left few sources of their own. The various arches and columns of the Romans show a great variety of conquered or submissive peoples: Jews, Gauls, Germans, Dacians, and various peoples of Africa and the Middle East.

Realism:
The realism of Roman portrait busts is often mirrored in the portrayal of battle scenes. Greek art, although certainly capable of realism, tends to idealize warfare. The Romans, however, had a taste for the details of battle.

The triumphal monuments often provide important information about the tactics and weapons of the Romans and their enemies, information that can often be checked against other sources.

Roman military art also portrays more than battles. For example, Trajan's Column shows soldiers building fortifications, which emphasizes an important truth about the Roman army. For much of its life, the Roman Empire's boundaries expanded very little. The Roman army depended as much on its engineering as on its weapons.

FOCUS QUESTIONS

1. Why did many small farmers lose their land at a time when the Roman Empire was expanding so successfully?
2. Why could the Roman republic not reform itself?
3. Why did the gap between rich and poor widen as Rome expanded its empire?
4. Why did the Roman army become such an important political force during the last century of the republic?
5. When Augustus finally brought stability to the Roman world, what were his most important reforms?

ASSIGNMENTS & ACTIVITIES

IN CONTEXT

Themes and issues that set Unit Five in context with earlier or later programs include the following:

- In its early days Rome was a city-state. As Rome conquered the rest of Italy, however, the other cities and regions were granted generous terms of government, which allowed them a good deal of independence. Contrast Roman policy to the wartime policies of the Greek cities. In following units we learn that Rome did not extend this generous policy to all of its later conquests.

- The Roman army had once consisted of citizen-soldiers who were highly trained but who were also property holders with a stake in the commonwealth. Compare the Roman soldiers with the hoplites of the Greek city-states. In Unit Five you learn how the social basis of the Roman army changed as Rome became an imperial power. In later units look for problems faced by the Romans toward the end of the Western Empire as they tried to staff the armies they needed to defend their frontiers against barbarians.

- Professor Weber emphasizes that some Romans actually suffered as a result of the great wealth that came into Italy from Rome's conquests. Compare this development to the economic changes that came about in the great Mesopotamian empires. In later units look for ways in which the Roman Empire would be weakened by the impoverishment of an important section of the Roman population.

- As he tried to stabilize the Roman Empire, Augustus revived or preserved many of the old forms of the republic but in fact he created a new kind of bureaucratic empire. How did his reforms of the army reflect the problems Rome suffered in the previous century? In the following units look for ways in which reform of the army was important to other rulers, especially to the emperor Diocletian.

TEXTBOOK ASSIGNMENT

Read the following pages in your assigned textbook:

Text: *Western Civilizations*, Fifteenth Edition (Norton, 2005)
Read: Chapter 5, "Roman Civilization," pp. 166-203.

Text: *The Western Experience*, Eighth Edition (McGraw-Hill, 2003)
Read: Chapter 4, "The Roman Republic," pp. 104-135.

Text: *The Western Heritage,* Ninth Edition (Prentice Hall, 2007)
Read: Chapter 4, "Rome: From Republic to Empire," pp. 108-143.

Text: *The Western Heritage,* TLC, Fifth Edition (Prentice Hall, 2007)
Read: Chapter 4, "Rome: From Republic to Empire," pp. 88-113.

ISSUES FOR CLARIFICATION

The Republic

The word *republic* comes from the Latin words *res publica*, which mean "the public thing," although a word like *commonwealth* is a better translation. Historians sometimes leave the impression that once Augustus had achieved undivided power, he simply became emperor and discarded the old republican forms. In fact, however, the Roman emperors retained nearly all of the trappings and offices of the old republic, and some opponents of the emperors for several more generations continued to think that there was a serious possibility of reviving the republic.

Tax Farming

Professor Weber mentions tax farming as a serious abuse throughout the Roman Empire. Like all states without a strong bureaucracy, the Roman Empire had enormous difficulties in collecting taxes. One solution practiced by many nations into modern times was tax farming. A wealthy man or a group of investors agreed to pay the government a lump sum in return for the right to collect taxes in a given area. Although the government received money quickly and easily, the system was always open to abuse. To receive the greatest return on their investment, the tax farmers had every incentive to tax their area as heavily and ruthlessly as possible. In many cases the population paid huge amounts, of which only a small amount went to the government.

GLOSSARY

Carthage: Great trading city in North Africa. Originally founded by the Phoenicians, Carthage fought three deadly wars with Rome resulting in Roman domination of the Mediterranean world.

Cohort: Group of three maniples, approximately three hundred men.

Consul: Highest executive office under the republic. Although consuls had extensive powers, they always held office in pairs for a term of only one year.

Etruscans: A people originally from Asia Minor who settled in central Italy and dominated much of Italy in the early days of Roman history.

Fides: Roman virtue of being true to responsibilities.

Gauls: In Roman times a group of barbarian peoples, many of whom lived in what is now France.

Gravitas: Sober seriousness of a real man.

Legion: Group of ten cohorts, approximately three thousand men.

Lexus: Root of the word *luxury, luxus* originally meant weeds and other plants that choke crops.

Maniple: Unit of one hundred infantrymen, the maniple was more flexible than the older phalanx.

Parthians:	People who founded a great empire in the east that encompassed much of the old Persian Empire.
Patricians:	Aristocrats of Rome. For much of Rome's history, they monopolized public office.
Pax Romana:	"Roman peace" that began in the reign of Augustus.
Phalanx:	A tight infantry formation similar to the Greek model mentioned in Unit Four.
Pietas:	Roman virtue of respect for established authority and tradition.
Plebians:	Class of commoners. Not all of them were poor.
Pontifex:	Originally the guardian of the bridge over the Tiber, the pontiff eventually became a high priest in the Roman state religion.
Praetorian guard:	The emperor's household troops. One of the few large bodies of soldiers not stationed on the frontiers of the empire.
Proletariat:	The landless poor.
Punic wars:	The collective name for the three wars Rome fought with Carthage for domination of the Mediterranean.
Religio:	The common beliefs that hold a community together.
Samnites:	A mountain people living southeast of Rome. During their war with the Samnites, the Romans developed more flexible infantry tactics.
Senate:	The highest legislative body in Rome.
Virtus:	Often translated as "virtue," *virtus* really means "manliness" or "courage."

TIMELINE

Place each of the following events on the timeline. In some cases you may have to specify a roughly defined period of time rather than a precise date.

1. Beginning of the war that first made great changes in the Roman army
2. Hannibal leaves Spain to invade Italy
3. Death of Julius Caesar
4. Battle of Actium
5. Era of civil wars at the end of the republic
6. Hannibal nearly captures Rome
7. Reign of Augustus
8. Tiberius Gracchus takes up cause of the poor
9. Marius introduces changes in the Roman army
10. Foundation of the Roman republic

600 B.C.	1 B.C.

The Western Tradition: Unit Five

MAP EXERCISE

Find the following locations on the map.

1. Carthage
2. Pyrenees
3. Tiber River
4. Sicily
5. The Alps
6. Rome
7. Sardinia
8. Spain
9. Corsica
10. Area of Greek cities needing protection from Carthage

SELF-TEST

Part I of the self-test asks about important factual material. Part II is interpretive. The answers in Part II are keyed to Professor Weber's interpretations. If you disagree with an answer, be prepared to defend your own understanding of the material. Check your answers at the end of Unit Five.

Part I

1. Romulus and his brother ___ _____ were the legendary founders of Rome.

2. Tiberius and Caius _____ were two Roman brothers who tried to aid the Roman poor, especially small farmers who had lost their land.

3. During the first century B.C. which of the following peoples was *not* a threat to the borders of Roman territory?
   a. Carthaginians
   b. Parthians
   c. Germanic peoples
   d. Arabs

4. _____, an ally of Marc Antony's at the battle of Actium, was the last Ptolemaic ruler of Egypt.

5. Which Roman general transformed the Roman army by abolishing the property requirement for enlistment?
   a. Sulla
   b. Marius
   c. Pompey
   d. Caesar

Part II

1. Which Roman ruler established the Roman Empire on a firm foundation and began the long *Pax Romana*?
   a. Pompey
   b. Julius Caesar
   c. Augustus
   d. Marc Antony

2. The long series of wars with _____ left Rome the most important power in the Mediterranean.

3. Which of the following was *not* an important consequence of Roman expansion under the republic?
   a. Importation of cheap grain into Italy
   b. Impoverishment of small farmers
   c. Importation of slaves from conquered territories
   d. Reform of the Roman civil service

4. Which of the following was *not* an important reason for Hannibal's failure to conquer Rome?
   a. Rome's superior infantry tactics as developed in the war against the Samnites
   b. The loyalty of the other Italian cities to Rome
   c. Roman naval power
   d. Roman attacks in North Africa

5. Which of the following was *not* an important source of trouble in the administration of provinces under the republic?
   a. Tax farming
   b. Rome's attempt to create complete religious unity throughout the empire
   c. Lack of a permanent civil service
   d. Tendency of administrators to enrich themselves from the local people

OPTIONAL ACTIVITIES

Although the following activities are not required for the course unless assigned by the instructor, students are encouraged to read them as sources of interesting material for further study.

Art and Architecture
At first sight, the Romans appear to be simple imitators of the Greeks, with little to add of their own. As you view Programs 9 and 10, consider your impressions of Greek art as seen in Programs 7 and 8. As you look more closely, determine whether the Romans still seem to be simple imitators.

You may wish to look at two special areas of Roman art. First, consider the public buildings of the Romans in contrast to those of the Greeks. What sort of statements about their nations and governments were these two peoples making? (*The Art of Rome* by Mortimer Wheeler is a good source of images and ideas.) Second, consider the one area of art where disputes about originality do not exist: portraiture.

Write a paper of 3–5 pages in which you analyze one building or portrait. What does the work you consider reveal about Roman society and culture?

Literature
Professor Weber mentions that to reawaken Romans to their civic duties, Augustus promoted the study of the Roman past. The most important work to come out of this revival was Virgil's *Aeneid*, which describes the trials of the Trojan hero Aeneas, whose descendants were the legendary founders of Rome.

Write a paper of 3–5 pages in which you analyze a brief passage to uncover some of the values that the *Aeneid* was supposed to promote. You might look at Book VI, in which Aeneas descends to the underworld and has a vision in which the history of Rome unfolds before him. Was this the way in which Romans of Augustus's generation liked to imagine themselves?

REVIEW QUESTIONS

The following questions are designed to help you think critically and to construct explanations from factual knowledge. Remember that whenever you learn a new piece of information you should ask yourself "so what?" In one sense or another these are all "so what?" questions.

1. Professor Weber discusses the virtues admired by the Romans of the early republic. Many Romans, and many historians since that time, have blamed the troubles of the late republic and empire on a decline of virtue. Does this interpretation make sense to you? In what sense were the Romans of the late republic less virtuous than their ancestors? What social and economic factors created a society that in some sense seemed less virtuous than the world of its predecessors?

2. Many Romans of the republic, especially Tiberius Gracchus, believed that small farmers were the heart of the Roman army. When these farmers were badly hit by economic forces, the Roman army drastically changed. Explain.

3. What were some of the principal features of Roman policy toward conquered nations? How did the policies change during the period under discussion? Why?

4. Although Tiberius and Caius Gracchus founded a popular party that fought for the interests of the poor, Rome did not become a more democratic state. If anything, precisely the reverse occurred. Explain.

5. Although Rome had possessed strong armies for centuries, in the first century B.C. Roman politics were suddenly dominated by the quarrels of powerful generals. Why did the army begin to play such an important role in politics?

6. Professor Weber argues that the Roman republic had become incapable of reforming itself. State your reasons for agreeing or disagreeing. Was there anything special about Augustus's reforms that would have prevented the Senate from carrying out similar measures?

FURTHER READING

Graves, Robert. *I, Claudius* (1934).

———*Claudius, the God* (1934). Especially good historical text that covers the reigns of Augustus and his next three successors. For Graves, politics in the Roman Empire seems to be mostly family squabbling.

Livy. *The Early History of Rome*, trans. (1971), Aubrey de Selincourt, *War with Hannibal* trans. (1965), Aubrey de Selincourt, *Rome and the Mediterranean* trans. (1976), Henry Bettenson, *Rome and Italy* trans. (1982), Betty Radice. Livy intended to promote ancient Roman virtues that Augustus thought were necessary to revitalize the Roman Empire.

Pallatino, M. *The Etruscans* (1974). An excellent study of archeological sources.

Stockton, D. *The Gracchi* (1974). A study of the family who transformed Roman popular politics.

FILMS AVAILABLE ON VIDEO

Antony and Cleopatra (1981). A good version of Shakespeare's play, against the background of the Roman civil wars.

Caesar and Cleopatra (1946). An excellent adaptation of George Bernard Shaw's play.

I, Claudius (1976). A BBC production of the novels of Robert Graves, *I, Claudius* and *Claudius the God*, chronicles the early years of the Roman Empire through the reign of the emperor Claudius.

Julius Caesar (1953). An excellent adaptation of Shakespeare's play.

ANSWER KEY

Timeline

1. 295 B.C.; war with the Samnites.
2. 218 B.C.
3. 44 B.C.
4. 31 B.C.
5. First century B.C. to approximately 30 B.C.
6. 216 B.C.
7. 31 B.C.–14 A.D.
8. 133 B.C.
9. 107 B.C.
10. Sixth century B.C.

Self-Test

Part I
1. Remus
2. Gracchus
3. (a) Carthaginians
4. Cleopatra
5. (b) Marius

Part II
1. (c) Augustus
2. Carthage
3. (d) Reform of the Roman civil service
4. (a) Rome's superior infantry tactics as developed in the war against the Samnites
5. (b) Rome's attempt to create complete religious unity throughout the empire

Unit 6

Program 11: Early Christianity

Program 12: The Rise of the Church

LEARNING OBJECTIVES

After completing Unit Six students should understand the following issues:

- The important features of Roman humanism. Use your textbook to supplement Professor Weber's description. Try to distinguish the origins of different elements, such as Stoicism and native Roman traditions.

- The sources of long-term instability in the Roman Empire. Compare the ways in which Professor Weber and your textbook fit their different explanations together.

- The sources of instability and uncertainty that led many people in the Roman Empire to seek consolation in religious creeds. How does your textbook supplement or contradict Professor Weber's discussion? What kinds of people were attracted to different sorts of religions?

- Reasons for the rise of Christianity.

- The discussions in the lectures and your textbook of the continuities between Judaism and Christianity.

- The similarities and contrasts between Christianity and the mystery religions.

- The reasons behind Christian intolerance toward other religions and toward Christian dissenters within the church.

TV INSTRUCTION

OVERVIEW
PROGRAM 11: EARLY CHRISTIANITY

Despite a certain number of vicious or insane emperors, the first two centuries A.D. were generally a time of confidence and prosperity for the Roman Empire. In the third century, however, under the pressure of civil war and barbarian attack, the empire was badly shaken. Although administrative reforms saved the empire for another two centuries, Romans never recovered their earlier confidence. Professor Weber argues that this loss of confidence led to a decline of older stoic beliefs and to a growth of new religions.

I. In the second century B.C., when Rome became open to Greek ideas, Stoic philosophy became enormously influential.
   A. The Stoics based morality on conformity with nature:
     1. conformity with one's human nature,
     2. and conformity with the divine world order.
   B. The Romans adapted this philosophy by emphasizing
     1. self-mastery.
     2. temperance.
     3. courage.
     4. dedication.
   C. The Romans also learned the universal, humanitarian ideals of Stoicism, as practiced by such men as
     1. Cicero (106–43 B.C.).
     2. Seneca (4? B.C.–65 A.D.).
   D. The Stoics argued that superior men were responsible for taking responsibility in government.
     1. The Stoic creed was well-suited to the men who carried out Augustus's reforms.
     2. Stoicism became the creed of the ruling elite.
     3. It justified Augustus's attempt to restore old moral values.

II. As a ruling philosophy, however, Stoicism was precarious.
   A. It depended on there being a supply of honest, capable administrators who were not always available.
   B. Stoicism was always an elitist philosophy; it never appealed to the masses.
   C. In hard times even the ruling elites often took little comfort in Stoicism. The emperor Commodus, for instance, abandoned the Stoic teachings of his father, Marcus Aurelius, and sought the protection of a variety of oriental deities:
     1. Cybele, the Great Mother, from Asia Minor.
     2. Mithras, from Persia.
     3. Isis, from Egypt.

III. When security collapsed, stoicism was often replaced by more personal and more accessible beliefs.
   A. Christianity was one religion among many that offered personal salvation.
   B. Even before the birth of Christ, the dominant Hellenistic culture had been deeply touched by oriental beliefs.
     1. According to Professor Weber many of these cults were especially popular among women and the lower classes.
     2. The cults themselves were not new but they were becoming increasingly important in the Greco-Roman world.

The Western Tradition: Unit Six

    C. In the Hellenistic world the Jews had probably preserved their traditional beliefs better than any other people.
      1. They worshipped only one God, Jehovah, a deity of universal power and significance.
      2. As a people, they had a unique and exclusive relationship with their God.
      3. Their religious beliefs had been a source of strength in times of persecution.
        a. In 175 B.C., for instance, Antiochus IV, ruler of Syria and Palestine, had tried to abolish competing religions.
        b. In 164 B.C., however, the Jews began a war of revolt to preserve their religion.
    D. In its resistance Judaism strengthened itself as a distinct, self-conscious belief.
      1. Judaism adopted ideas about immortality from the gnostics.
        a. Such beliefs gave people courage in times of persecution,
        b. and made them fearful of offending Jehovah by surrendering to the demands of Antiochus.
      2. The sect of the Pharisees became especially influential among the Jews. The Pharisees were given to
        a. strict observance of Jewish law.
        b. earnest prayer.
        c. interpreting Jewish law in the context of changing situations.
      3. Jewish observance in general now centered around the synagogue where the law and scriptures were
        a. read.
        b. discussed.
        c. interpreted.
      4. Professor Weber argues that these practices made people
        a. think for themselves.
        b. listen to people around them.
        c. adopt such current notions as belief in
          1. an immortal soul.
          2. angelic spirits.
          3. personal resurrection.
          4. free will.
    E. The ethical beliefs of the Pharisees anticipated many of the teachings of Christ, such as
      1. forgiveness of enemies.
      2. the command to seek peace.
      3. The Pharisee work *The Testament of the Twelve Patriarchs* (109–107 B.C.) was
        a. popular with Saint Paul.
        b. probably known to Christ.

IV. Christ did not believe that he was making a break with Judaism.
    A. Christ was continuing and fulfilling the prophecies of the Old Testament.
    B. Christ was the Messiah who would redeem Israel.

KEY TO THE IMAGES

Mixture of religions:
Many of the cults, especially the mystery religions of the Hellenistic Age, continued or increased in popularity under the Roman Empire. The Roman peace and the Roman roads allowed many of these religions to spread far from their original sources. Program 11 shows images of Cybele, Isis, and Mithras. The cult of Mithras was especially widespread because it was popular in the army.

Mixture of cultures:
The cosmopolitanism of the Roman Empire was not confined to religion. One image in Program 11 shows the mad Emperor Conunodus glorifying himself by wearing the lion's head of the Greek hero Hercules. Another image shows a statue that at first sight seems to be a relic of ancient Egypt, but in fact portrays Antinous, the lover of the Emperor Hadrian, dressed in Egyptian costume.

Witchcraft:
The Romans, like many of their contemporaries, were haunted by fears of witchcraft. Many of the mystery religions, such as the cult of Isis, owed much of their popularity to the protection they were thought to offer against witchcraft. One of the most striking images in Program 11 is a magical hand adorned with charms against magic.

On the other hand, Romans tried to use the supernatural for their own purposes. One painting in Program 11 shows a consultation with a sorceress. Although the subject of this particular consultation is not clear, sorceresses were frequently asked to predict the future.

FOCUS QUESTIONS

1. How successful was the Emperor Augustus in his attempts to restore traditional Roman values and to introduce an elitist philosophy of public service?
2. What were the signs of long-term instability in the Roman Empire? When did they begin to appear?
3. Why did many people reject Greco-Roman rationalism in troubled times?
4. What were the principal features of Jewish religion in the two centuries before the birth of Christ?
5. In what ways did Christianity claim to be a fulfillment of Jewish traditions?
6. Why did the Roman Empire last as long as it did?

OVERVIEW
PROGRAM 12: THE RISE OF THE CHURCH

Christianity was originally a continuation of fulfillment of Judasim rather than a break. In the generations after the crucifixion, however, the two faiths became increasingly hostile toward one another. By the early fourth century A.D. the organization of the church had made it a considerable social power in the cities. When the Emperor Constantine granted the Christians toleration and later converted himself, Christianity was well on the way to becoming the official religion of the empire.

I. Christ and His disciples had preached a sort of reformed Judaism to their fellow Jews.
   A. Earlier Jewish prophets had announced the coming of a Messiah who would deliver Israel from its enemies.
   B. Christ, however, seems to have preached a Day of Judgment that was coming very soon, when
      1. the wicked would be punished.
      2. the righteous would be rewarded.
   C. Christ's message was to abandon sin while there was still time.

II. Saint Paul greatly modified the structure of the Christian church.
   A. Paul was a Pharisee and a Roman Citizen from the city of Tarsus in Asia Minor.
   B. Originally a persecutor of Christians, Paul was converted around 35 A.D.

C. By recruiting gentiles to the faith, Paul greatly expanded the scope of Christianity and, in Professor Weber's works, "made it competitive with other religions."
 1. Unlike the first Christian leaders, he did not demand that gentile converts follow Jewish law in such matters as
  a. circumcision.
  b. dietary laws.
 2. He may have eased such regulations because he believed that the end of the world was so close at hand that it was necessary to make as many converts as possible.

III. In some respects Paul's work was made easier by the political and cultural structure of the Roman world.
 A. The Roman peace and the Roman roads made it possible for him to travel throughout the empire.
 B. In the Koine dialect of Greek, which was used as a *lingua franca* throughout the Mediterranean world, a traveler could make himself understood in most parts of the Roman empire.
  1. The New Testament, including Paul's letters to various churches, was written in the Koine.
  2. The Old Testament had already been translated into the Koine in a version known as the Septuagint.

IV. As time passed Judaism and Christianity became increasingly hostile toward one another.
 A. The Jews considered the Christians heretics.
 B. The Christians considered the Jews willfully blind because they did not acknowledge Jesus as the fulfillment of the Old Testament prophecies.
 C. In the second half of the first century A.D. the Jews undertook a great revolt against Rome.
  1. Anti-Semitism swept through the Mediterranean at about the same time.
  2. In 70 A.D. the Roman general Titus, later emperor, put down the rising and sacked Jerusalem.
 D. At this point Christians still considered themselves part of the Jewish community and shared in the humiliation of the defeat.
  1. Christians developed a deep hatred for secular power.
  2. The temporary collapse of orthodox Judaism, however, made it easier for Christians to become independent.

V. For generations Christians argued that believers should take no part in earthly affairs but should concern themselves only with the kingdom of heaven.
 A. The Christian teacher Origen (185?–254? A.D.) made some of the greatest demands on Christian renunciation.
  1. Christians should take no part in government.
  2. He advocated complete chastity.
 B. Many churchmen renounced and punished the flesh with the greatest mortification. They:
  1. gave away their property.
  2. fasted.
  3. flagellated themselves.
 C. Monastic communities were established to separate believers from the temptations and dangers of the world.
  1. Here Christians could concentrate on personal salvation.
  2. They could spend their lives
   a. in contemplation.
   b. in penitence for their sins.

VI. Many respectable pagans were revolted by the Christians.
 A. Christian renunciation looked like a cowardly or selfish refusal to face the problems of the world.
 B. Educated pagans saw nothing but ignorance or superstition in such Christian beliefs as
  1. the Resurrection of Christ.
  2. the Ascension.
  3. the Incarnation.

C. Perhaps most dangerous of all, the Christians seemed to be sowers of discord.
   1. They insisted that all people were brothers and sisters.
   2. They insisted that in the eyes of God a beggar or a slave was as good as a solid citizen.
   3. Christians denied the final power of the emperor.
      a. They did not rise against him in revolt,
      b. but they recognized a higher power than the state.

VII. Some aspects of Christianity, however, were quite compatible with other beliefs in the ancient world.
   A. The Stoics, for instance, had also emphasized
      1. individual salvation.
      2. the model of a Heavenly City or Kingdom.
      3. the rejection of social or national differences.
      4. high moral values.
   B. The mystery religions also shared certain characteristics with Christianity, such as its
      1. special revelation.
      2. special road to salvation.

VIII. Professor Weber argues that Christians' greatest strength was their tight organization.
   A. Because Christianity was a religion of a book, from the very beginning Christians met regularly to discuss the scriptures, much as the Jews did in their synagogues.
      1. In times of persecution Christians organized themselves as burial societies and often held meetings in their catacombs, or burial tunnels,
      2. because even the fiercest persecutors were reluctant to desecrate tombs.
   B. Christianity was also a relatively cheap religion to join, unlike
      1. the cult of Mithras, in which the initiate had to pay for the sacrifice of a bull.
      2. the cult of Isis, which demanded a great number of gifts and sacrifices.
   C. Many Christians did, however, contribute alms to the church because
      1. charity was pleasing to God.
      2. charity might help the donor win salvation in the next world.
   D. The bishops who administered the alms dispensed a great deal of charity.
      1. This wealth made them important men in a world of increasing misery where
         a. the cities were crowded with the starving poor.
         b. people lost their work.
         c. people were thrown off their land by
            1. barbarians.
            2. nobles.
            3. tax collectors.
      2. The bishops dispensed charity to Christians and non-Christians alike, which
         a. made them more acceptable to the community.
         b. sometimes made new converts.
      3. The Christian bishops, according to Professor Weber, were often the only honest, powerful men around.
         a. Provincial governors were often aristocratic nonentities appointed for only a year or two,
         b. as the figureheads of corrupt staffs.
      4. The bishops also administered free, honest courts that could be used by Christians and pagans alike.

IX. Finally, the Emperor Constantine (reigned 306–337 A.D.) granted official toleration to Christians.
   A. A vision told Constantine that the sign of the cross would bring him victory over one of his enemies.
      1. In 312 A.D., he defeated Maxentius, his chief rival, at the battle of the Milvian Bridge.
      2. Soon afterward, probably in early 313 A.D., Constantine issued the Edict of Milan, which granted Christians freedom of worship.

B. Within a century Christianity became the official religion of the Roman Empire.
   1. Christians were now suppressing pagan worship.
   2. Christians persecuted Jews.
C. The church led campaigns against heretical Christians.
   1. There was much disagreement in the church about theological issues, such as the doctrines of the Trinity and Incarnation.
      a. Was Christ a man who became God?
      b. Or a God who became man?
      c. Was He equal to God the Father?
      d. Or was He subordinate, as a son should be?
   2. These theological differences often reflected regional differences between various parts of the empire.
      a. Constantinople, for instance, believed that Christ combined two natures, one human and one divine.
      b. Alexandria argued that Christ possessed only one nature.
D. The struggle for Christian truth had become a struggle with other Christians.

KEY TO THE IMAGES

Fall of Jerusalem:
Between 66 and 70 A.D., Judea rose in revolt against Roman occupation. Finally, in 70 A.D. Jerusalem fell to the Roman general Titus, who later succeeded his father Vespasian as emperor. The Arch of Titus portrays the Roman victory in great detail. This triumph was so important to the Romans that they minted a special coin portraying Judea taken captive.

Art of the catacombs:
Because Christianity was a persecuted religion during its early history, Christians were in no position to build elaborate churches and as a result much of their early art has failed to survive. Christian art does survive, however, in the wall paintings of the catacombs, or burial chambers, where Christians sometimes took refuge.

Good Shepherd:
In the New Testament Christ often referred to Himself as a Good Shepherd who had come to save His flock from sin. Many of the earliest Christian images portray Him as this Good Shepherd, a motif that was also found in some of the mystery religions, which often portrayed their redeemers in this way.

Images of the Apocalypse:
The first generations of Christians believed that they were living in the last days of the world. After His resurrection, Christ prophesied that He would return again within the lifetimes of some of His listeners. Early Christian art, therefore, contains many images drawn from the apocalypse, or revelation, that contained these prophecies.

FOCUS QUESTIONS

1. Why did Paul feel it necessary to broaden the message of Christianity?
2. In what ways did the politics and culture of the Roman Empire contribute to the spread of Christianity, even though Christians were being persecuted during much of this time?
3. What were the reasons for tensions between Christians and Jews? How were the tensions different from those between pagans and Christians?
4. In what ways did Christians accept or reject participation in ordinary political and social life?
5. Why did many pagans and Jews consider Christianity a social threat?
6. How did Christian officials, especially the bishops, become important figures in the cities of the Roman Empire? How could this happen even before Christianity became the official religion of the empire?
7. Why was Christianity intolerant of other religions?

ASSIGNMENTS & ACTIVITIES

IN CONTEXT

Themes and issues that set Unit Six in context with earlier or later units include the following:

- Many religions and religious cults discussed in earlier sections were limited to a restricted number of people. The Jews, for instance, believed that God had made his covenant only with them. The mystery religions did make converts but the mysteries were revealed only to a limited number of initiates. Christianity, on the other hand, tried to spread its message to the entire world. In later units think of these issues as you look at the success and intolerance of the church.

- Nearly all of the first Christians were Jews, who continued to think of themselves as Jews. To them, Jesus was the Messiah promised by the prophets. Christianity's roots in Judaism were an important source of anti-Semitism. Christians were angered that a people who had already received the message of the Old Testament would nevertheless refuse to become Christians. In the following units look for these Christian outbreaks of anti-Semitism. Be careful, however, to distinguish religious anti-Semitism from anti-Semitism on racial grounds.

- Professor Weber discusses the attempt of Augustus to promote an elitist philosophy of public service. Until the conversion of the emperor Constantine three centuries later, Christians took no part in public life. Once Europe was dominated by Christian rulers, however, a Christian philosophy of public service began to develop. In later units, especially those dealing with the Middle Ages (Programs 19–22), look carefully at the ways in which Christians discussed public duties and political authority.

- Many pagans and Jews considered Christians to be a threat to public order, especially because Christians refused to take part in civic cults and were so intolerant of other religions. In later units ask yourself whether the fears of the pagans and Jews came true after the Christians rose to power.
- Both Christians and Jews revered the Old Testament as a holy book. In later units we learn that Muslims accepted both the Old and New Testaments. Look for ways in which this common

foundation in scripture promoted understanding or tolerance. In what ways did these common origins aggravate religious tension?

- Professor Weber emphasizes the administrative problems of the Roman emperors. In units that follow look for ways in which the church took over many of the responsibilities of the secular authorities. Trace the growth of the church into something more than a purely religious organization.

TEXTBOOK ASSIGNMENT

Read the following pages in your assigned textbook:

    Text: *Western Civilizations*, Fifteenth Edition (Norton, 2007)
    Read: Chapter 6, "Christianity and the Transformation of the Roman World," pp. 204-239.

    Text: *The Western Experience*, Eighth Edition (McGraw-Hill, 2003)
    Read: Chapter 5, "The Empire and Christianity," pp. 138-175.

    Text: *The Western Heritage*, Ninth Edition (Prentice Hall, 2007)
    Read: Chapter 5, "The Roman Empire," pp. 144-187.

    Text: *The Western Heritage*, TLC, Fifth Edition (Prentice Hall, 2007)
    Read: Chapter 5, "The Roman Empire," pp. 114-143.

ISSUES FOR CLARIFICATION

Exclusiveness

Christianity shared many features with Judaism and the mystery religions but it differed from them all in one important respect. The mystery religions had no desire to spread their doctrines to the world at large. They believed that only small, devoted bands of initiates should be allowed access to the wisdom and rites that could bring salvation.

Judaism was less exclusive in that it expected all Jews, of whatever class or spiritual condition, to participate in the rituals of the faith. Nevertheless, Judaism was a religion of one people: the Jews. Jews considered themselves a chosen people with a special relation to their God. They were not concerned with the spiritual state of gentiles.

Christ Himself was a Jew, and He preached His message almost entirely to His people. The very first Christians, in fact, still considered themselves Jews. They believed that Christ was the Messiah promised in the Old Testament. Soon after the death of Christ, however, Paul spread the Christian gospel to gentiles as well as Jews. Unlike other early Christians, Paul did not believe that gentiles should have to follow Jewish rituals to become Christians. Christianity had now become a religion that would try to spread its message to all peoples.

The Incarnation

The doctrine of the Incarnation created intellectual problems for pagans and Christians alike, even though similar beliefs had existed in the Mediterranean world for centuries. Many pagan religions, for instance, told of gods who assumed the form of human beings. There were also stories of human beings who became gods. The state religion of the Roman Empire even claimed that many Roman emperors had become gods after their deaths.

Christians, however, believed something different from these older beliefs. According to the church, Christ had been both God and man simultaneously: not a man who became a god, not a god in human form. Even Christians disagreed on the explanation for this seeming contradiction.

The doctrine of the Incarnation has remained a focus of disagreement throughout the history of the Christian church. Although it was a source of intellectual controversy, the doctrine of the Incarnation was also a source of comfort, for it emphasized that God so loved the world and the people He had created that He actually suffered and died for them.

Theology

Christians began the systematic study of religious doctrines at an early point in the history of the church, partly because such doctrines as the Incarnation were so complex and partly to explain Christian beliefs to the unconverted.

Many of the most serious controversies within the church centered on delicate points of theology. The Arians, for instance, tried to simplify the doctrine of the Incarnation. Instead of claiming that Christ was God and man simultaneously, they believed that Christ was simply a human being who had received a divine mission.

The church claimed that it had the right to formulate orthodox beliefs and to condemn deviations from orthodox theology as heresy.

GLOSSARY

Antiochus IV: Ruler of the Seleucid Empire in Syria and Palestine. In 175 B.C. he started a campaign to unify his realm by wiping out competing religions. His persecution of the Jews led to the Maccabean revolt in 164 B.C.

Ascension: Christian belief that Jesus bodily rose to heaven after His mission in this world.

Catacombs: Burial tunnels. In times of persecution Christians often took refuge in their catacombs because the Roman authorities were generally reluctant to desecrate tombs.

Cicero: Important orator, statesman, and Stoic philosopher. His writings and especially
(106–43 B.C.) his speeches became an important part of education in the west. His opposition to the state led to his death in 43 B.C.

Constantine: Roman emperor from 306–337 A.D. In the Edict of Milan he gave Christians freedom of worship.

Day of judgment: The Jews believed that the Messiah would come to establish the Kingdom of God on earth. Jesus seems to have preached that instead of the Kingdom there would be a Day of Judgment, coming very soon, when the wicked would be punished and the good rewarded.

Diocletian: Roman emperor from 284–305 A.D. Most of the third century had been a time of trouble and civil war. His military and political reforms gave the Roman Empire another century of relative stability.

Edict of Milan: Decree by which the Emperor Constantine granted Christians freedom
(ca. early 313) of worship.

Gnosis: Knowledge of spiritual mysteries. In a number of mystery cults *gnosis* was considered to be the key to salvation.

Hypatia: An Alexandrian woman, learned in philosophy and mathematics. She was murdered by a Christian mob in 415.

Incarnation: Christian belief that God became a human being. The Incarnation was the center of much theological debate because it was not clear how Christ could have simultaneously been both God and man.

Jehovah: For the Jews, a god of supreme universal significance and power. The Jews, who believed themselves Jehovah's chosen people, had a unique and exclusive relationship with their god. For the most part they remained aloof from other religious influences.

Maccabean Revolt: A long and bloody war beginning in 164 B.C. in which the Jews defended their religion from persecution by the Seleucid Empire.

Messiah: The Old Testament promised that one day a redeemer, the Messiah, would appear to make Israel and the Jewish people triumph over their enemies. Christians believed that Jesus Christ was this Messiah.

Origen: Christian teacher who lived in Alexandria in the third century. He believed that Christians should be concerned only with the church and should take no part in government.

Paul: Pharisee and originally a persecutor of Christians. Around 35 A.D. he converted to Christianity and became a missionary throughout much of the Mediterranean world. He insisted that non-Jewish converts to Christianity should not be made to follow Jewish ritual laws.

Pharisees: Jewish sect that was especially strict in following Jewish law. Their ethical and social ideas were influential with early Christians.

Pogrom: Organized anti-Semitic massacre.

Resurrection: Christian belief that Jesus came back to life after His death on the cross.

Romulus Augustulus: Last emperor to rule from Rome over the western part of the empire. He retired in 476 A.D.

Salus: Originally the Latin word for "good physical health." Under the influence of various religious movements, *salus* came to mean "the health of the soul," or "salvation."

Semites: A people who moved from the Arabian Desert into Mesopotamia some time before 2000 B.C. Both Arabs and Jews are Semitic peoples.

Seneca: Important Stoic writer and philosopher. He was the tutor and later councilor of the Emperor Nero. In 65 A.D. Nero accused Seneca of conspiracy and ordered him to commit suicide.

Septuagint: A translation of the Old Testament into Greek made two centuries before the birth of Christ. Because Greek was the most widely spoken language in the Roman Empire, the Septuagint was an important resource for Christian missionaries.

Titus: Roman general, later emperor, who sacked Jerusalem in 70 A.D.

TIMELINE

Place each of the following events on the timeline. In some cases you may have to specify a roughly defined period of time rather than a precise date.

1. The death of Christ
2. Retirement of Romulus Augustulus
3. Beginning of the Revolt of the Maccabees
4. Decree granting Christians freedom of worship
5. Sack of Jerusalem by the Romans
6. Suppression of public paganism
7. Murder of Hypatia
8. Reign of Diocletian

|200 B.C.   500 A.D.|

MAP EXERCISE

Find the following locations on the map.

1. Rome
2. Tarsus
3. Jerusalem
4. Borders of the Roman Empire (ca. 150)
5. Roman province of Palestine
6. Milan
7. Arabian Desert
8. Alexandria
9. Syria

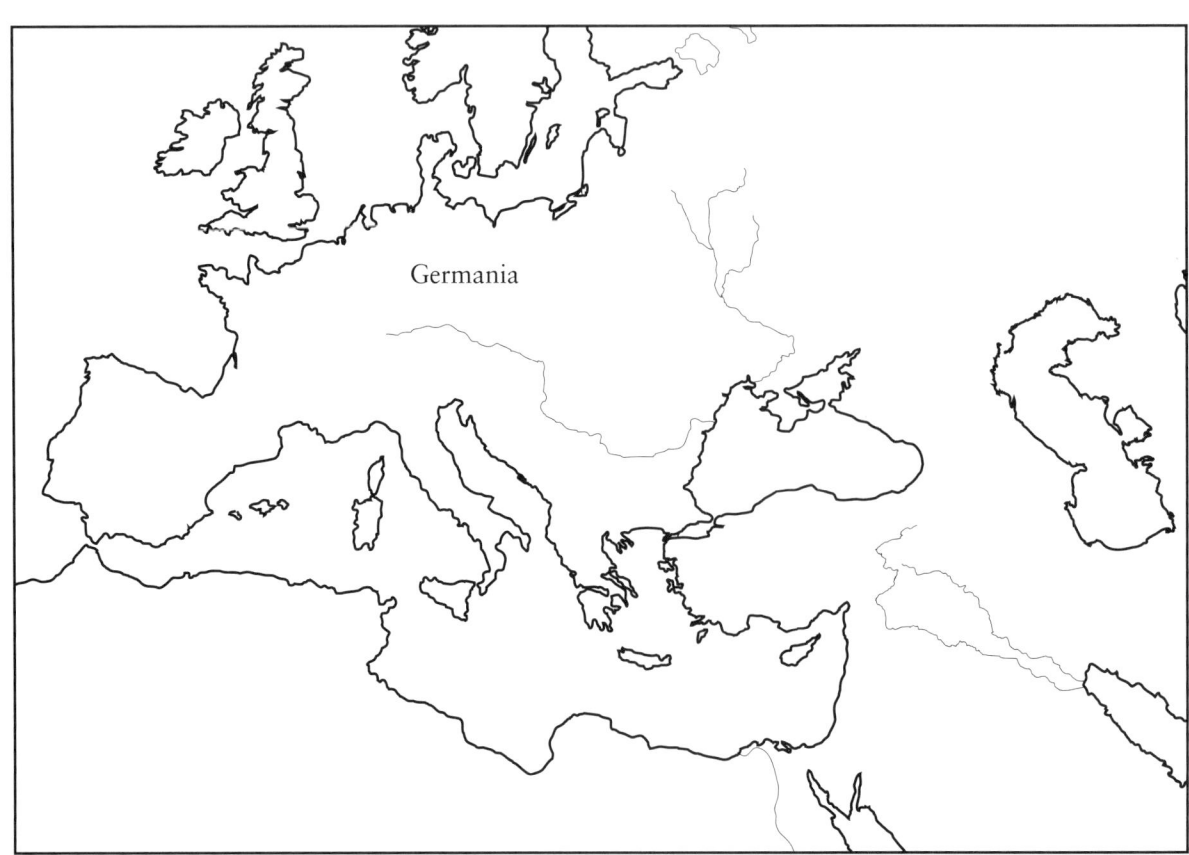

SELF-TEST

Part I of the self-test asks about important factual material. Part II is interpretive. The answers in Part II are keyed to Professor Weber's interpretations. If you disagree with an answer, be prepared to defend your own understanding of the material. Check your answers at the end of Unit Six.

Part I

1. Mark the false completion. As part of his reforms, the Emperor Augustus
   a. imposed religious uniformity throughout the Roman Empire.
   b. attempted to restore old moral values.
   c. reaffirmed the importance of marriage and the family.
   d. trained a ruling elite, educated on the principles of Greco-Roman humanism.

2. From Augustus's victory at Actium until the retirement of Romulus Augustulus, the Roman Empire lasted approximately how long?

3. Stoicism broadened and enriched Roman morality into a new humanism. All but one of the following men attempted to follow this ideal in political life. Mark the exception.
   a. Cicero
   b. Seneca
   c. Marcus Aurelius
   d. Commodus

4. Nearly all of Jesus's first followers were Jews. A few years after His death, however, _____ began to preach the Christian message to gentiles as well as Jews.

5. Christianity owed a great deal to the ethical teachings of a Jewish sect known as the
   a. Pharisees.
   b. Maccabees.
   c. Patriarchs.
   d. Messianics.

Part II

1. In Program 11 Professor Weber cites the following passage from T. E. Lawrence: "Their thoughts were at ease only in extremes... Their largest manufacture was of creeds; almost, they were monopolists of revealed religions... The common basis of all [their] creeds, winners or losers, was the ever-present idea of world-worthlessness." What people is Lawrence describing?
   a. Greeks
   b. Romans
   c. Semites
   d. barbarians attacking the Roman Empire

2. Professor Weber describes the Greco-Roman world as materialistic, skeptical, and tolerant. Above all, it was a cosmopolitan world in which tribes and races continually intermingled. In the midst of this empire, _____ were the people who best preserved their own identity and outlook.

3. Mark the false completion. The spread of Christianity was greatly helped
   a. by the Christian practice of giving charity to believers and nonbelievers alike.
   b. by the fact that pagan intellectuals readily accepted such doctrines as the Incarnation, the Resurrection, and the Ascension of Christ.
   c. by the unity of the Roman Empire.
   d. by the use of the Koine as a *lingua franca* throughout much of the Roman Empire.

4. The Edict of Milan, which was promulgated by the Emperor _____, granted Christians full toleration and freedom of worship.
   a. Trajan
   b. Marcus Aurelius
   c. Constantine
   d. Romulus Augustulus

5. Mark the false completion. By about 400 A.D.,
   a. public paganism had been suppressed.
   b. Christians had settled most of their theological disagreements.
   c. Christians were organizing massacres of Jews.
   d. many of the pagan schools of philosophy were being closed.

OPTIONAL ACTIVITIES

Although the following activities are not required for the course unless assigned by the instructor, students are encouraged to read them as sources of interesting material for further study.

Pagan Perceptions of Christianity

If you have already studied *The Golden Ass* for the Optional Activity in Unit Four, go back to the book and look for references to Christianity. Note that the author, who belonged to the cult of Isis, regarded Christianity as a rather inferior sort of mystery religion.

Write a paper of 3–5 pages in which you compare the author's perceptions of early Christianity to what you have learned from other sources. Concentrate on the following issues:

- What did cultivated pagans find so repulsive about Christianity?
- What does *The Golden Ass* tell you about the psychological and religious background of the time?

E. R. Dodds' work, *Pagan and Christian in an Age of Anxiety*, provides useful insights for this issue.

Comparison of Sources

The first four books of the New Testament—Matthew, Mark, Luke, and John—provide excellent opportunities for comparing differing accounts of the same events.

The first three books—Matthew, Mark, and Luke—are known as the Synoptic Gospels because their accounts are fairly consistent and they probably derive from a common source.

The Gospel of John, however, provides rather different accounts.

Choose some section of the gospel story, such as the account of the Last Supper, the Crucifixion, or the Resurrection. First read the story in one of the Synoptic Gospels. Then read the corresponding account in the Gospel of John.

Write a paper of 3–5 pages in which you contrast similarities and differences. Are there real contradictions in the accounts or only differences of emphasis? How would our views of Christ differ if only the Gospel of John had survived?

REVIEW QUESTIONS

The following questions are designed to help you think critically and to construct explanations from factual knowledge. Remember that whenever you learn new information you should ask yourself "so what?" In one sense or another these are all "so what?" questions.

1. Professor Weber argues that during the second century A.D. the Romans "shifted from confidence and stability to anxious uncertainty." What were some of the political and military causes of this loss of confidence? How did "anxious uncertainty" affect Roman philosophy and religion?

2. The combination of Stoicism with ancient Roman moral values created the ideal of the exceptional man: in Professor Weber's words, "a man with a mission who sets out to reestablish and secure the balance and harmony that was threatened by excess and corruption." In many ways this ideal was impressive in its rationalism and devotion to public service. Nevertheless, in the troubles of the later empire, many people turned away from this ideal to seek consolation in other creeds. What were some of the limits on Roman rationalism? What were some of the other creeds that gained followers at its expense?

3. In what ways did the religious beliefs of the Jews differ from those of other peoples in the Roman Empire? In what ways did the Jews defend their religion during this period?

4. In what ways are the teachings of Christ a continuation of earlier Jewish traditions? What were some of the reasons that Christianity was able to spread outside the Jewish community? What features did Christianity share with religious traditions other than Judaism? What features were new?

5. What were some of the reasons why Christianity was intolerant of other religions? What were some of the groups persecuted by the church after Christianity became the official religion of the Roman Empire?

FURTHER READING

Saint Augustine. *The Confessions* (1972). Augustine was one of the great teachers in the church during the fourth and fifth centuries. This autobiography is especially important for its intellectual and psychological insights.

Brown, Peter. *The World of Late Antiquity* (1971). A brilliant short study by one of the great historians of early Christianity.

Burgess, Anthony. *The Kingdom of the Wicked* (1985). An amusing novel about the first generation of Christians.

Cochrane, C. M. *Christianity and Classical Culture* (1975). Especially important in its description of the merging of two such different cultures.

Dodds, E. R. *Pagan and Christian in an Age of Anxiety* (1965). An important study of the psychological background of this age.

Gibbon, Edward. *The Decline and Fall of the Roman Empire* (1980), ed. Dero A. Saunders. An abridgment of one of the greatest works of historical writing. Especially controversial on the influence of Christianity. Gibbon is also one of the greatest prose writers in English.

Pagels, Elaine. *The Gnostic Gospels* (1979). A good discussion of an early variety of Christianity ultimately condemned by the church. The Gnostics had important intellectual roots in Greek philosophy.

Vidal, Gore. *Julian* (1964). An excellent historical novel about the last pagan Roman emperor.

FILMS AVAILABLE ON VIDEO

Barabbas (1962). Hollywood spectacular about the criminal who was released by Pontius Pilate when Christ was sentenced to die.

The Gospel According to Saint Matthew (1964). Using nonprofessional actors, the director Pier Paolo Pasolini created one of the greatest films of his career.

Jesus of Nazareth (1976). A television series created by the Italian director Franco Zeffirelli.

The Last Temptation of Christ (1988). Martin Scorsese's controversial adaptation of the novel by Nikos Kazantzakis.

Quo Vadis? (1985). A fairly recent version of the novel by Henryk Sienkiewicz about the persecution of Christians in the reign of the emperor Nero.

ANSWER KEY

Timeline

1. Approximately 30 A.D.
2. 476 A.D.
3. 164 B.C.
4. Probably early in 313 A.D.
5. 70 A.D.
6. Approximately 400 A.D.
7. 415 A.D.
8. 284–305 A.D.

Self-Test

Part I
1. (a) imposed religious uniformity throughout the Roman Empire.
2. Five hundred years
3. (d) Commodus
4. (Saint) Paul
5. (a) Pharisees

Part II
1. (c) Semites
2. the Jews
3. (b) by the fact that pagan intellectuals readily accepted such doctrines as the Incarnation, the Resurrection, and the Ascension of Christ.
4. (c) Constantine
5. (b) Christians had settled most of their theological disagreements.

Unit 7

Program 13: The Decline of Rome

Program 14: The Fall of Rome

LEARNING OBJECTIVES

After completing Unit Seven students should understand the following issues:

- The economic, administrative, and military causes behind the Fall of the Western Empire. Does your textbook explain the interplay of causes differently from Professor Weber?

- The economic and political relationship between cities and countryside in the Roman Empire.

- The causes that tempted or forced barbarians to invade the Roman Empire. According to your textbook, in which parts of the empire did the invasions do the most damage?

- The characteristics of the various barbarian peoples. Which tribes were quickest to adopt the empire's customs?

- The successes and failures of the Roman Empire's attempts to save itself in the third and fourth centuries. Use your textbook to trace the pattern of the empire's victories and defeats.

- The beginnings of the manorial system in western Europe.

- The development of a western Europe culture distinct from the culture that survived in the eastern half of the Roman Empire.

TV INSTRUCTION

OVERVIEW
PROGRAM 13: THE DECLINE OF ROME

By the sixth century A.D. the western half of the Roman Empire had collapsed as various barbarian tribes contended for power. Ever since that time, historians have been trying to explain the reasons behind the destruction of the empire. Some historians, like Edward Gibbon, have emphasized religious issues; others have looked at political, economic, and administrative problems.

I. By the middle of the fifth century B.C. the western half of the Roman Empire had been almost completely destroyed.
   A. Nearly all the territory from Hadrian's Wall in Britain to the Adriatic Sea was dominated by a series of warlike tribes, most of them Germanic.
   B. The emperor still sat in Constantinople and his armies held a few Italian ports, but otherwise he exercised almost no power in the west.

II. Before asking why the Roman Empire fell, it should be noted that the empire had been surrounded by dangerous enemies for centuries before its final collapse.
   A. From at least the second century onward, the empire had been faced with hosts of tribes across
      1. the River Tyne in England.
      2. the Rhine.
      3. the Danube.
      4. the mountains and deserts of Africa and Asia.
   B. Much of the time these tribes were held in check,
      1. in which case they often fought one another.
      2. Individuals, however, often wandered into the empire:
         a. to find work.
         b. to fight for the Romans as mercenaries.
         c. to settle down and become partially Romanized.
   C. Sometimes, however, the barbarians broke through the frontiers in force.
      1. They raided and looted as a tribe.
      2. In some cases they occupied some of the lands of the empire.

III. After the middle of the third century this process stepped up.
   A. The raids became invasions.
   B. Protecting the boundaries of the empire now became the emperor's principal task.
      1. Sometimes the Romans hired barbarians to fight as mercenaries in the service of the empire.
      2. Roman diplomacy sometimes inveigled the barbarians into fighting one another instead of attacking the empire.

IV. The roots of the barbarian attacks were too deep, however, to be treated by temporary measures.
   A. Early in the third century A.D. the Chinese improved their defenses against a confederation of Mongol tribes known as the Huns.
   B. The Huns then began to migrate west, pushing before them other warlike tribes such as
      1. the Goths.
      2. the Vandals.
   C. In the late fourth century the Goths broke through the boundaries of the empire and raided
      1. the Balkans.
      2. Italy.

D. Around the year 406 Vandals crossed the Rhine to ravage
1. Gaul.
2. Spain.
3. North Africa.
E. Finally, the Huns invaded the empire, bringing even worse destruction.

V. For the most part these invasions were less a matter of conventional warfare than of looting, robbery, and rape on a huge and seemingly endless scale.
A. Cities were sacked.
B. Populations were massacred or enslaved.
C. Open countryside was devastated.

VI. In explaining the decline and fall of the Roman Empire, the eighteenth-century historian Edward Gibbon lays much of the blame on Christianity,
A. which had caused needless fighting within the empire,
B. and had destroyed Rome's civic virtues.
C. Whatever the merits of Gibbon's interpretation, it should be pointed out that the empire did not fall until four and a half centuries after the beginning of Christianity. If Christianity poisoned the empire, the poison did not act very quickly.

VII. Modern historians emphasize social, economic, or constitutional issues.
A. One theory argues that most of the fertile, well-drained areas of the Roman Empire had passed into the hands of large landowners using slave labor.
1. Peasants were left with the poorer, marshier areas, which were often infested with malaria.
2. Disease and poverty then forced the peasants into the towns, where they spread the disease.
3. Then the disease, perhaps in combination with smallpox, spread throughout the empire,
a. decimating the garrisons.
b. depopulating the towns.
c. leaving the empire unable to defend itself.
4. Although disease may have played a part in weakening the Roman Empire, this theory is by no means a complete explanation.
B. Another explanation argues that shortsighted farming methods exhausted the soil,
1. impoverishing small landholders.
2. depopulating the countryside.
3. Therefore, little was left for the tax-collectors,
4. and it became increasingly difficult to pay for the army.
C. A similar view argues that the need for defense raised taxes.
1. Taxes became so burdensome that many small farmers were driven off the land,
2. and the tax base grew progressively smaller.
D. Points B and C have considerable merit but neither provides a total explanation because
1. some important areas remained quite lush, such as
a. Gaul.
b. Egypt.
2. Some provinces were able to pay their taxes without undue strain.

VIII. One problem, however, affected Hellenistic society in general and the late Roman Empire in particular: the cities were an economic drain on the countryside.
A. Because the cities were politically volatile, governments took great care to keep the urban population quiet.
1. There were massive subsidies of
a. wine.
b. grain.
c. oil.
d. money.

2. There were massive displays of public entertainment:
   a. gladiatorial contests.
   b. fights with wild animals.
   c. races.
   d. theater.
3. Many of these displays were enormously bloody.
   a. The Christians were able to mitigate some of the bloodshed,
   b. but the massive public expense remained.
   B. Because the cities produced little themselves, the programs had to be paid for by taxing the countryside.
   1. In prosperous times taxation may have been bearable,
   2. but as the barbarian invasions stepped up, the burden became much more serious.

IX. The Roman Empire's economy began to crack during the second and third centuries.
   A. The emperors needed heavier and heavier taxes,
      1. to maintain the army.
      2. to pay off the barbarians.
   B. As the economy entered a downward spiral, there were fewer and fewer people who could pay such taxes.
      1. Inflation and debasement of the currency drove gold and silver out of circulation.
      2. Much of the economy now operated on barter rather than on the exchange of cash.

X. Professor Weber argues that the Roman Empire, like all the great states of the ancient world, suffered from hypertrophy.
   A. As the state expanded, the sheer cost of army and administration became overwhelming.
   B. As communications broke down, armies could no longer be controlled from the center.
   C. Distant provinces were sometimes broken off by rebels or invaders.

XI. In the 280s the Emperor Diocletian took effective measures against these problems.
   A. He divided the empire into an eastern and a western half, each governed by an Augustus.
      1. Each Augustus took a vice-emperor, called a Caesar.
      2. The administration of the empire was split into four parts.
   B. This quartet of rulers, known as the tetrarchy, did not last, but the split between east and west remained.
   C. In 323 the Emperor Constantine moved the capital of the eastern empire to the Greek city of Byzantium, which he renamed Constantinople.
   D. These problems of scale did not go away but some historians have argued that the reforms gave the empire breathing space.
      1. The Western Empire survived until 476.
      2. Emperors lasted at Constantinople until 1453.

XII. The economic problems of the Roman Empire aggravated one another.
   A. Because the cities never became productive centers, they were a constant drain on the countryside.
   B. As exchange broke down, people in the countryside tried to become as self-sufficient as possible, depressing trade even further.
   C. The cities were divided between the very rich and the very poor.
      1. The urban poor lived in cramped quarters, where they spent as little time as possible.
      2. They mostly ate bread and vegetables. They drank little wine and ate little meat.

XIII. Even though the ancient world had impressive accomplishments in science and engineering, they were never exploited to increase economic productivity.
   A. Hero of Alexandria, for instance, designed a practical steam engine that remained an impressive toy.

B. Roman engineers were highly accomplished, building
   1. aqueducts.
   2. sewers.
   3. public baths.
C. But no industrial use was ever made of these skills.
   1. Perhaps because cheap labor in the form of slaves left the Romans no incentives to improve productivity.
   2. Perhaps because they accorded little respect to manual labor.
D. The ancient economy was not flexible. When it came under pressure, the emperors could only try to freeze things in place to
   1. raise taxes.
   2. increase the army.
E. Sometimes these solutions made the problems even worse.

KEY TO THE IMAGES

Games and circuses:
Games, races, and gladiatorial contests had been an important part of Roman life since the time of the republic. These spectacles were provided by the emperors or by other wealthy Romans who wanted to win favor with the populace or at least to keep them quiet. As can be seen from many of the images in Program 13, these games were enormously bloody, especially in the gladiatorial contests and the fights with animals.

After Christianity became the established religion, some of the bloodier games were abolished but the races remained as popular as ever. One image, from around 425, shows the Lampadius family presiding over the circus races it had provided.

Such racing remained popular in the west as long as there were families wealthy enough to be sponsors. The Byzantines remained fanatically devoted to racing for centuries to come.

Pompeii and Herculaneum:
In 79 A.D. an eruption of Mount Vesuvius on the Bay of Naples buried the cities of Pompeii and Herculaneum. The volcanic ash preserved much of the cities intact. Many of the wall paintings shown in the programs on Rome were preserved here. The site shows the layout of the streets and the architecture of many buildings. In some places the ash preserves the outline of the victim's bodies. There is even a bakery where the ash outlined the shapes of the loaves of bread.

FOCUS QUESTIONS

1. What are some of the explanations given by historians for the fall of Rome?
2. How did economic disorder contribute to the fall of the Western Empire?
3. In what ways did the cities of the Roman Empire drain the wealth of the countryside?
4. What were the different stages in the mounting pressure of barbarian attacks?
5. How did the imperial government reorganize itself in the third and fourth centuries?
6. In what ways did the eastern and western halves of the Roman Empire become increasingly different from one another?
7. By the sixth century what were the barbarian kingdoms that controlled the area once ruled by the western half of the Roman Empire?

OVERVIEW
PROGRAM 14: THE FALL OF ROME

In the course of trying to preserve itself from barbarian invasions the Roman Empire transformed itself socially and politically. Once the Romans had lost the social and economic underpinning of their armies they were forced to transform their society or to create a new kind of army. In defending itself the empire often debased the lives of its inhabitants to a level even lower than that of the barbarian tribes.

I. The Roman Empire consisted of a thin population spread over an enormous area.
   A. In the third and fourth centuries the empire included between fifty and sixty-five million people, from the Euphrates to the River Tyne in northern England.
   B. Even a fairly small number of tribesmen could badly damage a population that was spread out over such a vast area.
      1. Most tribes of Germans and Huns probably included between fifty and one hundred thousand people, of whom five to ten thousand were warriors.
      2. The Roman armies were also small and they could not be everywhere at once.

II. After the mid-third century, the barbarian invasions, or infiltrations, permanently crippled urban life.
   A. Towns had once been large, open centers of life and culture.
   B. They were now forced to shrink their boundaries to areas that could be easily defended, as was the case with such towns as
      1. Bordeaux, France.
      2. Silchester, England.
   C. The decay of urban life was visible in the decline of Roman art.
      1. Statues were sometimes made from a standardized body that would fit almost any man and to which was added an individualized head.
      2. The elegance of Hellenism was being replaced by something stiffer and rougher.

III. Much of the aristocracy left the towns and withdrew to fortified estates in the countryside.
   A. Here the local landowner was a little king.
      1. No one could force him to pay taxes.
      2. He paid his own guards and men-at-arms.
      3. He administered law on his own estates.
      4. He protected his clients, who were really his subjects.
   B. A way of life was emerging that would be followed by country gentlemen for at least the next thousand years.

IV. Even in good times the imperial system had always depended too much on the personality of the emperor.
   A. In the second century, after the murder of the despotic Emperor Domitian in 96, the empire was fortunate enough to be served by a series of good emperors.
      1. Nerva (reigned 96–98)
      2. Trajan (reigned 98–117)
      3. Hadrian (reigned 117–138)
      4. Antoninus Pius (reigned 138–161)
      5. Marcus Aurelius (reigned 161–180)
   B. Marcus Aurelius, however, allowed family feelings to overcome good judgment and named his son Commodus to succeed him.
      1. Commodus was a megalomaniac, who at times believed he was the mythological hero Hercules.

2. He wasted the empire's resources on
   a. an enormous harem.
   b. huge gladiatorial contests.
3. Commodus was finally assassinated.

C. Many emperors tried to follow the advice of Septimius Severus (reigned 193–211): "Be united, enrich the soldiers, and scorn the rest."

D. Unfortunately, this good advice did not save his son and grandson from being murdered by their own troops.

V. Much of the third century was passed in plots as the praetorian guard and the provincial armies contended to place their own candidates on the imperial throne.
   A. The empire was up for auction to whomever offered the soldiers the highest bribes.
   B. Important social divisions lay behind the ambitions of the army.
      1. From the beginning of the third century the armies consisted largely of peasants from the less civilized parts of the empire.
      2. These peasants violently opposed the urban aristocracy and middle class that governed the empire.
   C. This problem was further complicated by the policy that made each legion responsible for its own recruiting.
      1. Because most legions were stationed on the frontier, they naturally recruited from their own locality,
      2. and even more likely from the barbarians on the far side of the border.
   D. This system aggravated local differences throughout the empire.
      1. The army of Illyria, for instance, might have very different desires from the army of Gaul.
      2. The old cosmopolitan patriotism had vanished.

VI. By the end of the third century Diocletian had reorganized the empire into a fairly workable despotism.
    A. Lip service was paid to old Roman traditions but the government was carried on by members of a special caste.
       1. Soldiers were appointed to most positions of authority in the central and provincial administration.
       2. This military aristocracy was continually renewed with barbarian recruits.
    B. Professor Weber argues that the later empire was a police state with the trappings of an oriental despotism.

VII. Under the pressure of barbarian invasions the emperors thought they needed the strongest measures: despotic government, social regimentation, and extortionate taxes.
     A. The average civilian, however, came to feel that he had less and less that was worth defending.
     B. In some cases the barbarians were less extortionate than the government.

VIII. By the fourth century the old Roman army had vanished.
      A. The barbarian infantry lacked the discipline needed for complicated maneuvers.
      B. In 378, in one of the worst defeats suffered by Rome since the days of Hannibal, the Emperor Valens was killed in a battle against mailed Gothic cavalry.
      C. His successor Theodosius decided that infantry had become obsolete and hired bands of Gothic cavalry.
      D. The Roman military tradition had now been replaced by Gothic warlords and their heavily mailed cavalry.

IX. Professor Weber argues that the military strength of the Roman Empire had been based on the small farmers who manned the infantry.
   A. Once those farmers had disappeared, the legions were bound to decay or become transformed.
   B. The "Roman" soldiers were now barbarians, hired to fight other barbarians.
      1. Even generals and high officials were likely to be barbarians,
      2. such as Stilicho, the brother-in-law of the Emperor Theodosius.

X. By the beginning of the fifth century the military situation had become desperate in the Western Empire.
   A. In 402 Stilicho moved the western capital from Rome to Ravenna in northern Italy,
      1. which was easier to defend behind its marshes,
      2. and where the court could escape by sea if the enemy came too close.
   B. Without the court, Rome was helpless.
      1. In 410, Alaric the Goth sacked the city.
      2. To many it seemed that the world was literally coming to an end.

XI. Explanations for the disaster began on the day the city fell and have continued to the present.
   A. Professor Weber argues that Rome fell as the result of a long process that began when an oriental despotism finally triumphed over the city-state.
      1. The urban citizen class was crushed by the pressure of centralization and bureaucracy.
      2. Rome destroyed the social foundations of its army.
   B. Further, the Roman Empire never truly possessed a homogeneous culture.
      1. The empire was really an amalgamation of differing social organisms held together by military and administrative organization.
         a. The east inherited the debris of oriental and Hellenistic despotism.
         b. The west conquered and assimilated the tribal societies of European barbarians.
      2. There was a community of culture in the cities,
         a. but it was superficial,
         b. and generally limited to the privileged classes.
   C. When this privileged class was ruined by the economic crises of the third century and by the loss of its privileges, the differences between east and west emerged as strong as ever.

XII. The empire in the east survived,
   A. partly because it was more compact,
   B. and partly because the autocratic traditions of the east were better suited to running an empire than the divisive tribalism of the west.
   C. When Constantine installed himself at Constantinople, he was adopting many of the principles of the eastern semidivine ruler.
      1. As a Christian he did not claim to be a god.
      2. But as emperor he claimed to be God's representative on earth.

XIII. The empire had endured for many centuries.
   A. When it fell, many believed that the world had come to an end.
   B. The tradition of the eternal empire would lead to attempts to revive it hundreds of years in the future: on Christmas Day 800 A.D., when Charlemagne was crowned emperor in Rome.

KEY TO THE IMAGES

Villas:
As the countryside of the Roman Empire suffered under the pressure of civil war and barbarian attack, the villas of the upper classes began to change. One image from fourth-century Tunisia shows some of the most important developments. Villas were less sprawling now. The lower stories tended to have solid walls and towers were built at strategic points. These buildings might not stand up to an army but they could provide protection against marauding gangs. It is easy to see how such buildings might come to resemble castles.

Aerial archeology:
One of the most revealing images in Program 14 shows an aerial photograph of a field in modern England. At first sight there seems to be nothing but an expanse of grass. A closer look, however, shows a faint grid pattern in the vegetation, which reveals the remains of a Roman city.

Aerial photography has become an important tool for archeologists by revealing patterns that may not be visible at ground level. In this area, for instance, there was nothing to be seen but grass. At higher altitudes, however, new patterns appeared.

In places where the earth covered a road or wall the grass was a bit shorter because the roots could not go down as deep. In places where there was once a hole or ditch the grass was taller because the earth was more loosely packed and the roots could grow more easily These variations in the height of the grass were too slight to be seen on the ground, but clearly visible from the air.

Images of barbarians:
Long before the end of the western empire, artwork reveals the barbarian pressure. The Arch of Septimius Severus portrays battles with barbarians. A sarcophagus displayed in Program 14 is elaborately carved with battle scenes between barbarians and the Roman army. A close look at the artwork of the late empire reveals that many of the Roman soldiers were barbarians themselves, not much different in culture or customs from the people they were fighting.

FOCUS QUESTIONS

1. Why did the fate of the Roman Empire depend so much on the personal character of the emperor?
2. As more and more barbarians entered Roman service, what were the most important changes in the Roman army?
3. As the Western Empire collapsed, in what ways did great landowners create a new political system?
4. As the Roman Empire broke apart, what were the most important cultural and political differences between the eastern and western halves?
5. In what ways did the eastern emperors emphasize their divine mission?

ASSIGNMENTS & ACTIVITIES

IN CONTEXT

Themes and issues that set Unit Seven in context with other units include the following:

- The Western Empire finally crumbled during the period covered by Unit Seven. Look back to Units Five and Six. In the second half of the third century the empire was also in desperate trouble, torn by civil war and fighting along the frontier. In that period, however, the reforms of Diocletian helped give the empire another century and a half of life. In units to come look for survivals of the Roman Empire in art, politics, and culture. Look especially carefully at the Roman Catholic church and at the Holy Roman Empire.

- Professor Weber argues that during this period the economic and cultural center of Europe shifted away from the cities to the countryside. In later units we learn that long-distance trade drastically decreased all over Europe and that European intellectual life was now based in monasteries. When you study Units 10–12 on the High Middle Ages, watch for new economic and cultural patterns as the cities revive after the year 1000 A.D.

- Emperors in Constantinople continued to rule over the eastern half of the Roman Empire. In earlier units we learn of the important cultural, religious, and political differences between east and west. Now that the west was dominated by barbarian kingdoms, these differences became even more important. In later units look for conflicts, especially in religion, between eastern and western Europe. The iconoclastic controversy and the split between the Orthodox and the Roman Catholic churches were results of these tensions.

- Professor Weber has argued that a new form of political and economic life was beginning to dominate the countryside. In later units Professor Weber discusses the relationship between lord and vassal, between landlord and peasant. When you come to these areas, consider these relationships as responses to economic and political problems that had their roots in the period covered by Unit Seven.

TEXTBOOK ASSIGNMENT

Read the following pages in your assigned textbook:

   Text: *Western Civilizations,* Fifteenth Edition (Norton, 2005)
  Read: Review from Chapter 5, "Roman Civilization," pp. 166-203; and Chapter 6, "Christianity and the Transformation of the Roman World," pp. 204-239.

   Text: *The Western Experience,* Eighth Edition (McGraw-Hill, 2003)
  Read: Review from Chapter 5, "The Empire and Christianity," pp. 138-152.

   Text: *The Western Heritage,* Ninth Edition (Prentice Hall, 2007)
  Read: Review from Chapter 5, "The Roman Empire," pp. 144-187.

   Text: *The Western Heritage,* TLC, Fifth Edition (Prentice Hall, 2007)
  Read: Review from Chapter 5, "The Roman Empire," pp. 114-143.

ISSUES FOR CLARIFICATION

Feudalism

Professor Weber argues that by the time the Western Empire fell, the roots of feudalism were already developing. Because the term *feudalism* reappears in the lectures and readings, you should keep a few points in mind. First, the term *feudalism* was coined in the seventeenth century. It was never used during the Middle Ages at the height of "the Feudal Order." "Feudalism" was never a system. The following discussion mentions only a few of the most important points.

In the countryside the center of economic and political life was the manor, whose lord had judicial as well as economic power over the peasants who worked his lands. These peasants might be personally free or they might be bound to the land, in which case they were called serfs. These serfs could not be bought and sold like slaves but they could not leave the land.

The lord of the manor was often a warrior and might well have a lord to whom he himself paid homage. If a lord could not fight himself, he might be responsible for providing warriors or might have to pay money to provide for such warriors.

The Tetrarchy

By the middle of the third century the Roman Empire faced a seemingly insoluble dilemma. Barbarian forces were now capable of attacking in strength along borders that were thousands of miles long. The only way to repel these attacks was to give local generals strong forces to use at their own discretion, without having to consult a headquarters that might be many weeks' travel away.

This solution, however, created its own problems. When generals were given too much independence they became ambitious. Instead of fighting barbarians they devoted their energies to fighting one another for the throne. Much of the third century was devastated by a combination of civil war and invasion.

Diocletian designed the tetrarchy to solve both these problems. He split the empire into two parts, each governed by an Augustus. Further, each Augustus appointed a Caesar as his successor who also assisted in the government of his half of the empire.

In effect, the Roman Empire was now ruled by four men, each of whom had great independence in his own area of operations. Further, because the line of succession was set, Diocletian hoped to eliminate civil war.

On the whole, the system worked. Civil wars did not come to an end, especially when the tetrarchs fought each other, but the imperial thrones were more stable than in the worst years of the third century.

The tetrarchy did not prevent the ultimate Fall of the Western Empire but a certain amount of time had been bought. Moreoever, the tetrarchy provided the basis for government in the Eastern Empire, which would survive for nearly a thousand years.

GLOSSARY

Alaric:	Gothic king who sacked Rome in 410.
Attila the Hun:	Died 453. Leader of the Huns, one of the most destructive of the barbarian peoples.
Augustus:	After Diocletian's reorganization, "Augustus" was the title given to the ruler of each half of the empire.
Caesar:	Title given to the assistant and successor of an Augustus.
Constantine: (ruled 306–337)	The emperor who moved the capital of the Eastern Empire to Byzantium, which was renamed Constantinople.
Diocletian: (ruled 284–305)	The emperor who reorganized the empire as the tetrarchy.
Edward Gibbon: (1734–1794)	Author of *The Decline and Fall of the Roman Empire*, one of the great historical works in English. Gibbon believed that Christianity had contributed to the Fall of the Western Empire by weakening the Roman spirit.
Hadrian's Wall:	A defensive line across northern England, it marked the northwest limit of the Roman Empire.
Hero of Alexandria:	Lived early in the Christian era. He invented a workable steam engine.
Huns:	Originally a federation of Mongol tribes that began moving westward from Central Asia in the third century. Among the most destructive of the barbarian invaders, the Huns drove other tribes such as the Goths before them.
Malaria:	An infectious disease carried by the female anopheles mosquito. It may have been endemic in marshy areas throughout the empire.
Praetorian guard:	A corps of troops who formed the emperor's bodyguard. In times of unrest the praetorian guard often carried out coups to depose the emperor.
Romulus Augustulus:	The last emperor to rule the Western Empire from Rome. Deposed in 476.
Septimius Severus: (reigned 193–211)	An intelligent, ruthless emperor. He made clear his policy to win favor with the army.
Stilicho: (359?–408)	A Vandal and a Roman general. In 402 he moved the western capital from Rome to Ravenna.
Tetrarchy:	Reorganization of the empire started by Diocletian. The empire was split into an eastern and a western half, each of which was ruled by an Augustus. Each Augustus appointed an assistant called a Caesar, who would also succeed him. Each of these four men was responsible for the direct administration of a quarter of the empire.
Theodosius: (ruled 379–395)	Succeeded Valens as eastern emperor. Under his rule, Gothic heavy cavalry units became the main force of the Roman army, overshadowing the infantry.
Valens: (ruled 364–378)	Eastern emperor killed in battle against the Goths at Adrianople.

The Western Tradition: Unit Seven   115

TIMELINE

Place each of the following events on the timeline. In some cases you may have to specify a roughly defined period of time rather than a precise date.

1. Constantine moves his capital to Constantinople
2. Deposition of Romulus Augustulus
3. Death of Marcus Aurelius
4. Alaric's sack of Rome
5. Reign of Diocletian
6. Vandals cross into Gaul, later to Spain and North Africa
7. Stilicho moves imperial court to Ravenna
8. Beginning of pressure from the Huns on other barbarian peoples

|1 A.D.   500 A.D.|

MAP EXERCISE

Find the following locations on the map.

1. Gaul
2. The Danube
3. Two areas of the empire invaded between 375 and 425
4. Constantinople
5. The Rhine
6. Boundaries of the empire (ca. 150)
7. Illyria
8. Ravenna
9. Antioch
10. City sacked by Alaric in 410
11. Bordeaux
12. Balkans
13. Adriatic
14. Bosporous
15. The River Tyne

SELF-TEST

Part I

1. _____ invented a workable steam engine in the Classical period.

2. What was the population of the Roman Empire in the third and Fourth centuries A.D.?

3. The _____ were a federation of Mongol tribes. As they migrated westward they drove other tribes before them.

4. In the year _____ an army led by the Emperor _____ was annihilated by the Goths.

5. _____, the last emperor to rule the Western Empire from Rome, was deposed in the year _____.

Part II

1. Mark the false completion. The tetrarchy
    a. was intended to solve the problem of overextended administration.
    b. was accompanied by a great elaboration of court ritual.
    c. was accompanied by the growth of a military ruling class.
    d. ended fighting between rivals for the throne.

2. Mark the false completion. The agricultural crisis in the countryside
    a. caused small farmers to lose their land.
    b. was intensified because the cities drained wealth from the countryside.
    c. forced small holders into slavery.
    d. resulted in declining tax revenues.

3. Mark the false completion. As the Western Empire broke up, many towns
    a. became strongholds for the wealthy who fled to the cities for protection.
    b. drastically shrank in area.
    c. heavily fortified themselves.
    d. lost their importance as centers of culture.

4. Mark the false completion. In the fourth century A.D. the Roman army
    a. was increasingly made up of barbarians.
    b. was often in conflict with civilian administrators.
    c. contained a low proportion of troops from the center of the empire.
    d. refused to make the transition from emphasis on infantry to emphasis on cavalry.

5. In 402 A.D., Stilicho moved the Western capital from Rome to _____.
   Explain why:

OPTIONAL ACTIVITIES

Although the following activities are not required for the course unless assigned by the instructor, students are encouraged to read them as sources of interesting topics for further study.

Ancient Sources

Sources on the barbarian invasions and the collapse of the Western Empire are often difficult to use because many of them were written long after the events described. For this assignment read one of the following sources and write a paper of 3–5 pages in which you comment on the events of the fifth and sixth centuries as seen by the respective writers.

- Gregory of Tours, *The History of the Franks* (1974), trans. Lewis Thorpe, available in a Penguin Edition, is an important source for the Dark Ages, covered in Unit Nine. Book I, however, describes the last days of the empire as seen from a perspective several centuries later. How does Gregory account for the fall of Rome? What events does he choose to emphasize? Gregory was an important churchman. How does this perspective affect his narrative?

- *The Nibelungenlied* (1969), trans. A. T. Hatto, available in a Modern Library Edition, was written in the early thirteenth century, although the events it describes took place in the fifth century when the Huns destroyed the barbarian Kingdom of Burgundy. What can you deduce from this source about the values and psychology of the barbarian invaders? If you read this selection, remember that you are reading from a perspective almost eight centuries after the events described. How does the perspective affect the narrative? This reading is also useful for Units Nine and Ten.

- Edward Gibbon's *The History of the Decline and Fall of the Roman Empire*, written at the end of the eighteenth century, is still one of the classic accounts of the fall of Rome. For this assignment read one of the chapters of Volume One in which Gibbon discusses the latter days of the Western Empire (Chapter 15, Gibbon's indictment of the Christians, is especially recommended). Write a paper of 3–5 pages in which you discuss at least one of the following issues:

  - How does Gibbon's account differ from those you have found in the lectures and the textbook?
  - What kind of bias do you find in Gibbon or your other sources?
  - Do these biases invalidate their explanations?
  - How do these biases lead your sources to give more emphasis to some explanations and less to others?

REVIEW QUESTIONS

1. In discussing the fall of the Western Empire Professor Weber raises the issue of hypertrophy. He believes that the empire had grown so large that it collapsed under its own weight. Examine this claim in detail. Why, for instance, did the empire collapse in the fifth century? After all, the empire had reached its greatest extent three centuries earlier. Why did hypertrophy take so long to act? Professor Weber claims that most large empires suffer from similar problems. How did hypertrophy weaken or fail to weaken the empires of Egypt and Mesopotamia? Alexander's empire?

2. What are the explanations Professor Weber cites for the fall of the Western Empire? Do these explanations contradict one another? Do at least some of them complement one another? Some of these explanations apply to the whole empire but only the west collapsed. How can you explain the different fates of the two halves of the empire?

3. The ancient world possessed great technical skills and important thinkers in science and mathematics, yet technology never transformed the ancient economy. Why not?

4. In what ways did the Roman army reflect larger social problems within the empire? Examine the following two issues in detail:
   a. What caused increased hostility between soldiers and civilian administrators?
   b. Why was the Roman infantry, once the best in the known world, considered obsolete by the end of the fourth century?
5. In the course of the barbarian invasions how did cities change in the western half of the empire? What were the most important changes in the countryside? In what ways was a new political system forming in the countryside?
6. One of the most important weaknesses of the empire was that too much depended on the personal character of the emperor. Why did so much power become concentrated in his hands? Why could the empire not devise a less personal system of rule?

FURTHER READING

Sources

Weber, Eugen, *The Western Tradition*. 2nd ed. 1965 Julius Caesar: "The Germans," p. 183

Ammianus Marcellinus: "Roman Policy Toward the Germans," p. 184

St. Jerome: "Letters," p. 186

Appolinaris Sidonius: "Letters," p. 194

Gregory of Tours: "History of the Franks," p. 194

Studies

Balsdon, J. P. *Roman Women* (1962). Important text on social history.

Brown, Peter. *The World of Late Antiquity.* (1971). One of the best comprehensive summaries of the period.

Bury, J. B. *The Invasion of Europe by the Barbarians* (1928). Written by one of the great historians of the ancient world.

Jones, A. H. M. *The Decline of the Ancient World* (1966).

Kagan, Donald, ed. *The End of the Roman Empire: Decline or Transformation?* (1978). A collection of essays on different aspects of the end of the empire.

Katz, Solomon. *The Decline of Rome* (1955). A good short introduction.

L'Orange, H. P. *Art Forms and Civic Life in the Late Roman Empire* (1965). An important study of the impact of civic life on the art of late antiquity.

Lot, Ferdinand. *The End of the Ancient World* (1931). Treats political developments in detail.

Luttwak, E. N. *The Grand Strategy of the Roman Empire* (1976). Rather than concentrating on individual battles, Luttwak concentrates on the overall goals of the Roman Empire.

Macmullen, R. *Enemies of the Roman Order* (1966). A study of internal opposition to the emperors.

Rand, E. K. *Founders of the Middle Ages* (1928). Discusses the reactions of early Christians to the classics.

Seredy, Kate. *The White Stag* (1979). One of the few texts on the period written on the point of view of the Huns.

White, Lynn. *The Transformation of the Roman World* (1966). Interconnected essays.

FILMS AVAILABLE ON VIDEO

The Fall of the Roman Empire (1964). Hollywood epic with a good cast.

ANSWER KEY

Timeline

1. 330 A.D.
2. 476 A.D.
3. 180 A.D.
4. 410 A.D.
5. 285–385 A.D.
6. 406 A.D.
7. 402 A.D.
8. Mid-third century A.D.

Map Exercise

3. Italy, the Balkans, Gaul, North Africa, and Spain are all good answers.
10. Rome.

Self-Test

Part I
1. Hero of Alexandria
2. Between fifty and sixty-five million people
3. Huns
4. 378 A.D.; Valens
5. Romulus Augustulus; 476 A.D.

Part II
1. (d) ended fighting between rivals for the throne.
2. (c) forced small holders into slavery
3. (a) became strongholds for the wealthy who fled to the cities for protection.
4. (d) refused to make the transition from emphasis on infantry to emphasis on cavalry.
5. Ravenna. Ravenna could be more easily defended behind its marshes and could be readily evacuated by sea.

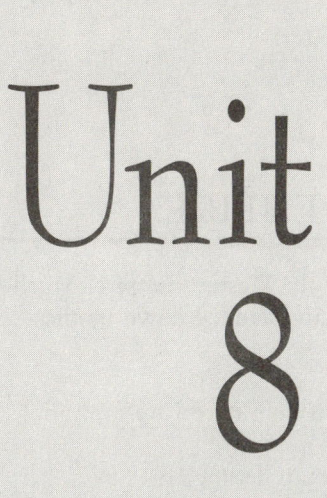

Unit 8

Program 15: The Byzantine Empire

Program 16: The Fall of Byzantium

LEARNING OBJECTIVES

After completing Unit Eight students should understand the following issues:

- The principal differences among Islam, Orthodox Christianity, and Roman Catholicism. Do Professor Weber and your textbook explain the bitterness with which these creeds have fought one another throughout so much of their history?

- The political consequences that derived from these differences. How do Professor Weber and your textbook assess the sources of strength and weakness of these religions?

- The ways in which the Byzantine and Islamic empires preserved and transmitted culture. Use your textbook to specify which sorts of knowledge were transmitted by the Byzantines and by the Islamic powers.

- The strengths and weaknesses of the Byzantine emperors.

- The military strengths and weaknesses of the Byzantine and Islamic empires. Compare the assessments in the lectures and in your textbook.

TV INSTRUCTION

OVERVIEW
PROGRAM 15: THE BYZANTINE EMPIRE

Emperors reigned at Constantinople for a thousand years after the fall of the Western Empire. Much of the heritage of Greece and Rome survived only because it was preserved and handed down by the Byzantine Empire.

I. When the Emperor Constantine transferred the capital of the Eastern Empire to Constantinople, he founded a second Rome.
   A. The Byzantines copied and preserved much of the Greek and Roman heritage in
      1. art.
      2. literature.
      3. law.
   B. Byzantine missionaries converted the eastern Slavs from the Balkans to the Baltic Sea.
   C. From 330, when Byzantium was rechristened Constantinople, until 1453, when the city fell to the Turks, the Byzantine state endured for a longer time than any other political institution in the Western tradition, with the exception of Egypt.

II. Although Constantinople aspired to rule the old Roman Mediterranean Empire, the city was not well situated for such a role.
   A. The average ship needed two weeks to cross the Mediterranean from north to south.
   B. A journey from east to west could require two or three months.
   C. Despite these obstacles, in the sixth century the Emperor Justinian regained
      1. Italy from the Goths.
      2. North Africa from the Vandals.
   D. But the effort was so great that
      1. he exhausted the resources of Byzantium.
      2. he destroyed the Italian economy.
      3. he killed a great part of the Italian population.
   E. Further, these reconquests were short-lived.

III. Byzantium reached its high point from the eighth to the twelfth centuries, after the empire had shrunk and become more defensible.
   A. It had lost outlying possessions to
      1. the Arabs.
      2. the Slavs.
   B. But the empire itself survived waves of barbarian attacks.

IV. Constantinople lay at the crossroads between Europe and Asia.
   A. Built on a high peninsula on the Bosphorus, the city was very close to the Asian shore.
   B. It commanded the route from the Caucasus and the Russian steppes to the Mediterranean.
   C. It was a link between the valleys of the Danube and the Euphrates.

V. Professor Weber argues that perhaps the most important factor in the empire's survival was the conviction that the empire had been willed by God.
   A. Byzantine wars were fought like Crusades, with troops marching behind holy icons.

B. This religious conviction may also explain Byzantium's political conservatism: What reason could there be to change a political system that had been ordained by God?
C. Although the emperor was God's anointed,
1. many emperors were murdered.
2. A change in rulers, however, did not mean a change in basic policies.

VI. The political history of Byzantium was very different from that of the Western Empire.
A. Many separate states arose from the ruins of the Western Empire.
1. In the west people lived under many different law codes:
a. tribal law.
b. local law.
c. manorial law.
d. the law of the central or would-be central state.
2. The authority of the central government fought a continuous battle for recognition in the countryside.
B. In the east, however, the single state was preserved.
1. There was only one law, Roman law.
2. Even decisions of the church councils needed the emperor's approval.
a. Unlike the Pope, the Patriarch of Constantinople always lived in the shadow of the imperial ruler.
b. This political system is called Caesaropapism, in which the ruler of the state is also the effective ruler of the church.

VII. According to Professor Weber, the power of the Byzantine emperor represented the triumph of the Hellenistic view of the emperor's position.
A. Some aspects of this view went as far back as Alexander the Great.
B. The Emperor Diocletian had explicitly claimed such power.
C. Because the emperor was God's anointed, the Byzantines were ready to acknowledge emperors who had come to power in a variety of ways:
1. by election.
2. through royal descent.
3. by seizing power in a coup.
D. Some of the emperors had come from humble backgrounds.
E. Once a man became emperor, he could not be deposed except through successful revolution.
1. Failed revolutionaries were horribly punished.
2. But a successful rebel would be granted complete authority,
3. because his victory was considered to be a sign of God's approval.
a. Approximately one-third of all the emperors were usurpers.
b. Approximately the same number died in violent circumstances.

VIII. The sanctity and reverence that surrounded the emperor were not always a sign of his real strength.
A. In the third through the fifth centuries, when the personal position of the emperor was especially weak, imperial ceremonies stiffened and increased the distance between ruler and ruled.
B. The emperors may have hoped that awe would save them from at least their more impressionable subjects.
C. Ceremony and splendor were also useful for impressing ambassadors and other rulers, especially those from less sophisticated parts of the world.

IX. The Byzantines acted on the principle that diplomacy was cheaper than war.
A. Friendly rulers were sometimes given Byzantine princesses in marriage to create a dynastic relationship with the imperial house.
B. Bishops of the Orthodox Church were sent out to maintain both religious and political interests in foreign parts.

X. The Byzantine Empire was strong only when it could maintain a strong fiscal structure.
   A. In the third century the economy of both parts of the empire collapsed.
      1. Inflation soared.
      2. The economy threatened to lapse into barter.
   B. In the fourth century, however, reforms restored the value of money and taxation was reestablished.
      1. Ultimately, these reforms were not enough to save the western part of the empire.
      2. But the eastern half survived on a firm economic foundation.

XI. The ability of the government to raise taxes allowed the Eastern Empire to maintain a highly trained army and navy.
   A. Because war was a matter of survival for the Byzantines, they were constantly developing strategies and practical improvements:
      1. drill.
      2. special tactics.
      3. secret weapons such as Greek fire.
   B. These matters gave the Byzantines an important advantage when they were fighting armies such as those in the west whose commanders neglected such matters.
   C. Such improvements allowed the Byzantines to do great things with relatively small numbers.
      1. Belisarius, for instance, reconquered North Africa from the Vandals with about 15,000 men.
      2. He needed only 8,000 men to reconquer Italy.
      3. By the tenth century the grand total of Byzantine military forces was at most 140,000.

XII. Professor Weber argues that the Orthodox faith was even more important to survival than the army.
   A. The empire never had a common nationality.
   B. But the Orthodox faith provided a unifying bond.
   C. The church was crucial to the state in ways that were very different from the position of the church in the west.

KEY TO THE IMAGES

Greek fire:
For a millennium after the fall of the Western Empire, emperors ruled at Constantinople, often under pressure from enemies who greatly outnumbered them. The Byzantines owed their survival to an efficient and innovative army and navy and to the system of taxation that provided regular support.

The Byzantines also possessed secret weapons, the most prominent of which was known as Greek fire. This was a flammable mixture of quicklime, sulfur, and petroleum that could be sprayed from tubes onto enemy ships and armies. Although Greek fire was by no means the only key to Byzantine survival, it greatly impressed contemporaries and is often portrayed in battle scenes, particularly scenes of naval battles.

Divine sanction:
Byzantine emperors always claimed to have been chosen by God to rule the empire. Even a successful rebel or usurper could claim divine sanction. Victory was a sign of God's approval.

The depth of this attitude appears most clearly in Byzantine art. Rulers did not hesitate to have themselves portrayed in the same picture with Christ or the Virgin. This program shows the Virgin and Child enthroned between the Emperors Constantine I and Justinian I. This tendency lasted throughout the history of the empire. Sometime between 1028 and 1034, the Emperor Constantine IX and the Empress Zoo were portrayed on either side of Christ.

The attempt to associate oneself with divinity was imitated by rulers in other parts of Europe. An image from Sicily portrays William II offering the church of Monreale to the Virgin.

The Western Tradition: Unit Eight 125

FOCUS QUESTIONS

1. In what ways did the Byzantine Empire preserve and pass on the heritage of Greece and Rome?
2. How were the Byzantines able to rule an extensive empire for such a long period of time?
3. How did religious conflicts weaken the empire? How did the Orthodox religion strengthen the empire?
4. How did Byzantine emperors use rituals and art to elevate themselves to semidivine status?
5. How did the different economies of the east and west affect the ability of these areas to defend themselves and wage war?

OVERVIEW
PROGRAM 16: THE FALL OF BYZANTIUM

Throughout its history the Byzantine state was intimately tied to the Greek Orthodox church. Although the piety of its subjects often strengthened the government, this close relationship had important dangers, for religious controversies could tear the empire apart. Religious disagreements weakened the empire as it faced the Islamic invasions and the religious split between the Greek Orthodox and the Roman Catholic churches was an important stage in the tensions between east and west.

I. Unlike the Latin church, which never quite identified itself with the Western Empire, the Greek Orthodox church was practically one with the state.
   A. Orthodox missionaries, for instance, were also ambassadors of the Byzantine state.
   B. When pagan rulers converted they usually became political allies.
   C. Much of the Slavic world was converted from Byzantium.
      1. In the ninth century Saints Cyril and Methodius produced a script and a liturgy that was used by
         a. the Bulgarians.
         b. the Slavs of the Balkans.
      2. In the tenth century this script and liturgy were adopted by the Russians.

II. Because the church was so important to the state, theological disputes often became political quarrels.
   A. For instance, the Orthodox church insisted that Christ had two natures:
      1. human.
      2. divine.
   B. Another group of Christians, however, the Monophysites—literally the "one naturists"—argued that Christ had only one nature, totally divine.
   C. The theological quarrel was intensified because many Monophysites lived in areas that resented the central government in Constantinople, areas such as
      1. Egypt.
      2. Syria.
   D. The dispute became especially bitter at a time when the empire badly needed unity.

III. The Prophet Mohammed had announced a new religious revelation in Arabia.
   A. Mohammed recognized that other men had been prophets from God, or Allah, prophets such as
      1. Moses.
      2. Jesus.
   B. He claimed, however, to be the last prophet, the only one to reveal Allah's complete truth. He taught
      1. strict monotheism.

2. a straightforward ritual
   a. similar to Jewish ritual.
   b. emphasizing cleanliness.
3. Basic virtues such as
   a. courage.
   b. charity.
   c. hospitality.
4. The promise that those who died for the faith would immediately enter paradise.

IV. Within a few generations Islam had conquered much of the known world.
   A. By his death in 632, Mohammed had united all the tribes of Arabia.
   B. By 644, his followers had conquered
      1. Egypt.
      2. Libya.
      3. Syria.
      4. Iraq.
      5. Persia.
   C. By the end of the century Muslims had continued their conquests by
      1. conquering the remnants of the Persian Empire.
      2. laying siege to Constantinople.
   D. Within another fifteen years Islam had spread from India to Spain.

V. In part the Muslims were successful because much of their religion and culture fit in with other traditions.
   A. Mohammed himself came from crossroads of Middle Eastern culture.
      1. He was a merchant of Mecca, a great trading town.
      2. He found support in Medina, another trading center.
   B. Mohammad also drew a great deal from Judaism and Christianity.
      1. He considered the Old and New Testaments to be holy books.
      2. He taught that Jesus and the prophets of the Old Testament had been true messengers of God.
   C. The Arabs themselves shared a culture similar to that of people throughout the Middle East.
      1. Arabic was closely related to Aramaic, which was spoken by common people from
         a. Iraq
         b. to Palestine.
      2. Eventually Arabic would become a *lingua franca* extending from
         a. Spain
         b. to India.

VI. Perhaps the greatest reason for their success was that the Arabs were relatively tolerant in religious matters.
   A. Muslims asserted that Mohammed had brought a higher revelation than those of Christianity or Judaism. Therefore,
      1. Muslims enjoyed special privileges.
      2. only Muslims could enter paradise.
   B. Nonbelievers, however, were not exterminated and were allowed to practice their religion, although they did have special obligations:
      1. only non-Muslims paid taxes.
         a. This arrangement encouraged conversion.
         b. At the same time, however, Muslims had fiscal reasons for tolerating nonbelievers.
   C. Despite these obligations, nonbelievers often felt less burdened under Muslim rule than they had under the Byzantines.
      1. Even though they paid the entire tax burden, they paid no more than they had under the Byzantines and often less.
      2. Christian dissenters such as the Monophysites of Syria and Egypt had more freedom of worship.

VII. The Muslims were quick to learn from other cultures.
   A. They developed bureaucratic and authoritarian institutions similar to those of
      1. Byzantium.
      2. Persia.
   B. They preserved and developed the heritage of Greece and Persia:
      1. philosophy.
         a. They passed on the works of Plato
         b. and Aristotle.
      2. geography.
      3. astronomy.
      4. mathematics.
         a. they borrowed "Arabic" numerals from the Hindus and introduced them to the west.
         b. they passed on the concept of zero in arithmetic.
         c. they made important contributions to algebra.
      5. chemistry.
      6. medicine: in the tenth century, when the first medical school was founded in the west, at Salerno, it was staffed by Muslims.
      7. architecture.
         a. the minarets of their mosques.
         b. the belltowers of western churches.
   C. They created an international network of letters and science that extended from Spain to India.
   D. In the eighth century the Muslim advance was checked along certain fronts.
      1. In 718 the Arabs failed to take Constantinople after a year-long siege.
      2. In 733 they were driven out of Gaul by the Franks.

VIII. The iconoclastic controversy divided Christians throughout this period.
   A. Holy images, or icons, were venerated throughout much of the Christian world.
      1. These images depicted
         a. Christ.
         b. the Virgin Mary
         c. many of the saints.
      2. These icons were believed to have miraculous powers of
         a. healing.
         b. protection.
   B. Holy images were especially venerated in the western church.
   C. In the eastern church, however, a substantial body of opinion considered these images to be sacrilege.
      1. Iconoclasm was especially strong in areas where the church hoped to make converts among
         a. Jews.
         b. Muslims.
      2. Because these people found images repugnant
   D. Between 726 and 843 the eastern church banned icons.
      1. Because images were venerated in the west, a split developed between the church of Rome and the church of Constantinople.
      2. In the west the popes no longer looked to Byzantium for military support but now looked for aid to the Franks, who had driven the Arabs from Gaul.

IX. Eventually the split between the eastern and western churches developed into a complete rupture.
   A. Even after icons were restored in the east, the churches disagreed on many issues:
      1. Should priests marry?
      2. Should priests wear beards?
      3. Should the bread in the sacrament be leavened or unleavened?
   B. The official reason for the split in 1054 was a disagreement over the creed.

C. Apart from theological considerations the split resulted for several political and cultural reasons.
   1. Greek contempt for the barbarian west.
   2. Western disdain for the Greeks.
   3. The cultures of east and west had become so different that they no longer provided a sense of unity or common purpose.

X. Throughout this period Constantinople was the great cosmopolitan center of the western world.
   A. As many as a million people may have lived there.
   B. It contained wonders seen in few other places in the world:
      1. miles of paved streets.
      2. arcades of shops.
      3. running water in every neighborhood.
      4. a hippodrome greater than the Colosseum.
      5. the cathedral of Santa Sophia.

XI. For much of this period the west was poor and backward.
   A. In exchange for the riches of Byzantium the west could only offer
      1. iron.
      2. timber.
      3. slaves.
      4. woolens.
   B. Byzantium was eventually beset from all quarters by
      1. Turks in Anatolia.
      2. Normans in
         a. Italy
         b. Greece.
      3. Italian sea powers, especially
         a. Genoa.
         b. Venice.
   C. In 1204 the city was captured not by Muslims but by Christian Crusaders, who had been persuaded by the Venetians to attack the city.
      1. Venice came to dominate the eastern Mediterranean.
      2. Although a Greek dynasty eventually regained the throne, the Byzantine Empire was permanently crippled.

XII. Despite enormous obstacles the Byzantines were responsible for achievements seen in few other parts of the world.
   A. The pressures on Byzantium were unending:
      1. ruthless taxation.
      2. tyrannical government.
      3. land-grabbing nobility.
      4. barbarian attacks.
   B. Nevertheless, the Byzantines created many institutions that embodied charity and social justice.
      1. Hospitals that cared for
         a. lepers.
         b. the aged.
         c. other ailments.
      2. Hostels for
         a. pilgrims.
         b. strangers.
         c. old people.

3. maternity homes.
   4. refuges for
      a. abandoned children.
      b. the poor.
C. The city finally fell to a Turkish attack in 1453.

KEY TO THE IMAGES

Images of Christ:
Throughout the history of the church Christ has been portrayed in many different ways. In the early days he was often portrayed as the Good Shepherd protecting his flock of souls. After the empire became Christian, however, other images of Christ began to appear as well. Christ often appears on a throne in the image of a great ruler. In representations of the Last Judgment he appears as more of a judge than a savior. Christ was portrayed as both judge and savior but emphasis varied widely.

Christ and Mohammed:
Although Christians denounced Mohammed as a false prophet, Muslims had a different view of Christ. According to Mohammed, Christ and the prophets of the Old Testament had all been true messengers from God. Mohammed was the last and greatest of a long line.

This attitude appears in a Turkish miniature seen in Program 16 showing Christ on a donkey riding side by side with Mohammed, who is mounted on a camel. The two prophets appear to be colleagues rather than rivals.

The iconoclasts:
During the eighth and ninth centuries the eastern church was torn by the struggle over holy images. When the iconoclasts were in power, much religious art was destroyed or defaced. One of the images in the show portrays a group of bishops defacing an image of Christ.

Christian and Muslim architecture:
The cathedral of Santa Sophia in Constantinople was one of the greatest churches in Christendom. It is clear, however, from such buildings as the Mohammed Ali mosque in Cairo that the influence of Santa Sophia was not limited to the Christian world.

Borrowing, however, went on in both directions. The minarets, or towers of mosques from which the *muezzin* called the faithful to prayer, clearly influenced the spires and bell towers of Christian churches.

FOCUS QUESTIONS

1. What were the consequences of the close association between the Byzantine Empire and the Orthodox church?
2. Why did Islam spread so extensively in the century after the death of Mohammed?
3. What issues led to the division between the Orthodox and Roman Catholic churches?
4. What were some of the features that made Constantinople the leading city of Christendom for so many centuries?
5. In what concrete ways did the Byzantine state embody the principles of Christian charity?
6. Why were the Byzantines able to develop a bureaucracy and a diplomatic service long before such institutions appeared in Western Europe?

ASSIGNMENTS & ACTIVITIES

IN CONTEXT

Themes and issues that set Unit Eight in context with other units include the following:

- The Orthodox and Roman Catholic churches separated in 1054, in part as a result of a theological dispute about the nature of the trinity. Look back to earlier units to the monophysite and Arian heresies. In later units look at the issues that separated the Protestant reformers from the theology of the Catholic church.

- The Orthodox church considered the Byzantine emperor to be God's deputy on earth. Look back to earlier units in which we learn Hellenistic and Roman rulers sometimes claimed to be gods in their own right. As a Christian, the Byzantine emperor could not make this claim, but examine the religious claims he did make to support his authority. In later units watch for arguments made by secular rulers in western Europe to provide a religious underpinning for their authority.

- Both Islam and Christianity played important roles as transmitters of Greek and Roman learning. Look back to Units Five through Seven on the Roman Empire. In what ways were the Romans themselves transmitting or spreading the learning of earlier times? Look ahead to Unit Thirteen on the Renaissance. Watch for ways in which learning would eventually be carried on by secular as well as religious scholars.

- Throughout the period covered by Unit Eight the Byzantine Empire acted as a buffer between western Europe and much of Islam. In later units on the Crusades, watch for ways in which the Crusaders began to exert their power in the east. How would the Crusaders strengthen or weaken the Byzantine Empire?

- The Byzantine Empire possessed a bureaucracy and a corps of diplomats long before these institutions appeared in the west. Look back to the institutions of the Roman Empire. In what ways were the Byzantines simply following procedures laid down long before? In what ways were they innovators? Look ahead to units on the fifteenth century, when the states of western Europe developed similar institutions. Did these states follow the Byzantine model or did they create their own institutions quite independently?

TEXTBOOK ASSIGNMENT

Read the following pages in your assigned textbook:

Text: *Western Civilizations*, Fifteenth Edition (Norton, 2005)
Read: Chapter 7, "Rome's Three Heirs: The Byzantine, Islamic, and Early-Medieval Western Worlds," pp. 246-285.

Text: *The Western Experience*, Eighth Edition (McGraw-Hill, 2003)
Read: From Chapter 7, "The Empires of the Early Middle Ages (800–1000): Creation and Erosion," pp. 210-219, 228-245; and from Chapter 10, "The Urban Economy and the Consolidation of States," pp. 340-349.

The Western Tradition: Unit Eight

Text: *The Western Heritage,* Ninth Edition (Prentice Hall, 2007)
Read: From Chapter 6, "Late Antiquity and the Early Middle Ages: Creating a New European Society and Culture (476-1000)," pp. 194-200.

Text: *The Western Heritage,* TLC, Fifth Edition (Prentice Hall, 2007)
Read: From Chapter 6, "Late Antiquity and the Early Middle Ages: Creating a New European Society and Culture (476-1000)," pp. 146-171.

ISSUES FOR CLARIFICATION

Iconoclasm

The second of the Ten Commandments given to Moses reads: "Thou shalt not make unto thee any graven image, or any likeness of any thing that is in heaven above, or that is in the earth beneath, or that is in the water under the earth."

Throughout much of their history Jews and Muslims have interpreted this commandment as a strict prohibition against making any kind of figurative representation, even the holiest of images. Christians, however, have usually interpreted the passage more broadly, claiming that God only forbids the making of idols or images of false gods. Most Christians at most times have accepted holy images and in many periods these images have been objects of great veneration.

In some sections of the Byzantine Empire, however, Christians believed that the commandment should be interpreted more strictly. Because Jews and Muslims found images repugnant, the Byzantines often promoted iconoclasm in areas where they hoped to make converts. Between 726 and 843 the Byzantine emperors actually forbade holy images in churches. This period of iconoclasm, which literally means "the breaking of images," led to great turmoil within the empire.

Because the Latin church held images in great veneration, iconoclasm also created great tensions between the popes and the Byzantine emperors.

Monophysites

Christians believe that Christ is God and man simultaneously: not a man who became a god, not a god in human form. Throughout the early history of the Church there were many explanations of this seeming paradox. The position eventually adopted by church councils was that Christ embodied two natures, one human and one divine, that were inextricably combined. Many Christians, however, disagreed with this interpretation. Among them were the Monophysites, who were especially strong in Egypt and Syria. The Monophysites believed that Christ had only one nature, which was both human and divine. Because the Byzantine Empire tried to impose theological consistency, Monophysites were often persecuted. After the Islamic conquests, many Monophysites preferred living under Muslim rule because they enjoyed more toleration than they had under the Byzantine Empire.

GLOSSARY

Basileus: Greek title meaning "royal king"; the title of the Byzantine emperor.

Bosporus: Strait between the Black Sea and the Sea of Marmora. Constantinople stood on the western shore.

Byzantium: Greek city on the Bosporus, renamed Constantinople.

Caesaropapism:	System of government in which the head of the secular government is also head of the church.
Coptic church:	Christian Church in Egypt, whose members were Monophysites, believing that Christ embodied only one nature rather than the two natures claimed by Orthodox theologians. The Copts were persecuted by Constantinople and in many cases were better off after Egypt was conquered by Islamic forces.
Saint Cyril:	Byzantine missionary sent with Saint Methodius to convert the Slavs in the ninth century. The two missionaries produced a script for writing slavic languages.
Goths:	Germanic people with whom the Byzantines fought a long war in the sixth century. This war temporarily restored much of the Mediterranean to the Byzantine Empire.
Greek fire:	A flammable oil-based compound used as a secret weapon by the Byzantine army and navy.
Icon:	Holy image that becomes an object of veneration.
Iconoclasm:	Movement within the Eastern Orthodox church that ordered the destruction of icons. Iconoclasm was the official policy of the Orthodox church between 726 and 843.
Islam:	In Arabic, "submission to God's will." *Islam* is the preferred term for the religion founded by Mohammed. Muslims feel that the term *Mohammedism* falsely suggests that Muslims worship Mohammed as God in the same way that Christians worship Christ.
Justinian:	Byzantine emperor from 527–565. During his reign the church of Santa Sophia was rebuilt, the Roman Law was recodified, and Italy and North Africa were temporarily reconquered for the empire.
Mecca:	Trading city in Arabia, the home of Mohammed. Now the holiest city in Islam.
Saint Methodius:	Byzantine missionary sent with Saint Cyril to convert the Slavs in the ninth century. The two missionaries produced a script for writing slavic languages.
Minarets:	Spires from which a Muslim crier, called a *Muezzin*, summons the faithful to prayer.
Mohammed:	Founder of Islam. Muslims do not worship Mohammed as God but rather venerate him as the last and greatest of God's prophets.
Monophysites:	Movement especially strong in Egypt and Syria that believed that Christ embodied only one nature. This doctrine contradicted the teaching of the Orthodox church and Monophysites were often persecuted in Byzantine lands.
Patriarch of Constantinople:	Bishop of Constantinople. Until 1054, the Patriarch acknowledged the superior authority of the Pope. After that time the Patriarch became the highest clergyman in the Eastern Orthodox church.
Pope:	Bishop of Rome. Until 1054, the Pope was the nominal leader of both the Latin and Greek churches.
Santa Sophia:	Church of the Holy Wisdom in Constantinople. Perhaps the greatest example of Byzantine architecture.
Vandals:	Germanic people from whom the Byzantines reconquered much of North Africa in the sixth century.
Venice:	Great Italian trading city at the head of the Adriatic. By the thirteenth century Venice had become an important commercial rival of Constantinople.

TIMELINE

Place each of the following events on the timeline. In some cases you may have to specify a roughly defined period of time rather than a precise date.

1. Fall of Constantinople to the Turks
2. Constantinople becomes the imperial capital
3. Start of schism between Orthodox and Roman Catholic churches
4. Death of Mohammed
5. Constantinople falls to western Crusaders
6. Arabs driven out of Gaul by the Franks
7. Height of Iconoclastic controversy
8. Beginning of missionary activity to the Slavs
9. Period of most rapid Arab expansion
10. Period of Byzantine's Mediterranean Empire

|300 A.D.   1500 A.D.|

MAP EXERCISE

Find the following locations on the map.

1. Alexandria
2. Arabia
3. Mecca
4. Spain
5. Libya
6. Genoa
7. Venice
8. Balkans
9. Syria
10. Iraq
11. Bosporus
12. Caucasus

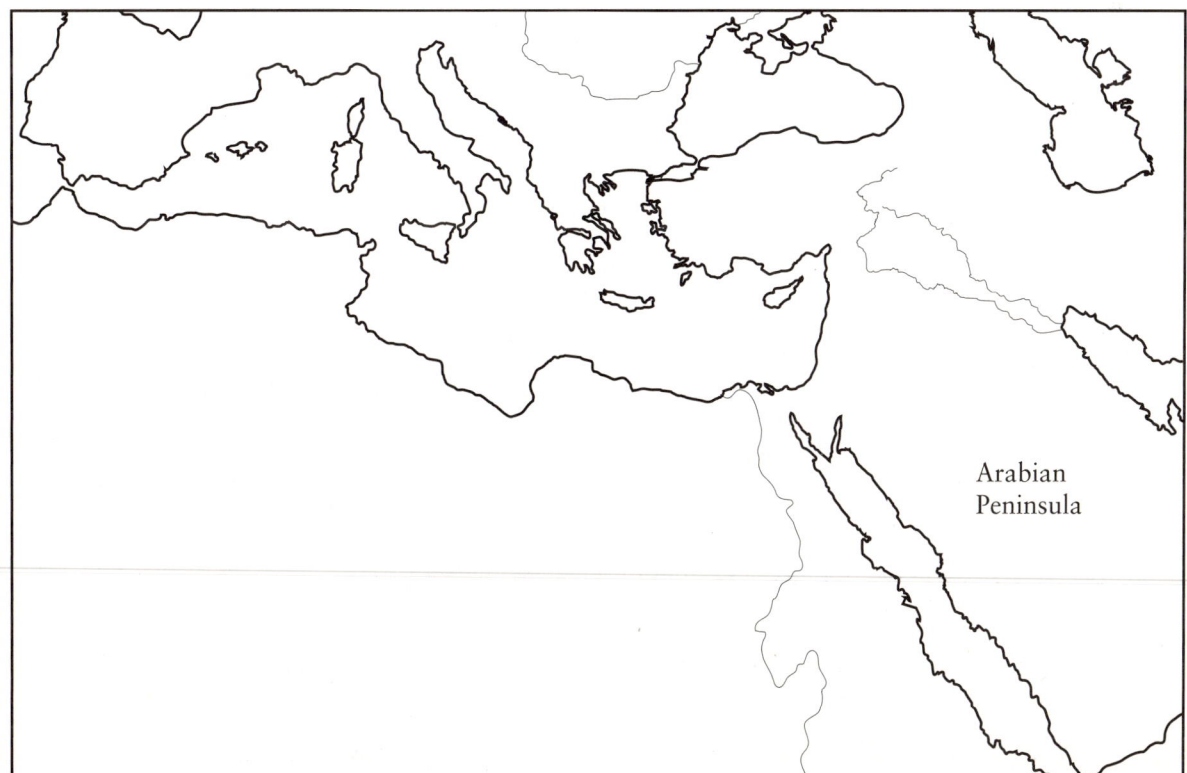

SELF-TEST

Part I

1. The Emperor, who died in 337, removed the imperial capital to Byzantium.
    a. Diocletian
    b. Constantine
    c. Julian
    d. Valens

2. In 1054 the Pope and the Patriarch of Constantinople excommunicated each other,
    a. because the Patriarch refused to give up iconoclasm.
    b. as a result of a theological disagreement over the nature of the trinity.
    c. because both the Pope and the Patriarch claimed supremacy over the whole Christian world.
    d. because the Patriarch was suspected of showing too much sympathy with Islam.

3. In _____ Constantinople fell to western Crusaders, and in 1453 the city fell to _____.

4. In which of the following areas were the Islamic armies turned back soon after their initial conquests?
    a. Egypt
    b. Gaul
    c. Syria
    d. Lybia

5. _____ was the movement that demanded the removal or destruction of religious images in churches.

Part II

1. Mark the false completion. The following factors were important advantages enjoyed by the Byzantines in preserving their empire:
    a. the ability of the economy to pay taxes.
    b. a well-trained, professional army.
    c. the Byzantine policy of religious toleration.
    d. an extensive bureaucracy and corps of diplomats.

2. Mark the false completion. Islam
    a. took no interest in preserving the culture of Greece or Rome.
    b. borrowed important elements of ritual from the Jews.
    c. imposed a greater burden of taxation on non-Muslims than on Muslims.
    d. recognized the Hebrew prophets as true messengers of God.

3. Mark the true completion. The Greek Orthodox church
    a. was largely free of political pressure from the emperors.
    b. unlike Islam was not effective in spreading its religion.
    c. tried to impose a uniform theology throughout the empire.
    d. tried to heal the split with Rome by acknowledging western political leaders as the equals of the emperor.

4. Mark the false completion. The elaborate rituals surrounding the Byzantine emperors
   a. were intended to impress the ambassadors of foreign powers by making the emperor seem to be almost a god.
   b. owed a great deal to the emperor worship of the pagan Roman Empire.
   c. effectively prevented attempts on the emperor's life.
   d. were imitated by Islamic rulers.

5. Mark the true completion. The eastern and western halves of what had been the old united Roman Empire
   a. were both able to develop systems of taxation able to maintain a well-trained army.
   b. remained united in theological terms, although they disagreed on many other matters.
   c. both participated in the struggle against Islam.
   d. maintained a similar separation between secular and religious powers.

OPTIONAL ACTIVITY

Although the following activity is not required for the course unless assigned by the instructor, students are encouraged to read it as a source of further study Using Biased Sources.

One of the most common problems facing historians is to find ways of using sources that display an obvious bias. *The Secret History of Procopius* is an especially good example (see Further Reading). Much of the book consists of lurid tales of Byzantine politics, including many accounts of the supernatural. Although the book is fascinating, how can it be used as a historical source when so much of it is untrue or even impossible? Write an account of 3–4 pages on Procopius's treatment of one Byzantine emperor. The sections on Justinian are especially good. What do these scandalous tales tell you about the psychology of the Byzantine world?

REVIEW QUESTIONS

1. Islam has much in common with Judaism and Christianity. What are the most important resemblances? What are the most important differences? Compare the Jewish Messiah, Christ, and Mohammed. How do their respective religions view these central figures?

2. Throughout Byzantine history religious struggles were translated into politics and vice versa. Name two episodes in which religious issues affected the politics of the empire.

3. What was special about the Byzantine Empire that brought religion and politics so close together? In what earlier states were religion and politics so closely entwined?

4. The Byzantine Empire greatly expanded and contracted throughout its history. What military advantages did the empire enjoy? What disadvantages? In what ways did religion help or hinder Byzantine efforts to control their empire?

5. How did Byzantine art and ceremony exalt the emperor? Why did emperors find it necessary to assume such majesty? As you look at the images in Programs 15 and 16, what are some of the most important ways of portraying the emperor? How did these images symbolize his power?

6. In what ways did the Byzantine and Islamic empires preserve and transmit the learning of the ancient world? In what ways did the two empires spread their respective religions?

FURTHER READING

Geankopolos, Deno J. *Byzantine East and Latin West* (1966). Especially good on the different evolutions of the two halves of the old empire.

Gibb, Hamilton A. *Mohammedism: An Historical Survey* (1953).

Hodgson, M. *The Venture of Islam.* Three volumes (1974). A masterpiece of scholarship.

Kennedy, Hugh. *The Prophet and the Age of the Caliphates* (1986). The political history of Islam from the sixth through the eleventh centuries.

Khaldun, Tbn. *The Muqqaddimah* (1969). Ibn Khaldun was one of the great Islamic scholars in the Middle Ages. This work is his introduction to world history.

Lewis, Bernard. "The Arabs in History" (1966). A short, comprehensive essay.

Mango, Cyril. *Byzantium: The Empire of New Rome* (1981). One of the most comprehensive surveys. Stresses continuities with the older empire.

Ostrogorski, George. *History of the Byzantine State* (1969). The standard political history.

Ostrogorsky, George. *History of the Byzantine State* (1957). Detailed political history.

Pelikan, Jaroslav. *The Christian Tradition; Volume II: The Spirit of Eastern Christendom* (1974). Detailed treatment of religious doctrines.

Procopius. *Secret History* (1961). Written in the early Middle Ages, the book is full of scandal about Byzantine history.

Runciman, Steven. *Byzantine Civilization* (1970). Succinct and thorough. Runciman is a graceful stylist.

Vasiliev, A. A. *History of the Byzantine Empire* (1952). Comprehensive but dry. Best used for reference on individual topics. Strong on cultural history.

ANSWER KEY

Timeline

1. 1453
2. 330
3. 1054
4. 632
5. 1204
6. 732
7. 726–843 (only an approximate answer is necessary)
8. Ninth century
9. Early seventh century to the mid-eighth century
10. Sixth century

Self-Test

Part I
1. (b) Constantine
2. (b) as a result of a theological disagreement over the nature of the trinity
3. 1204; the Turks
4. (b) Gaul
5. Iconoclasm

Part II
1. (c) the Byzantine policy of religious toleration.
2. (a) took no interest in preserving the culture of Greece or Rome.
3. (c) tried to impose a uniform theology throughout the empire.
4. (c) effectively prevented attempts on the emperor's life.
5. (c) both participated in the struggle against Islam.

Unit 9

Program 17: The Dark Ages

Program 18: The Age of Charlemagne

LEARNING OBJECTIVES

After completing Unit Nine students should understand the following issues:

- The impact of Christianity on barbarian cultures. Use your textbook to supplement Professor Weber's discussion of the conversion of various barbarian peoples.

- The sources of the church's power within these cultures. Use your textbook to discover which of the barbarian peoples were most ready to accept Christianity.

- The ways in which the church promoted learning and education, especially in the monasteries.

- The most important economic developments of the period.

- The attempts of the Carolingians to create a new European empire. How does your textbook explain the successes of the Carolingian Empire? Why, however, would Europe not be safe from invasion for another two centuries? Compare your textbook with Professor Weber's interpretation.

- The effects of the barbarian invasions of the ninth and tenth centuries.

TV INSTRUCTION

OVERVIEW
PROGRAM 17: THE DARK AGES

During the fifth century the material and political structure of the Western Empire collapsed. Europe was now torn by the wars of a myriad of barbarian powers. Learning, culture, and whatever attempts there were at social welfare were now taken over by the church. Although the church eventually converted the barbarians, the barbarians themselves often corrupted the church. The new civilization in the west was slow to take root.

I. The material culture of the west was shattered along with the political structure.
   A. In some places lands in fertile valleys were abandoned because they were vulnerable to attack.
   B. People sometimes moved to upland areas that had not been inhabited since the Stone Age.
      1. These places did not provide a good living,
      2. but they were better protected from attack.

II. At the political level, barbarian kingdoms, many of them quite small, replaced the empire.
   A. Spain was dominated by the Visigoths, who were themselves conquered by the Arabs in the early eighth century.
   B. Italy was ruled by the Lombards, especially in the north.
   C. Gaul was dominated by
      1. Franks.
      2. Burgundians.
   D. England was conquered by
      1. Angles.
      2. Saxons.

III. As the barbarians were converted, the church took over many functions that had once been performed by the Roman state.
   A. The church was the primary moral authority.
   B. Nearly all learned people belonged to the clergy.
   C. The church carried on some of the traditions of the Roman name.
   D. Ordinary people usually looked to the bishop for leadership.

IV. The church, however, was also influenced by the barbarians, not always for the good.
   A. The standard of learning in the church was much lower than it had been in earlier times.
   B. Even priests and bishops shared the vices of the age. Some of the clergy
      1. lived in concubinage.
      2. oppressed the poor.
      3. carried on murderous feuds.

V. According to Professor Weber, holy water did not always soften the morals or customs of the barbarians.
   A. Gregory of Tours, for instance, recounts a long history of violence and treachery in the early Frankish kingdom.
   B. Among the most horrifying are his accounts of treachery among the nobility and royal family of the kingdom.

C. Even the barbaric virtues often broke down, such as
   1. loyalty.
   2. military honor.

VI. In such a world the church exploited the terror and awe inspired by its supernatural prestige.
   A. Professor Weber argues that barbarians could only be intimidated by the wrath of God and by the vengeance of the saints.
   B. Saints enjoyed enormous prestige as patrons and protectors.
      1. Saint Cuthbert, for instance, was the patron saint of fishermen.
      2. Every important city had a patron saint, often a local bishop or martyr.
         a. Saint Denys in Paris
         b. Saint Martin in Tours
      3. Saints were expected to provide practical help for all problems:
         a. to cure the sick.
         b. to provide protection from enemies.
   C. In principle any church could provide sanctuary for
      1. fugitive slaves.
      2. escaped criminals.
      3. outlaws.
   D. In fact, however, only the fear inspired by an especially prestigious saint could prevent a king or nobleman from profaning his church.
   E. The saints enjoyed great prestige in the countryside.
      1. This prestige was especially important because rural areas had been slower than the towns in converting to Christianity.
      2. In some cases the cult of a local saint was deliberately substituted for the cult of a local deity.

VII. Professor Weber argues that this sort of Christian mythology was necessary to introduce Christian faith and morals into a barbarian society.
   A. Peoples without philosophy, or even literacy, could not understand the profound theology of the church.
   B. Only displays of supernatural power could make an impression.

VIII. Women played important roles in strengthening the church.
   A. There were many women saints:
      1. Saint Hilda of Whitby inspired the first woman missionary to the Saxons.
      2. Saint Audrey, or Ethelreda, of Ely was another important English saint.
   B. At the political level women played an important role in the conversion of many areas.
      1. In 496, Clotilda of Burgundy married Clovis, King of the Franks, and helped convert him.
      2. One hundred years later her great-granddaughter Bertha married Ethelbert of Kent. Their offspring carried Christianity throughout England.
      3. In 987, Vladimir of Kiev married the sister of a Byzantine emperor and Christianity took hold in Russia.
      4. The process of conversion began in Hungary when Stephen, later Saint Stephen, was baptized by his mother and encouraged by his wife.

IX. Eventually the church's prohibition against marriage between close relatives affected the political structure of Europe.
   A. A network of royal marriages spread across the continent.
      1. Royal and noble families were no longer quite so inbred.
      2. Many of the most important ruling families were related, at least distantly, to one another.
   B. In theory, at least, the church's prohibition of polygamy excluded bastards from the throne.
      1. Although the ruling classes were slow to obey this rule,
      2. eventually, succession to the throne became clearer and more stable.

X. Although the church did much to shape society, its primary mission was not to civilize the world but rather to prepare it for the last judgment.
   A. The church preached that the world lived under an enormous burden of sin and guilt.
   B. Only faith in Christ the Redeemer could save people at the last judgment.
   C. Therefore, Christians should turn away from this world and prepare for the world to come.

XI. The patterns of Christian life and the traditions of Latin culture were no longer being preserved or developed in the cities, but rather in religious institutions, in the monasteries.
   A. From the third century on, pious men and women had withdrawn from the world to live lives of contemplation either
      1. as isolated hermits,
      2. or in groups.
   B. In the early days this was especially common in countries with warm climates such as
      1. Egypt.
      2. Syria.
   C. In colder countries, however, especially those where life was unsettled, a tighter degree of organization was often necessary.
   D. Saint Benedict was one of the most important monastic leaders in the west.
      1. In 520, he established his first monastery at Monte Cassino, south of Rome.
      2. In 529, he drew up his monastic rule.
   E. The Benedictine rule was widely imitated in the western church.
      1. Monks took a lifelong vow to observe
         a. poverty.
         b. chastity.
         c. obedience.
      2. They followed four main precepts:
         a. no private property.
         b. no eating of meat except when sick.
         c. steady manual labor.
         d. strict confinement to the monastery.
      3. Benedict recommended that three or four hours a day be spent reading devotional books, although he made allowances for the illiterate.
   F. Public prayer became increasingly important as time passed.
      1. Monks did less manual labor.
      2. More and more of a monk's time was devoted to praying for fellow Christians.
   G. In spite of repeated reforms monasteries became more business-like and worldly.

XII. Despite their imperfections, monasteries played an important part in the development of a Christian civilization.
   A. Monks copied manuscripts from the ancient world.
   B. Because most monasteries were in the countryside,
      1. monks played the largest role in converting the heathen population.
      2. monks probably introduced the agricultural and technological improvements that eventually transformed European life.

KEY TO THE IMAGES

Scenes of Judgment:
The church did much to preserve the culture of the ancient world and to develop a new culture among the barbarian peoples. Nevertheless, the church did not consider its principal mission to be the spreading of civilization. More than anything else, according to Professor Weber, the church was trying to redeem souls in preparation for the Last Judgment.

Many images in Program 17 illustrate this anxiety about the coming of Judgment. Souls are shown waiting for admission at the Gates of Paradise. Another soul is being weighed in a balance. An angel is seen locking the jaws of hell. These same concerns are reflected in the image of Christ as judge.

Images of saints:
The saints were heroes of holiness whose intervention with God could bring blessings or curses. The lives of the saints were repositories of holy stories. Along with scenes from the Bible, the lives of the saints were among the most popular themes of narrative art in the West. In England, Saint Cuthbert, who became the patron saint of sailors, was the subject of many book illuminations. In France, Saint Martin of Tours was among the most powerful of saints.

Reliquaries:
Churches wanted more than holy images of the saints. It was thought that even after the death of a saint or other holy person miracles could still be performed by objects associated with him during his life. Many churches, for instance, were thought to possess thorns from the crown of thorns that had once pressed down on Christ's head.

The bones of a saint were especially efficacious. To hold these relics many churches possessed special cases known as reliquaries. Part of the skull of Saint Yricix, for instance, was held in a reliquary fashioned as a portrait bust.

FOCUS QUESTIONS

1. In what ways did Christianity temper the moral standards of the barbarian kingdoms?
2. How did the barbarians affect the moral standards of the church?
3. In what ways did the supposed supernatural powers of the church help maintain its power in barbarian Europe?
4. What were some of the ways in which the church spread Christianity? In what parts of Europe were missionaries most active? How did women contribute to the spread of Christianity?
5. In what ways did the church spread and transform the heritage of the ancient world?
6. How did the monasteries provide at least some shelter or sanctuary from the outside world?
7. How did the monasteries spread learning and technology?
8. Why did the monasteries increase in size and influence?

OVERVIEW
PROGRAM 18: THE AGE OF CHARLEMAGNE

In the midst of the violence and chaos of the Dark Ages a number of advances in technology and agriculture were transforming material life. By 800 the Franks were trying to create a new Roman Empire in the west.

Unfortunately, they failed and Europe was tormented by another two centuries of barbarian raids and invasions. By around 1000 A.D., however, many parts of Europe had created states that could hold their own against invasion.

I. Between the sixth and the tenth centuries a number of technological inventions transformed material life.
   A. The heavy wheeled plow could dig deep into the soil and turn over furrows,
      1. instead of simply scratching the topsoil as lighter plows did.
      2. Heavier soils could now be cultivated.
   B. Productive power greatly increased.
      1. The invention of the crank made it possible to transmit motion to turn
         a. grindstones.
         b. handmills.
         c. pulleys.
      2. Waterpower was harnessed in mills to
         a. grind grain.
         b. cut logs.
      3. Animal power was used more efficiently through the use of
         a. nailed shoes for horses and other draft animals.
         b. the horsecollar, which allowed horses to use their shoulders more efficiently.
         c. harnesses that could harness one animal behind another.
         d. A team of animals could now pull three or four times the weight that a Roman team could manage.

II. Developments in agriculture were increasing the food supply.
   A. Systems of crop rotation developed
      1. that left a field fallow every two or three years.
      2. Sheep and cattle could graze on the fallow fields and on the stubble of harvested fields.
      3. The animals' manure improved crop yields.
   B. New crops were planted.
      1. New varieties of wheat that were
         a. more productive,
         b. easier to grow and process.
         c. Rye, which had been around for centuries, was planted on a greater scale, especially in cold climates.

III. Professor Weber argues that as a result of this increase in productivity Europe's economic center shifted from the shores of the Mediterranean to the plains between the Baltic, the North Sea, and the English Channel.
   A. Extra wheat and meat made northerners bigger and stronger.
   B. Extra oats made it possible for northerners to raise more horses.
   C. These horses could be used for the heavy cavalry that had become the backbone of armies.
      1. The invention of the stirrup, which braced a rider in the saddle, made cavalrymen even more effective.
      2. These cavalrymen were victorious over the Arabs at Poitiers in 732.

IV. Iron was crucial to warfare and the economy.
   A. Although iron was expensive everywhere, the north possessed a further advantage in its more plentiful supplies of ore.
   B. By the ninth century iron was available for tools and weapons:
      1. plow parts.
      2. spade tips.
      3. sickles.

V. According to Professor Weber, the Franks were the northern tribe to take greatest advantage of this new productivity.
   A. Charlemagne (reigned 768–814) campaigned successfully in
      1. Spain.
      2. Italy.
      3. Dalmatia.
      4. Germany.
      5. Bohemia.
   B. Charlemagne also provided his dominions with a fairly effective system of administration, consisting of
      1. literate clerks.
      2. royal officials and military commanders with territorial responsibilities.

VI. Charlemagne ruled a society that produced a small economic surplus. His reforms tried
   A. to increase that surplus, especially on royal estates,
   B. to skim off whatever surplus there was as efficiently as possible.
   C. Eventually, he was able to support armies as large as twenty thousand horsemen and sixty thousand footmen.

VII. On Christmas Day, 800, Charlemagne was crowned emperor in Rome by Pope Leo III. A Christian empire had been revived in the west.
   A. The Romanesque architecture of the empire showed the determination to revive Roman forms and to spread Rome's Christian message.
   B. Mural paintings in churches were one of the most effective ways of spreading the Christian message to a largely illiterate population.
      1. Because the iconoclastic struggle was going on in the Byzantine Empire in the eighth and ninth centuries, tensions between east and west grew over this issue.
      2. The popes were all the more ready to turn to the Franks for help, rather than to the emperor in Constantinople.

VIII. Charlemagne was a great patron of the church.
   A. Charlemagne encouraged literature and art.
      1. Illuminated manuscripts
      2. Endowments to
         a. clerks.
         b. scribes.
         c. illuminators.
   B. Charlemagne wanted the monasteries to supply a corps of literate administrators for his empire.
   C. Scores of new monasteries were built and hundreds of churches were built or restored.
      1. Towers and belltowers grew taller.
      2. Often these towers were watchtowers warning of advancing enemies.

IX. Most of the great monastic foundations disappeared in the time of troubles after Charlemagne's death.
   A. Saint Riquier's, for example, was built in the 790s, near Amiens, in northwest France.
      1. It housed three hundred monks.
      2. It ran a school with one hundred students.
      3. One hundred ten knights defended the foundation.
      4. A host of servants served the monastery.
   B. In 881, the Norsemen burned the abbey.
      1. Seven thousand five hundred people had once lived in the nearby town.
      2. Today a village of only one thousand people stands on the site.
   C. The plans for the renovation of the Abbey of St. Gall in Switzerland show what some of these great foundations were like.
      1. There were cloisters descended from the porticos of Greek and Roman times.
      2. Some of the rooms had quite modern conveniences.
         a. Heating facilities
         b. Bathrooms
         c. Drinking fountains
      3. There was an infirmary.
      4. They had a hostel.

X. Charlemagne's empire did not survive his death.
   A. After his death his lands were divided among several of his legitimate sons.
   B. His successors were incompetent and divided.
   C. From about 820, for more than a century, Europe was devastated by horrors even worse than those of the centuries before Charlemagne.
   D. The Saracens (the word comes from the Byzantine word for a Muslim Arab) attacked from the south and east.
      1. They attacked across
         a. the Adriatic.
         b. the Mediterranean.
         c. the Pyrenees.
      2. In 845, they sacked Rome.
   E. The Hungarians were a Turkic people who displaced the Huns from what is now Hungary. They attacked
      1. Germany.
      2. France.
      3. Italy.
      4. the area around Constantinople.

XI. The Saracens and Hungarians were raiders. The greatest threat to western Christendom came from the Norsemen or Vikings.
   A. For a while, after 800, Carolingian missionaries and diplomats staved off some of the Viking threat.
   B. In 845, however, the Vikings
      1. destroyed Hamburg;
      2. sacked Paris.
      3. The French king, Charles the Bald, paid a heavy ransom before they would leave.

XII. After 850, the Viking raids escalated from isolated raids to skillfully planned invasions aimed at conquest and plunder.
    A. Year after year the Vikings set up winter quarters along the Atlantic and the English Channel, from which they attacked
        1. Germany.
        2. The Netherlands.
        3. England.
        4. France.
    B. They were powerful enough to defeat most local armies, and their swift, shallow-draft ships made them enormously mobile.
    C. Swedish Vikings penetrated much of what is now Russia, along the rivers
        1. Dnieper.
        2. Volga.
    D. The Vikings or their descendants founded the first Russian states:
        1. Novgorod.
        2. Kiev.
    E. The Vikings were also traders who penetrated as far as Constantinople.
    F. In the 900s, the Vikings set out across the Atlantic and set up colonies in
        1. England.
        2. Ireland.
        3. Iceland.
        4. Greenland.
        5. as well as making landfalls in North America.

XIII. Perhaps the most important of the Viking settlements was in Normandy, in the lower valley of the Seine.
    A. In 911, it became the Duchy of Normandy.
    B. In 1066, the Duke of Normandy conquered England.

XIV. Viking pillaging and raiding redistributed Europe's wealth.
    A. With the loot they stole from the church
        1. they bought land.
        2. they set up trading expeditions.
    B. Much of the church's wealth now came back into circulation.

XV. By around 1000 A.D., a number of local rulers were able to defend their lands effectively:
    A. Eudes, Count of Paris.
    B. Rollo, Duke of Normandy.
    C. Henry, Duke of Saxony, and his son Otto, who finally defeated the Hungarians.
    D. Much suffering lay in the future but western Christendom was now fairly secure.

KEY TO THE IMAGES

Technology:
Many images in Program 18 reveal the new sources or uses of power that would eventually transform the economy of the west. You will see animals yoked one behind the other. The invention of stirrups allowed heavily armed knights to sit more securely in the saddle. Waterpower was being used to run sawmills and gristmills.

Images of Charlemagne:
Although Charlemagne did not revive the Western Empire, he was remembered in art and literature as the greatest western ruler in hundreds of years. In one image Saint James appears to the sleeping Charlemagne, promising him Galicia in Spain. An illustration from *The Song of Roland* shows him weeping for his knights who had fallen in battle.

Learning:
In Charlemagne's time, rulers and nobles in western Europe were often illiterate. Charlemagne, however, could read, although he never really learned to write. He did, however, patronize scholars. Many of our oldest manuscripts of Roman literature date from this period. The classical manuscripts have been lost, and without the Carolingian copies, much of the learning of the Roman world would have been lost.

One image in Program 18 shows a cleric dictating to a scribe. Another shows the scholar Einhard, who wrote Charlemagne's biography and was a student of classical literature.

FOCUS QUESTIONS

1. What were some of the most important agricultural innovations made during this period?
2. How were draft animals used more efficiently?
3. Why did the centers of military and economic power move north from the shores of the Mediterranean?
4. To what extent was Charlemagne able to create a new political and cultural order in Europe? To what extent did he fail?
5. How did art and architecture reflect the development of the Carolingian Empire?
6. What invaders attacked western Europe in the ninth and tenth centuries?
7. What enabled the western European states to hold their own against invaders?

ASSIGNMENTS & ACTIVITIES

IN CONTEXT

Themes and issues that set Unit Nine in context with other units include the following:

- Professor Weber emphasizes that the monasteries preserved much of the learning of the classical world. In fact, many of the oldest surviving manuscripts of Greek and Roman authors were written down during the Carolingian period. In later units, when you consider the enthusiasm for classical learning during the Renaissance, remember that without the efforts of Carolingian monks the Renaissance would have been deprived of many of its greatest texts.

- In Unit Nine Professor Weber emphasizes two important institutions in the countryside: the manor and the monastery. In later units, as you trace the revival of European cities, look for new centers of learning and religious revival in the church. In secular affairs look for new sources of political and military power. Once the cities became prosperous enough to supply large-scale revenues from taxation, rulers were no longer so dependent on their vassals for military service.

- During this period the rulers of western Europe began to hold their own against invasion. Look for the economic and military developments that gave European armies new strength. In the units on the High Middle Ages we learn that between 1000 and 1100 Europe began to expand militarily, in the Crusades, in the *reconquista* of the Iberian peninsula, and in the border fighting in eastern Europe.

- During this period most scholars and writers were members of the clergy. Throughout the Middle Ages the clergy would preserve its intellectual preeminence, but from the time of the High Middle Ages onward there would appear an increasing number of educated men and women among the laity. In later units watch for signs of this growing secular culture. Look for ways in which it harmonized or came in conflict with clerical culture.

- In Unit Nine Professor Weber emphasizes ways in which the supernatural powers of the church were able to impress barbarian peoples. These supernatural powers remained one of the church's sources of strength for centuries to come. Gradually, however, new attitudes toward the supernatural developed. By the time of the reformation in the sixteenth century, many Christians, although by no means all, were becoming skeptical of miracles, saints, and wonder-working relics. As you read Units Ten, Eleven, and Twelve on the Middle Ages, look for signs of growing skepticism. What sorts of people were most likely to be skeptical? What sorts of people retained the older faith in miracles?

TEXTBOOK ASSIGNMENT

Read the following pages in your assigned textbook:

Text: *Western Civilizations*, Fifteenth Edition (Norton, 2005)
Read: Review from Chapter 6, "Christianity and the Transformation of the Roman World," pp. 204-239; and from Chapter 7, "Rome's Three Heirs: The Byzantine, Islamic, and Early-Medieval Western Worlds," pp. 246-285.

Text: *The Western Experience*, Eighth Edition (McGraw-Hill, 2003)
Read: Chapter 6, "The Making of Western Europe," pp. 178-207.

Text: *The Western Heritage*, Ninth Edition (Prentice Hall, 2007)
Read: Review from Chapter 6, "Late Antiquity and the Early Middle Ages: Creating a New European Society and Culture (476-1000)," pp. 194-225.

Text: *The Western Heritage*, TLC, Fifth Edition (Prentice Hall, 2007)
Read: Review from Chapter 6, "Late Antiquity and the Early Middle Ages: Creating a New European Society and Culture (476-1000)," pp. 146-171.

ISSUE FOR CLARIFICATION

Saints

The saints were men and women whom the church considered to have lived especially holy lives and whose souls were presumed to be with God. It was thought that even after death the saints continued to watch over the affairs of human beings. Although the saints were not gods themselves, their intercession with God was supposed to be especially efficacious.

The three persons of the Trinity—God the Father, God the Son, and God the Holy Ghost—oftentimes seemed remote from the affairs of ordinary people. The saints, however, were more accessible. A believer who needed help prayed not only to God the Father and to Christ but also to various saints who would intercede with God.

As an example, consider the case of a man named Paolo who lived in Venice and worked as a musician. Because his name was Paolo, Saint Paul was his personal patron saint. In the Middle Ages people often paid little attention to dates of birth, but the feast day of a patron saint was a day of personal celebration, somewhat like a birthday. For civic affairs, Saint Mark was the patron saint of Venice; on his feast day the city government held great celebrations; and when the city was in danger, Venetians prayed to Saint Mark for deliverance. As a musician, Paolo also prayed to Saint Cecilia, the patron saint of music, and on her feast day the guild of musicians held special celebrations.

As time went on, through the Middle Ages and beyond, the cult of the saints became increasingly elaborate. Saints came to provide specialized kinds of help. On a journey, for instance, people prayed to Saint Christopher, the patron saint of travelers. Saint Jude was thought to be of special help in finding lost objects. Every sort of affliction was associated with a saint, who was thought to be of special help in bringing relief.

Objects associated with the saints were also thought to possess miraculous powers. Rome, for instance, was an especially holy city because the popes watched over the bones of Saint Peter and Saint Paul. Churches throughout Europe contended to possess the bones and other relics of the saints.

Although the saints may appear to have been worshipped as gods in their own right, it is important to note that the church insisted that only God Himself could perform miracles. The power of the saints came from the fact that God found their prayers especially pleasing.

GLOSSARY

Heavy plow: One of the most important inventions of the early Middle Ages. Heavy wheeled plows made it possible to cultivate heavy soils and to exploit lands cleared from forest.

Outlaws: In many parts of medieval Europe courts could punish criminals by declaring them to be outlaws. These people lost their legal rights and the protection of the law. It was not a crime to kill them.

Pagans: Literally, "people of the countryside." The word reflects the fact that in most parts of Europe, Christianity came to the countryside well after the cities had been converted.

Sanctuary: The right of churches, shrines, and other holy places to protect people from arrest.

TIMELINE

Place each of the following events on the timeline. In some cases you may have to specify a roughly defined period of time rather than a precise date.

1. Coronation of Charlemagne as Holy Roman Emperor
2. Marriage of Clotilda and Clovis
3. Conversion of Vladimir of Kiev to Christianity
4. Saint Benedict founds Monte Cassino
5. Norsemen sack Paris
6. Period of the Dark Ages
7. Arabs defeated at Poitiers
8. Reign of Charlemagne as King of Franks
9. End of Carolingian Empire
10. Saracens sack Rome

400 A.D. ——————————————————————— 1000 A.D.

MAP EXERCISE

Find the following locations on the map.

1. Tours
2. Baltic Sea
3. Two areas where Charlemagne campaigned
4. Kingdoms of the Angles and Saxons
5. Bohemia
6. Aachen
7. Two areas invaded by the Vikings
8. Kingdoms of the Visigoths
9. Dalmatia
10. North Sea
11. Pyrenees
12. Monte Cassino
13. Burgundy

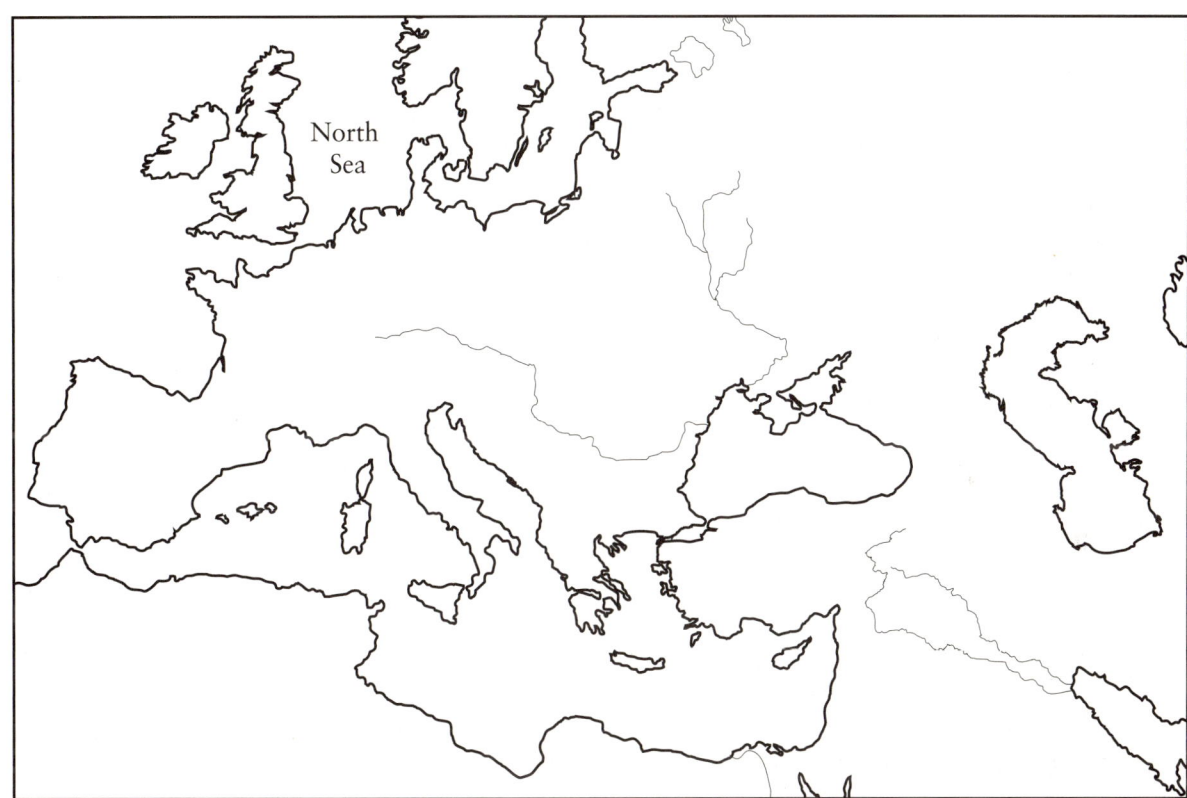

SELF-TEST

Part I

1. Between the sixth and the tenth centuries, which of the following innovations was *not* made in European agriculture?
    a. Introduction of the heavy plow.
    b. Introduction of more complex crop rotation.
    c. Introduction of large-scale irrigation.
    d. Introduction of new strains of wheat.

2. In 800 _____ was crowned emperor in Rome.

3. Which of the following innovations in animal management were *not* made during this period?
   a. Horseshoes
   b. Horsecollars
   c. Tandem harnesses
   d. Saddles

4. Approximately how large were Charlemagne's biggest armies?

5. The _____ was a power-transmitting device unknown to the ancients, which came into use during this period. It could be used with grindstones, pulleys, and so on.

Part II

1. For much of the period studied in Unit Nine, the Christian kingdoms were in great peril from barbarian invaders. At about what time did the Christian kingdoms begin to hold their own or to turn the tide against the invaders?

2. Mark the false completion. When the Christian church converted barbarian peoples,
   a. much of its power rested on its ability to impress or even terrify with its supernatural prestige.
   b. in some cases the cults of the saints borrowed features from pagan worship.
   c. few women took an active part in converting their peoples.
   d. the moral standards of the clergy often deteriorated.

3. Professor Weber claims that during this period the economic center of Europe shifted from the shores of the Mediterranean to the plains between the Baltic, the North Sea, and the English Channel. Northern Europe enjoyed an economic advantage over the south for all but one of the following reasons.
   a. The north had a greater abundance of iron ore.
   b. The north was better protected from barbarian raids.
   c. The north was able to feed its population better.
   d. The north was better able to raise draft animals such as horses and oxen.

4. Mark the false completion. Mural paintings were especially cherished in the churches of western Europe because
   a. they taught illiterate people stories of the Bible.
   b. they promoted better understanding between the eastern and western churches.
   c. they could promote the cults of the saints.
   d. they were a form of art in which all Christians could share.

5. Mark the false completion. The western European churches
   a. provided a class of literate administrators.
   b. promoted education.
   c. introduced agricultural improvements to peasants.
   d. preached an optimistic view of human progress.

OPTIONAL ACTIVITY

Although the following activity is not required for the course unless assigned by the instructor, students are encouraged to use it as a source of interesting topics for further study.

Biography and Imitation

Professor Weber emphasizes that the fall of the Western Empire was accompanied by a disastrous decline in learning. By the ninth century, however, learning was reviving, although sporadically, in different areas of Europe. One figure in this revival was Einhard, who wrote a biography of Charlemagne (a convenient edition is published by Penguin as *Einhard and Nottker the Stammerer: Two Lives of Charlemagne*, Baltimore, 1969).

As an example of the revival of classical learning, scholars believe that Einhard had studied Suetonius's *Lives of the Twelve Caesars* and that the life of Charlemagne is in part an imitation of Suetonius's life of Augustus.

Write a 3–5 page paper in which you describe similarities and differences in the two biographers. How do they organize their works? How do they explain events? (For instance, do they look for supernatural causes? Do they concentrate on personal characteristics? Do they look for impersonal explanations?)

Keep in mind that Einhard had actually known and worked with Charlemagne whereas Suetonius wrote several generations after Augustus. How well did each writer understand the personal characteristics of his subject? To what extent did each writer go out of his way to justify his subject or apologize for his actions?

REVIEW QUESTIONS

1. Professor Weber emphasizes the barbarity of many barbarian rulers, even after their conversion to Christianity. In what ways did the church try to mitigate this barbarity? In what ways did the church become corrupt itself?

2. Discuss the role of the saints in the Christian life of this period. In what ways did saints have affiliations with particular locations? How were saints supposed to help believers in their daily life? In what ways did the cult of the saints ease the transition from paganism to Christianity? How did the cult of the saints help the church protect itself in the barbarian kingdoms?

3. What role did women play in the spread of Christianity?

4. Professor Weber claims that the new culture of western Europe was born not in the cities but in the monasteries. What roles did monasteries play in political and intellectual life? How did western monasticism change in the centuries after Saint Benedict formulated his rule? Compare the interpretations in the lectures and in your textbook.

5. What were the principal improvements in agriculture made during this period?

6. Professor Weber claims that the economic center of Europe was now moving north. Why did these improvements have an especially strong impact in the North?

7. In what ways was Charlemagne more than just an especially successful barbarian chieftain? What were the most important features of his empire?

8. Discuss the role of holy images in the life of western Christianity. Why did these images seem essential to the western church? How did the issue of images increase tension between eastern and western Christianity?

9. In the ninth and tenth centuries the Christian kingdoms of western Europe found themselves under assault by invaders. Who were the most important of these invaders? Where did they attack?

FURTHER READING

Original Sources

Bede. *A History of the English Church and People* (1955). Written by one of the greatest intellectual figures of the early Middle Ages. Excellent source on the conversion of England.

Brentano, Robert, ed. *The Early Middle Ages: 500–1000* (1964). A good collection of sources. Good controversial commentary by the editor.

Einhard. *The Life of Charlemagne* (1969). A biography written by a younger contemporary of Charlemagne. (See Optional Activity.)

Gregory, Bishop of Tours. *History of the Franks* (1965). One of the most important sources for early medieval France. The source of many of Professor Weber's comments on the early Middle Ages.

Hillgarth, J. N., ed. *The Conversion of Western Europe: 350–750* (1969). Excellent collection of primary documents and sources.

Weber, Eugen. *The Western Tradition.* 2nd ed. (1965). Charlemagne

"Letter to the Pope," p. 204

"The Capitularies on the Army," p. 205

"Letter to Abbot Fulrad," p. 206

"Capitularies Relating to Education," p. 206

"Admonitio Generalis," p. 208

"General Capitulary for the Missi," p. 208

Studies

Barraclough, Geoffrey *The Crucible of Europe: The Ninth and Tenth Centuries in European History* (1976).

Bloch, Marc. *Feudal Society* (1971). Classic work on the social and economic structure of feudalism. Also important because Bloch is a founder of a new school of historiography.

Dawson, Christopher. *The Making of Europe* (1932). By one of England's finest Catholic historians.

Drew, K. F., ed. *The Barbarian Invasions: Catalyst of a New Order* (1977). Collection of essays that focus on different issues from different points of view. The essays view the Dark Ages as much more than a period of violent squalor.

Duby, Georges. *The Early Growth of the European Economy* (1974). Emphasizes the relationship of lords and peasants. Sophisticated economic analysis.

Horn, Walter W. and Born, Ernest. *The Plan of Saint Gall* (1979). Reconstructs the architecture and life of one of the most important Carolingian monasteries. Excellent source for exploring early medieval architecture.

Kitzinger, Ernst. *Early Medieval Art* (1983). A good short introduction.

Knowles, David. *Christian Monasticism* (1969). A broad survey of different kinds of monasticism. Good photographs.

Munz, Peter. *The Age of Charlemagne* (1971). Concentrates on social rather than military or political history.

Power, Eileen. *Medieval People* (1963). *Medieval Women* (1976). Lively case studies of individuals.

Sawyer, Peter. *The Age of the Vikings* (1962). One of the best surveys of the subject.

Wallace-Hadrill, J. M. *The Barbarian West, A.D. 400–1000* (1962). Excellent analyses of sources. Gives a good idea of scholarly controversies.

Wemple, Suzanne Fonay. *Women in Frankish Society: Marriage and the Cloister, 500 to 800* (1981). Excellent source for following up the course's remarks on the role of women in the conversion of pagans.

White, Lynn Jr. *Medieval Technology and Social Change* (1962). A good account not only of medieval inventions and techniques but also of their effects on material life.

Wolff, Philippe. *The Awakening of Europe* (1968). Very good on the relationship between intellectual developments and the changes in material life.

ANSWER KEY

Timeline

1. 800 A.D.
2. 496 A.D.
3. 987 A.D., 988 A.D., 989 A.D. are all given in different sources. Your answer may vary depending on your textbook.
4. 520 A.D.
5. 845 A.D.
6. 500–800 A.D. (Some interpretations may define the period as extending from 500–1000 A.D.).
7. 732 A.D.
8. 768–814 A.D.
9. 987 A.D.
10. 845 A.D.

Map Exercise

3. France, Italy, Dalmatia, Germany, and Bohemia are all good answers.
4. England and southern Scotland
7. Germany, the Netherlands, Russia, England, France, and Ireland are all good answers.
8. Spain

Self-Test

Part I
1. (c) Introduction of large-scale irrigation.
2. Charlemagne
3. (d) Saddles
4. Approximately eighty thousand soldiers (twenty thousand horsemen, sixty thousand foot soldiers).
5. crank

Part II
1. The middle of the tenth century
2. (c) few women took an active part in converting their peoples.
3. (b) The north was better protected from barbarian raids.
4. (b) they promoted better understanding between the eastern and western churches.
5. (d) preached an optimistic view of human progress.

Unit 10

Program 19: The Middle Ages

Program 20: The Feudal Order

LEARNING OBJECTIVES

After completing Unit Ten students should understand the following issues:

- The conditions in the European countryside that created feudal relations. Your textbook will supplement Professor Weber's discussion of changing political and economic relationships in the countryside.

- The economic and military factors that affected feudal relations.

- The difficulties faced by medieval rulers who tried to maintain large states or empires. How does your textbook discuss the administrative problems of Charlemagne and of the later Holy Roman emperors?

- The changes that developed as Europe became more prosperous in the years after 1000. Use your textbook to trace the relationship between military power and economic prosperity.

- The goals and achievements of the various Crusades. Does your textbook agree with Professor Weber's interpretation of the changing motives of the Crusaders?

- The growth of an increasingly secular culture in the cities and at the courts of rulers.

TV INSTRUCTION

- The ways in which class structure became increasingly complex.

OVERVIEW
PROGRAM 19: THE MIDDLE AGES

The political and economic arrangements of the Middle Ages grew up in a society where land was almost the only source of wealth and where protection against violence was a constant need. Gradually, a series of personal relationships based on service in return for gifts grew up to meet these needs. As a money economy eventually reasserted itself, these relationships became less personal and more subject to abstract rules.

I. Even before the fall of the Western Empire, social and demographic slumps had worn down the superstructure of the Roman world.
   A. The network of roads and cities decaying
   B. Professor Weber argues that as urban society cracked, the precolonial, rural substructure reappeared.
      1. In the countryside clans or gangs gathered around
         a. great landowners.
         b. village leaders.
         c. tribal chiefs
      2. These local lords were the real powers in the countryside.
   C. The countryside became the real base of the economy as it had been in pre-Roman days.
      1. This was a great change for the cities.
      2. But the change was less noticeable in the countryside, which had always lived according to its own rhythm, no matter who ruled it.

II. As the empire collapsed, barbarian ways of living met and mingled with those of the older inhabitants.
   A. The barbarian tribes carried cultural baggage of their own. They
      1. ate porridge.
      2. drank beer.
      3. were more warlike.
      4. were less disciplined.
      5. were more inclined to personal freedom.
      6. created art that was more abstract than that of the older inhabitants.
   B. The older inhabitants
      1. ate bread.
      2. drank wine.
      3. used cash.
      4. built with stone.
   C. Basically, however, the two societies had many similarities.
      1. They were rural.
      2. They owned slaves.
      3. They were dominated by aristocracies of comparable brutality.
   D. There was a certain amount of integration of the two groups, especially in the upper reaches of society.

III. Professor Weber argues that Europe now possessed an "agro-military" economy.
   A. Agricultural production remained at the subsistence level.
   B. The main source of profit was armed robbery and pillage, even though technological progress had been made with such inventions as
      1. the yoke.
      2. the heavy plow.
      3. the crank.
   C. This economic impetus created better-armed tribes who could build stronger states, such as:
      1. the Saxons in England.
      2. the Lombards in Italy.
      3. the Franks in Gaul.

IV. Of all these states, the Carolingian Empire under Charlemagne was the most prestigious.
   A. Despite its universal pretensions, however, the Carolingian Empire was a village chieftainship writ large.
      1. The empire did not create a solid administrative structure.
      2. When Charlemagne died, his successors could not carry on his work.
   B. Real power remained in the countryside.

V. Professor Weber argues that war was the major source of profit and revenue.
   A. The agricultural economy operated at the subsistence level.
   B. The kings collected little in the way of taxes.
   C. Kings and lords increased their wealth by robbing the subjects of other kings and lords.

VI. The economy was based on the exchange of gifts and services.
   A. The weak sought the protection of the powerful.
   B. The strong looked for subordinates who would
      1. work.
      2. fight.
   C. In such a violent society the most honorable form of service was fighting, especially on horseback with a sword or lance.
      1. Such a servant was called a vassal or liege, and was bound to his lord by
         a. oaths.
         b. the ceremony of homage.
      2. The relationship between lord and vassal lay at the heart of the social system.

VII. Even though this was a period of great violence, relatively few men could be fighters.
   A. Weapons were enormously expensive.
      1. A helmet might be as expensive as three oxen.
      2. A horse was worth eighteen or twenty cows.
   B. Fighting on horseback also required a long period of training.

VIII. By the end of the eighth century heavy cavalrymen dominated European armies.
   A. The stirrup allowed knights to sit firmly in the saddle to
      1. charge with a lance.
      2. rise in the saddle to fight with a sword.
   B. Riding horseback allowed a knight to wear heavy armor without becoming incapacitated.
      1. Armor protected him from infantry weapons.
      2. His horse gave him mobility to
         a. charge infantry head on.
         b. attack from the sides or the rear when the infantry was too powerful to engage frontally.
         c. cut off stragglers.
   C. All these advantages made Charlemagne increase the proportion of cavalry in his armies.

IX. Heavy cavalry became especially important after the collapse of the Carolingian Empire.
   A. Only solid mounted soldiers could counter
      1. the Vikings.
      2. the Saracens.
      3. the Hungarians.
   B. Such soldiers were difficult to maintain because
      1. trade had decayed.
      2. currency was scarce.
      3. even the supply of food was chancy.
   C. The solution was a set of relationships based on homage, centering on
      1. service.
      2. in exchange for grants of
         a. cash.
         b. loans.
         c. revenue from land.
         d. land itself.
   D. At first these grants were held at the will of the lord for the retainer's
      1. term of service.
      2. lifetime.
   E. By the eleventh century, however, these grants were becoming hereditary family property.

X. The value of these grants depended on how much could be squeezed out of the peasants who worked the land.
   A. Lords demanded payments in
      1. produce.
      2. food for livestock.
      3. labor.
      4. transport.
      5. other service.
   B. In addition the lord enjoyed many other privileges.
      1. Only he could hunt on his lands.
      2. He could force peasants to use his
         a. mills.
         b. ovens.
         c. fishponds.
      3. Most important was his local court where he could
         a. judge.
         b. punish.
         c. levy fines to raise money.

XI. Although a lord could maintain his vassals in a variety of ways, the most common grants were of land.
   A. This system of land tenure was suited to a society where power only extended over a local area.
      1. The lord needed armed retainers for aggression and defense.
      2. Further, he needed these retainers to be close by, although he could not maintain them permanently in his own castle.
   B. Money was scarce in the economy.
      1. In times of crisis kings and lords were often forced to melt down plates or sell jewels.
      2. Therefore, lords generally gave their retainers grants of land.
   C. With this land came rights over the peasants who farmed it.

XII. At first most tenants held their lands, or fiefs, only at the lord's will.
   A. When the tenant took possession of his new lands, he gave his lord a gift, called a relief.

B. The lands reverted to the lord when the tenant
   1. finished his term of service.
   2. died.

XIII. Gradually, however, the tenant's lands became hereditary family property.
   A. Because the lords were willing to accept the same services from the tenant's son or even son-in-law.
   B. Reliefs continued to be paid when a new tenant took possession but they were beginning to be considered something like a down payment.
   C. The lord now considered his fief more as a source of revenue than as a source of power.

XIV. The personal bonds between lord and tenant were becoming weaker.
   A. In theory a man should have only one lord, but in fact, through lands passed down through marriage, inheritance, or sale, many men held lands from several lords.
      1. Allegiance to any one lord became attenuated,
      2. especially when two of a man's lords went to war with one another.
   B. Abstract, legal relations took the place of the old personal ties.
      1. By the twelfth century, with the revival of the money economy, fees in cash were becoming increasingly common.
      2. By the thirteenth century written contracts spelled out the obligations of the contracting parties.
   C. Professor Weber argues that the older personal relationships had arisen in a society where cash was scarce. As the money economy revived, these personal relationships became anachronistic.

XV. The feudal bond, however, even when much of the reality had passed, remained a model for other personal relationships.
   A. In the twelfth century the poets of courtly love in southern France described the love between a man and his lady as being like the devotion of a liege to his lord.
   B. The perfect lover was the perfect vassal, as he swore allegiance to his lady on bended knee.
   C. The gesture of homage, with hands joined together, became the gesture of prayer still used today.

XVI. Within the society it was the clergy who recorded events, according to their own ideals, and advised rulers.
   A. The clergy persuaded Charlemagne to revive the Roman Empire.
      1. They encouraged him to imitate ancient architecture.
      2. They restored or preserved as much as possible of the ancient culture.
   B. The clergy looked to the Old Testament as a model, in which the king was appointed to carry out God's will. The king should
      1. lead his people to salvation.
      2. bring peace.
      3. maintain order.
      4. protect the weak.

XVII. The Old Testament model, however, contradicted the reality of royal power.
   A. A real prince of peace would lose his revenues and forfeit his hold on the lords.
   B. If he protected the weak and poor, he would offend the aristocracy in return for allies who were powerless to help him.
   C. The true masters of the Middle Ages were the men of war.
      1. According to Professor Weber, they offered their peasants little real protection.
      2. They often robbed the peasants of other lords.
   D. Three classes were taking shape, each with different interests and subject to different pressures:
      1. the lords and their retainers.
      2. the clergy.
      3. the peasants.

KEY TO THE IMAGES

Scenes of labor:
Although labor may not have been as highly honored as fighting or praying, a great deal of medieval art, especially miniatures from illuminated manuscripts, portrays people at work. In Program 19 we see images of peasants winnowing and threshing. These images of daily life often appear to illustrate the passing of time—plowing in the spring, harvesting in fall—a sign that the medieval sense of time was inextricably intertwined with the rhythms of the agricultural year.

Ceremonies:
Medieval art was fond of portraying the ceremonies that marked important stages in life: the dubbing of a knight, a vassal doing homage to his lord, or a soldier being honored for bravery in battle. Initially, most of these ceremonies involved aristocrats or clerics, but as the towns revived and some of the peasantry became prosperous, medieval art began to portray other ceremonies as well: citizens at their courts, freeholders before their lord's magistrates.

Sense of history:
Medieval artists often illustrated great works from the past. Their sense of historical accuracy, however, was often undeveloped. One thirteenth-century Bible that appears in Program 19 shows an Old Testament battle being fought with medieval siege weapons. In a medieval account of the Fall of Troy, the character Pyrrhus is portrayed as a medieval knight rather than as a Greek soldier.

FOCUS QUESTIONS

1. Even before the fall of the Western Roman Empire, barbarian society and the society of the Roman countryside were coming to resemble one another. Describe and explain.
2. What were some of the principal developments in warfare during this period? How did these developments affect political and social relationships?
3. How did the feudal fief eventually come to be regarded as a kind of hereditary family property?
4. What were some of the ways in which feudal lords extracted wealth from their peasants?
5. How did clerical writers of this period describe the ideal ruler? To what extent could real leaders have lived up to this ideal?

OVERVIEW
PROGRAM 20: THE FEUDAL ORDER

Despite the pillaging of the early Middle Ages, the church was increasing in wealth. After the year 1000, a cultural revival began, especially in architecture and literature. The church also developed a more sophisticated political theory, in which the different "estates" of a realm each made its own contribution to the overall good. As prosperity grew, an increasingly secular culture developed alongside the culture of the church.

I. The church had been acquiring wealth throughout the Middle Ages.
   A. It had been given lands to support monasteries and churches.
   B. The pious often left bequests to the church when they died.
   C. Further, the church as an institution could manage its wealth with more continuity than many secular lords.

The Western Tradition: Unit Ten

      D. Around 1000 A.D., the church began to build on a great scale.
         1. At first in the Romanesque style, which borrowed heavily from the styles of ancient Rome, although it was an original style in its own right.
         2. Later, Gothic architecture became popular, although Romanesque continued to flourish, especially in Italy.

II. The clergy now developed a more sophisticated model for the ideal political state.
    A. Society was divided into three orders or "estates," each of which made its own contribution to the whole.
        1. First came the clergy, who prayed for the souls of all Christians.
        2. Next came the warriors or nobles, who fought to protect society.
        3. Last came the rest of society, whose work supported the other two orders.
    B. The ideal of three orders or estates endured long after political reality had changed.
        1. As late as 1789, the French king convened his Estates General, divided into these three orders.
        2. Professor Weber argues that the model survived for such a long time because it provided a convenient justification for the privileges of the rulers and the upper classes.
    C. Professor Weber also argues that the model was used as a justification for idleness.
        1. Honorable people either
           a. prayed.
           b. fought.
        2. Productive labor was vulgar, fit only for those unworthy of a nobler calling.
    D. Some historians, however, argue that the Christian tradition had always recognized an honorable place for work.
        1. Christ Himself was a carpenter.
        2. Saint Benedict's rule for monks required manual labor.
    E. Professor Weber, however, argues that these provisions did not stem from a real respect for work.
        1. Saint Benedict called for work as a way of banishing boredom and idle thoughts.
        2. He also considered that work was a good way of teaching humility, precisely because it was a humbling experience.

III. The three-part model of society created frictions: bitterness that stemmed from the power relations it represented.
    A. The church tried to reduce this friction by teaching that social order was based on cooperation and mutual exchange of services.
    B. It used Saint Paul's image that society was like a human body in which the different parts were all necessary.
    C. The model, derived from even older sources in the Greco Roman world, became known as the organic theory of society and state.
    D. All three orders had to cooperate peacefully to prosper in accordance with God's will.

IV. After 1000, as Europe became more secure from attack, the countryside became more prosperous.
    A. More land came under cultivation.
        1. There were clearings of
           a. marsh.
           b. forest.
           c. fallow.
        2. New villages sprang up to clear and work new lands.
    B. Professor Weber argues that, because landowners were good at squeezing a surplus from the peasantry, most of the new wealth went into the hands of the upper classes.

C. The upper classes developed a taste for luxury.
   1. To satisfy this demand new specialized classes grew out of the indistinct mass of the peasantry:
      a. masons.
      b. vintners.
      c. artisans.
      d. traders.
   2. Further, the economy based on exchange grew stronger.
      a. Ancient cities revived.
      b. New market towns grew up at
         1. crossroads.
         2. river crossings.
         3. stops along the great roads.

V. By the end of the twelfth century, the towns of Europe, which had long been in eclipse, were regaining importance.
   A. Once again the towns were centers of
      1. economic life.
      2. political power.
      3. cultural creativity.
   B. The growth of urban life deeply affected each of the three social orders.
      1. In the church a split developed between
         a. the monastic orders, based largely in rural areas, and
         b. the urban clergy around the cathedrals.
      2. Among the aristocracy, a split opened up between
         a. the great lords who controlled market areas, and
         b. the great majority of knights and squires who were stuck on the land or who were becoming little better than employees of the great lords.
      3. The greatest revolution, however, took place among the Third Estate, who became increasingly diverse.

VI. During this period the third estate developed an enormously complex class structure.
   A. The great majority of people remained peasants but even in this class there was some social mobility.
   B. The greatest contrast was in towns with
      1. artisans.
      2. journeymen.
      3. small traders.
      4. large-scale merchants, a few of whom were true merchant princes.
   C. Professional organizations grew up.
      1. Guilds that defended the interests of a craft or trade
      2. Fraternities that looked after the interests of a parish
      3. Corporations of masters and students who formed schools. Some of these corporations became the first universities.

VII. In the midst of these social and economic changes came great political struggles, such as the struggle of King John of England with his rebellious barons.
   A. By the time John became king in 1199, royal administration was improving.
   B. Unfortunately, royal finances remained in disarray; John taxed his subjects and encroached on their rights so heavily that the country came to the verge of civil war.
   C. To placate the rebellious barons, in 1215, John issued the Magna Carta, spelling out the rights of Englishmen.
      1. For the most part this document concerned the rights of the clergy and feudal magnates.
      2. Nevertheless, some provisions were made for the merchants and towns.

VIII. Professor Weber argues that Europeans were beginning to believe that the world could actually become better. One sign of this increasing confidence was European expansion.
    A. Between the eleventh and the thirteenth centuries, eight major expeditions set out to rescue Jerusalem and the Holy Places from the infidel.
        1. The first Crusade captured Jerusalem in 1099 and established a kingdom that lasted for nearly one hundred years.
        2. The fourth Crusade, in 1204, was first directed against Egypt but turned aside instead to capture Constantinople, where a Latin kingdom was set up that lasted for sixty years.
    B. By this time, however, enthusiasm for the Crusades was dying out.
        1. The city of Acre fell to the Muslims in 1291.
        2. All the Crusader strongholds in Syria and Palestine had now been recaptured by Muslims.

IX. Some of the crusading spirit was turned against enemies of the church within Europe itself.
    A. In the thirteenth century a Crusade was launched against the Albigensians, or Cathars, in the Albi area of southwest France.
    B. The Albigensians were a serious threat because they believed that God and Satan, good and evil, were nearly equal in power.
        1. They believed that life was a constant struggle between the forces of good and evil.
        2. Further, they believed that the world and all matter had been created by evil. This meant that the most important institutions of the world were also creations of the devil:
            a. the church.
            b. the social and political structure.
    C. The Albigensians were destroyed in a great Crusade that devastated southwestern France.

X. The most popular kind of crusade, however, was fought to kill or convert the foreign heathen, especially when they were not too far from home.
    A. In the Iberian peninsula, from the ninth century onward, Christians fought against the Muslim conquerors.
        1. The effort began soon after Muslim conquest and lasted until the fall of Granada in 1492.
        2. Spain and Portugal eventually launched crusades of a sort to
            a. North Africa.
            b. America.
    B. From Germany expeditions were launched against the
        1. Slavs.
        2. Hungarians.
    C. In the eleventh century the pace of conquest stepped up. Settlers came with armies to settle
        1. in Prussia.
        2. in Transylvania.
        3. across the Pyrenees.

XI. By the twelfth century a profane secular culture was growing up alongside the culture of the church.
    A. Some of this new culture reflected the interests of the urban centers.
    B. Much of it reflected the desires of lords and ladies who simply wanted to enjoy each other.
        1. The games of love reflected a softening of manners.
        2. In some cases religion and morality were mocked.
    C. The romance of *Aucassin and Nicolette*, for instance, makes fun of nearly every religious and social convention.
        1. Aucassin declares that he would rather go to hell when he dies, as long as he can be with Nicolette.
        2. He turns against his own father who tries to keep him from Nicolette.

KEY TO THE IMAGES

Gothic architecture:
Among the characteristic features of Gothic architecture are the buttresses that support the walls of the great structures. In some buildings the buttresses are partly detached from the walls they support. These "flying buttresses" created a lacework pattern of enormous strength and complexity. With the additional strength that came from buttresses, the walls of Gothic buildings could be pierced for great stained glass windows. The windows themselves were among the most important parts of Gothic architecture, for they allowed the interior and the exterior of the churches to be of equal importance.

Middle classes:
The art of the Middle Ages continued to trace the growing importance of towns. An illustration from *The Chronicles of Hainaut* shows citizens receiving a charter for their town. These charters, which were issued by lords or rulers, granted the towns important privileges and immunities, usually for a considerable price. At this point, the towns were often relatively weak but as they grew in wealth the towns became essential to the power of rulers.

Organic Theory of Society:
According to the organic theory of society, the clergy, aristocracy, and Third Estate were like the organs of the body, each contributing to the good of the whole. Professor Weber explains how some classes benefited considerably more than others.

A few satirical pieces from the period show that contemporaries could also see the deficiencies of such theories. One of the most striking images shows society as a great tree. The representatives of different classes sit in the branches and quarrel with each other like birds fighting over their feeding grounds.

FOCUS QUESTIONS

1. What were some of the most important features of the cultural revival that began around the year 1000?
2. As Europe grew more prosperous, what were the most important effects on the clergy? On the nobles? On the laborers?
3. What was the organic theory of society? Why did it persist so long as a model of society?
4. What were the ostensible goals of the Crusades? To what extent did the Crusaders live up to these goals?
5. What was the Albigensian heresy? Why did the church take such strong measures to destroy it?
6. In what ways was an increasingly secular culture beginning to develop?

ASSIGNMENTS & ACTIVITIES

IN CONTEXT

Themes and issues that set Unit Ten in context with other units include the following:

- In Unit Ten, as well as in earlier units, Professor Weber examines feudal relationships as a response to the problems of maintaining order in the countryside, at a time when centralized power was weak or nonexistent. In Unit Ten and in later units, look for a changing balance of political and economic power as cities once again became important. How did cities and a money economy increase or decrease military power?

- During the period covered by Unit Ten the church launched a Crusade that annihilated the Albigensian heresy. Compare the Albigensian Crusade to the Crusades against the Muslims in the Holy Land. Why did the church find it necessary to take such strong measures against heresy? In later units look at the church's response to heresy in the Age of the Reformation.

- Professor Weber argues that increasing prosperity radically altered relationships among classes. Look carefully at the results of prosperity within the church. The wealth of the church led to great achievements in art and architecture during this period. In later units watch for ways in which the wealth of the church became a cause for resentment among certain classes.

- Feudal relations and obligations had once been based on personal relationships. As the money economy grew in strength, however, many feudal obligations were commuted into cash payments. In later units watch for the spread of the money economy into all areas of life. Professor Weber argues that capital accumulation was an important cause of the Protestant Reformation.

TEXTBOOK ASSIGNMENT

Read the following pages in your assigned textbook:

    Text: *Western Civilizations,* Fifteenth Edition (Norton, 2005)
    Read: Chapter 8, "The Expansion of Europe: Economy, Society, and Politics in the High Middle Ages, 1000–1300," pp. 286-327; and Chapter 9, "The High Middle Ages: Religious and Intellectual Developments, 1000–1300," pp. 330-365.

    Text: *The Western Experience,* Eighth Edition (McGraw-Hill, 2003)
    Read: Chapter 8, "Restoration of an Ordered Society," pp. 248-287; Chapter 9, "The Flowering of Medieval Civilization," pp. 290-327; and from Chapter 10, "The Urban Economy and the Consolidation of States," pp. 330-345.

    Text: *The Western Heritage,* Ninth Edition (Prentice Hall, 2007)
    Read: Chapter 7, "The High Middle Ages: The Rise of European Empires and States (1000–1300)," pp. 226-253, and Chapter 8, "Medieval Society: Hierarchies, Towns, Universities, and Families (1000–1300)," pp. 256-283.

    Text: *The Western Heritage,* TLC, Fifth Edition (Prentice Hall, 2007)
    Read: Chapter 7, "The High Middle Ages: The Rise of European Empires aned States (1000–1300)," pp. 172-193, and Chapter 8, "Medieval Society: Hierachries, Towns, Universities, and Families (1000–1300)," pp. 194-213.

ISSUES FOR CLARIFICATION

Wealth of the Church

The wealth of the church was closely tied to medieval beliefs about the afterlife. Even if a person died in a state of grace and escaped the pains of hell, it was believed that the soul did not usually go directly to heaven but rather to an intermediary state known as purgatory, where it endured great torments until it had been cleansed of its sins. Even pious, upright people believed that their souls would have to endure great suffering after death.

The church taught that these pains could be alleviated or even abolished by the prayers of faithful Christians. Pious people prayed continually for the souls of their dead relatives. Further, people often left bequests to the church to pay for masses and prayers to be said for their souls.

Oftentimes these bequests were in land, and over the centuries the church became one of the greatest landowners in Europe. Abbots and bishops, as well as being clergymen, were great landowners. The church took strong and effective measures to keep its wealth from being dissipated. The fact, for instance, that the Western clergy were supposed to be celibate reduced the tendency of clergymen to divert the wealth of the church to enrich their own families.

Serfdom

Keep in mind that by no means all peasants were serfs. The great distinction between serfs and other peasants was that serfs were not free to leave their land. They could not be sold separately from the land, but when a lord acquired a new manor, the serfs acquired a new master.

Free peasants and serfs, however, shared many of the same obligations. Apart from paying their master rent, they were required to work a specified number of days for their land. If the lord owned a mill, wine-press, or olive-press, the peasants would be required to use it, often paying rates considerably higher than were charged elsewhere.

Perhaps most important of the lord's rights was the court he held over his tenants. These courts were both administrative and judicial in nature and they gave the lord an important instrument of leverage in his relations with his tenants.

GLOSSARY

Dowry: Money, goods, or land that a woman brings to her husband in marriage. Although women could not perform military service, they could in fact bring land as part of their dowry. In such cases the husband was responsible for fulfilling the terms of tenure.

Homage: The ceremony that solemnized the bond between lord and vassal.

Vassal: Person in the feudal system who held land by paying homage to a lord and by performing certain prescribed services.

TIMELINE

Place each of the following events on the timeline. In some cases you may have to specify a roughly defined period of time rather than a precise date.

1. Period in which ancient cities revive and new market towns arise
2. Signing of the Magna Carta
3. Initial capture of Jerusalem by the Crusaders
4. Fall of the last Crusader stronghold in the Holy Land
5. Beginning of the Christian reconquest on the Iberian Peninsula
6. End of the last Crusade on the Iberian Peninsula

|800 A.D.   1500 A.D.|

MAP EXERCISE

Find the following locations on the map.

1. Two sites of universities founded in the twelfth century
2. Capital of the Latin Kingdom in the Holy Land
3. City captured by the Crusaders in 1204
4. Last Crusader stronghold capture
5. Country whose king signed the Magna Carta
6. Area of Albigensian Heresy
7. An area where Crusades were fought outside the Holy Land
8. A second area where Crusades were fought outside the Holy Land
9. Cologne

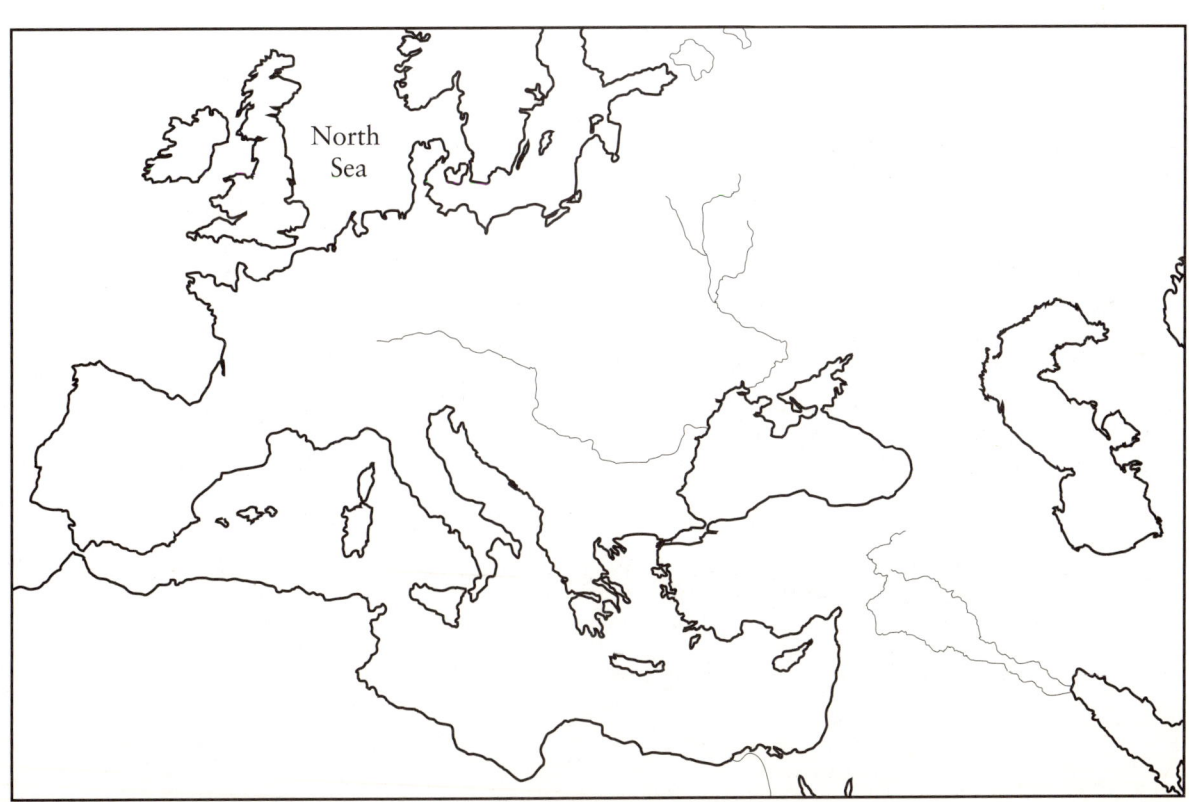

SELF-TEST

Part I

1. Medieval social theory divided people into three orders or estates. The first estate consisted of _____, the second estate of _____, and the third estate of those who worked to support the other two.

2. When a new vassal came into possession of his property, also known as a _____, he gave his lord a payment known as a _____.

3. Two of the most important architectural styles of the Middle Ages were _____ and _____.

4. Mark the false choice. By the thirteenth century universities had been founded at
   a. Paris.
   b. Bologna.
   c. London.
   d. Oxford.

5. Mark the false choice. In the thirteenth century a Crusade was launched in the south of France against heretics known as
   a. Cathars.
   b. Albigensians.
   c. Pure Ones.
   d. Monophysites.

Part II

1. Mark the false choice. The heavily armored cavalry of the Middle Ages enjoyed important advantages because
   a. the stirrup braced horsemen firmly enough to use lances and swords.
   b. they were able to charge infantry.
   c. their weapons were cheap.
   d. their mobility allowed them to outflank bodies of troops too large to assault frontally.

2. Mark the false choice. Feudal relationships grew up to cope with the problems of a violent society in which barter was the principal form of exchange. After the year 1000
   a. many feudal obligations were paid in cash.
   b. the growth of a money economy strengthened the personal bonds between lord and vassal.
   c. feudal obligations were often spelled out in contracts.
   d. rulers were increasingly able to raise taxes that allowed them to hire troops.

3. Mark the false choice. The organic theory of state and society
   a. gave special honor to economic productivity.
   b. divided society into three classes of people.
   c. was maintained in many places long after the Middle Ages.
   d. used Christian values to justify hierarchy and social order.

4. Mark the false choice. The Albigensians believed that
   a. Satan should be worshipped.
   b. God and Satan were locked in combat on nearly equal terms.
   c. the world had been created by the powers of evil.
   d. the Catholic church and the social system were creations of evil.

5. Mark the false choice. The Crusades
   a. were often accompanied by permanent colonization.
   b. were usually directed against heretics or non-Christians.
   c. were fought only in the Holy Land.
   d. lasted almost into the sixteenth century.

OPTIONAL ACTIVITY

Although the following activity is not required for the course unless assigned by the instructor, students are encouraged to use it as a source of interesting topics for further study. You may also wish to view some of the following films, which deal with matters discussed in this unit.

Literary Analysis of Chivalry

In Program 20 Professor Weber analyzes the love story of Aucassin and Nicolette. Taking his analysis as a model, write a 3–5 page paper in which you analyze the values to be found in one of the following works:

- Anonymous, *The Song of Roland*.
- Chretien de Troyes, *Lancelot*.
- Geoffrey Chaucer, "The Knight's Tale." Chaucer was one of the greatest English poets. If you find his Middle English too difficult, Penguin publishes a translation of *The Canterbury Tales*, which contains "The Knight's Tale."

These works were written at different times in the Middle Ages. Be sure to keep the date of composition in mind as you make your analysis.

- What does the work you have chosen reveal about the duties of a knight?
- What are the greatest difficulties for the protagonist?
- What are his greatest successes?
- What does the work reveal about the relationship between knights and the rest of society?

REVIEW QUESTIONS

1. In the early Middle Ages the church taught that God had appointed earthly rulers to carry out His will: to lead the people to salvation, to bring peace and maintain order, and to protect the poor. Professor Weber claims that any ruler who tried to follow this scheme closely would have fatally weakened his own power. Explain Professor Weber's line of reasoning. State your own reasons for agreeing or disagreeing. Look in your textbook for additional arguments for or against this interpretation.

2. Another political theory of the Middle Ages claims that clergy, nobles, and commoners were like bodily organs, each of which contributed to the good of the whole. In theory, what contribution did warriors make to the rest of society? To what extent did warriors live up to these responsibilities? What were the most conspicuous ways in which they succeeded or failed?

3. Professor Weber claims that around the year 1000 the church began to lead a new cultural revival. In what ways do the art and architecture of the period support or rebut this claim? Concentrate on a small number of buildings or works of art to formulate your answer. You should use images from your textbook as well as those presented in Programs 19 and 20. Review Unit Nine for some of the economic and political developments that were also taking place around this time.

4. As the level of economic productivity rose, what were the most important effects on different classes of people? How was the clergy affected? The nobles? The laborers? What were some of the effects on society as a whole? On the relationship between city and country?

5. As towns and cities became increasingly important, breaks opened up among different parts of the clergy and among different parts of the nobility. Which sections of the clergy and nobility profited? Which were hurt?

6. From the eleventh century onward (from the ninth century in the Iberian peninsula), a great number of Crusades were fought in which Europe expanded, especially to the south and east. What do these campaigns reveal about the military and economic strength of Europe? In what respects did these campaigns continue trends first discussed in Unit Nine?

7. In what ways did religious attitudes begin to change toward the end of the Middle Ages? How were these trends reflected in literature? What social developments may have encouraged these trends?

FURTHER READING

Original Sources

Capellanus, Andreas. *The Art of Courtly Love*. A medieval treatise on gallantry and love.

De Troyes, Chretien. *Arthurian Romances* (1958). (See Optional Activities for an extended description.)

Herlihy, David, ed. *The History of Feudalism* (1971). A comprehensive collection of documents.

Villehardouin and Joinville. *Chronicles of the Crusade* (1963). Includes important accounts by men who actually fought as Crusaders.

Weber, Eugen. *The Western Tradition*, 2nd ed. (1965) "Feudalism and Personal Dependence," pp. 212–224. "The Church in the Middle Ages," pp. 225–238. "The Crusades," pp. 240–249.

Studies

Duby, Georges. *Rural Economy and Country Life in the Medieval West* (1968). By one of greatest modern historians of the Middle Ages.

The Three Orders: *Feudal Society Imagined* (1981). Excellent on the structure of medieval society and the ways in which the society conceived itself.

Fuhrmann, Horst. *Germany in the High Middle Ages* (1986).

Male, Emile. *The Gothic Image: Religious Art in France in the Thirteenth Century* (1913). An especially influential work in art history.

Mayer, Hans Eberhard. *The Crusades* (1972). The best account in one volume.

Mayer, Hans Eberhard. *The Crusades* (1988). A good survey in one volume.

Pirenne, Henri. *Medieval Cities: Their Origin and the Revival of Trade* (1970). An older work but still important as a source of controversial issues.

Power, Eileen. *Medieval Women* (1975). Series of essays. Highly influential.

Rrig, Fritz. *The Medieval Town* (1971). Especially good on Northern Europe.

Shahar, Shulamith. *The Fourth Estate: A History of Women in the Middle Ages* (1983). An excellent survey.

Strayer, J. R. *On the Medieval Origins of the Modern State* (1970). Excellent history that looks forward to later developments.

Strayer, J. R. *Western Europe in the Middle Ages* (1982). Excellent short introduction.

FILMS AVAILABLE ON VIDEO

Edward II (1992). Derek Jarman's adaptation of Christopher Marlowe's play about one of the most hapless English kings of the Middle Ages.

King Richard II (1982). A good adaptation of Shakespeare's play about a devious yet remorseful king.

ANSWER KEY

Timeline

1. Eleventh and twelfth centuries
2. 1215 A.D.
3. 1099 A.D.
4. 1291 A.D.
5. Ninth century
6. 1492 A.D.

Map Exercise

1. Paris and Bologna are mentioned in the program.
2. Jerusalem
3. Constantinople
4. Acre
5. England
6. Mediterranean France.
7-8. The Liberian peninsula, the eastern shores of the Baltic, east from Germany into Slavic and Hungarian lands

Self-Test

Part I
1. clergy; warriors or nobles
2. fief; relief
3. Romanesque; Gothic
4. (c) London.
5. (d) Monophysites.

Part II
1. (c) their weapons were cheap.
2. (b) the growth of a money economy strengthened the personal bonds between lord and vassal.
3. (a) gave special honor to economic productivity.
4. (a) Satan should be worshipped.
5. (c) were fought only in the Holy Land.

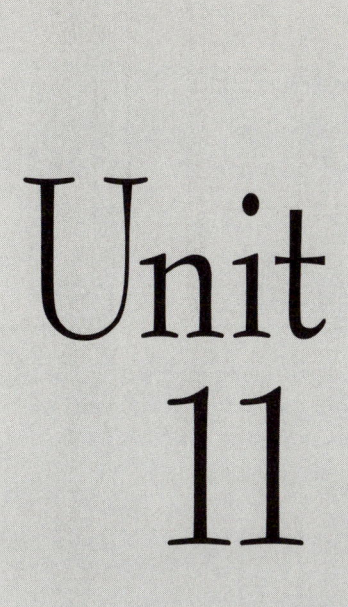

Unit 11

Program 21: Common Life in the Middle Ages

Program 22: Cities and Cathedrals

LEARNING OBJECTIVES

After completing Unit Eleven students should understand the following issues:

- The sources of conflict between the church and the secular powers in the Middle Ages. Use your textbook to supplement Professor Weber's discussion of the quarrels between secular rulers and the papacy.

- The limitations in food and shelter suffered during the Middle Ages. According to Professor Weber and your textbook, were these problems worse than in earlier periods?

- The standards of health and the patterns of disease to strike western Europe during the Middle Ages. Use your textbook to trace the pattern and timing of outbreaks of bubonic plague.

- The cultural and economic forces at work in the building of the great medieval churches. How does your textbook supplement or rebut Professor Weber's interpretation of the relationship between churchbuilding and economic prosperity?

- The important patterns and techniques for trading that developed in the late Middle Ages.

- The social and economic forces at work in the growth of European commerce.

TV INSTRUCTION

OVERVIEW
PROGRAM 21: COMMON LIFE IN THE MIDDLE AGES

As the Middle Ages wore on, the kings of many countries gradually increased their powers over their dominions. Expanding royal power led to conflicts with the church in numerous countries. Professor Weber argues that many medieval beliefs and practices were shaped by the constant insecurities of life: war, disease, and famine.

I. The kings of many European countries were gradually increasing their powers.
   A. After the eleventh century, royal power expanded in
      1. England.
      2. Catalonia.
      3. Castile.
   B. After the twelfth century, the French were also forging the judicial and administrative structures of enduring states.

II. After being anointed at his coronation, the king exercised semireligious powers.
   A. He was identified with powerful patron saints.
   B. His very touch was supposed to cure scrofula, known as the King's evil.

III. The king was the only lord in his realm who owed no allegiance to some higher lord.
   A. All the greatest lords owed him allegiance. He was in a good position to increase his domains if a vassal
      1. had no heirs.
      2. failed in his duties.
   B. He was supposed to be the protector of
      1. the church.
      2. non-nobles.

IV. The emperor possessed the prestigious Roman title and the memory of Charlemagne.
   A. In fact, however, the emperor was only the uncertain ruler of parts of
      1. Germany.
      2. Italy.
   B. His real power lay with his hereditary lands, not with his prestigious title.
   C. When the emperor was weak, he was ignored by
      1. his own subjects.
      2. rulers whose lands lay outside the empire, such as
         a. France.
         b. England.
         c. the Spanish kingdoms.
   D. Disunity was most acute in Germany, the emperor's own realm, because
      1. his title was controlled by the princes who elected him.
      2. wars were waged at times to depose him.
   E. In effect the emperor was merely the leader of a confederation of German princes.

V. Emperors and kings continually came in conflict with the power of the pope.
   A. Secular rulers, for instance, often argued that their sacred, religious character entitled them to

The Western Tradition: Unit Eleven 177

        1. rule priests as well as laymen.
        2. appoint, or invest, bishops.
        3. draw revenues from the church.
    B. The popes asserted that their powers transcended those of all earthly rulers.
    C. Two of the most important sources of conflict were the quarrel
        1. especially with the emperors, about the right to invest bishops.
        2. with the kings of France about their rights to tax the clergy.

VI. Ultimately the kings of France humiliated the popes.
    A. Pope Boniface VIII tried to prevent King Philip of France from taxing the clergy.
        1. In 1303, Philip sent an army to capture the pope at his summer retreat.
        2. Boniface died a few weeks later.
    B. The pope's successors took refuge in Avignon, in southern France.
        1. They did not return to Rome until 1378.
        2. Even after that the papal throne was disputed, with some claimants remaining in Avignon.
    C. Papal prestige was severely damaged by "Babylonian captivity," as it was described at the time.

VII. Nevertheless, rulers and clergy supported one another in most respects.
    A. Rulers helped to suppress heresy.
    B. The clergy preached obedience to secular authority.

VIII. Professor Weber argues that throughout the Middle Ages people were much less protected against nature than they are now.
    A. Much of the land was still true wilderness:
        1. moor.
        2. marsh.
        3. forest.
    B. Wild animals still roamed the land and sometimes even penetrated the cities:
        1. bears.
        2. boars.
        3. stags.
        4. wolves.
    C. People still depended on the wilderness for some of their food:
        1. meat from animals, when they could get it.
            a. In most places only the nobility could hunt,
            b. although poaching was common.
        2. wild fruits and herbs.
        3. honey.
    D. Cereal grains made up the biggest part of diets:
        1. wheat.
        2. rye.
        3. oats.

IX. Survival depended on the harvest.
    A. Famines sometimes killed as much as 10 percent of a population.
    B. Even a delay in grain shipments could be disastrous.

X. Professor Weber argues that the insecurity of life led to many characteristic beliefs and customs.
    A. The rich often overate. They were subject to
        1. stomach troubles.
        2. bad livers.
        3. high blood pressure.
        4. gout.

B. The poor fantasized about food, as in the poem "The Land of Cockaigne." Sometimes despair led to
  1. hallucinations, perhaps induced by
     a. hunger.
     b. food poisoning.
  2. appeals to magic.
C. The world was darker and colder than now.
  1. Chimney pieces were invented in the eleventh century but few people could afford stone to build them.
  2. Light remained a luxury.
     a. In the houses of the poor there was often no opening but the door.
     b. Even in palaces and castles windows remained small for reasons of security.
     c. Only the richest people could afford small panes of glass.

XI. Life expectancy was generally low.
  A. Sometimes half the babies born in a year died before the age of one.
  B. A high proportion of mothers died in childbirth.
  C. As only one example, life expectancy for Burgundian aristocrats was only twenty-one in the fifteenth century.
  D. Therefore, the average age of the population in the Middle Ages was much lower than now.

XII. Disease was one of the greatest dangers to life.
  A. Epidemics struck repeatedly:
    1. smallpox.
    2. dysentery.
    3. respiratory diseases.
    4. malaria, which was endemic in many areas.
    5. skin diseases, the worst of which was leprosy, which may have infected 5 percent of the population in the twelfth and thirteenth centuries.
  B. Perhaps the greatest killers were the great outbreaks of bubonic plague in the 1340s and 1370s.
    1. Perhaps one-third of Europe's population died.
    2. In the cities the death rate was 50 percent.

XIII. Professor Weber argues that this insecurity had deep consequences in religion and superstition.
  A. People looked for signs in
    1. dreams.
    2. visions.
  B. Monastic circles practiced
    1. fasts.
    2. repressions.
    3. rigid discipline.
  C. All in an attempt to focus on
    1. one's own inner world.
    2. the world of demons and angels.

XIV. Only gradually did the people of the Middle Ages learn to measure time precisely.
  A. Many medieval timepieces were inaccurate or unreliable.
    1. Sandclocks
    2. Waterclocks
    3. Sundials
  B. Even the calendar was only partly standardized.
    1. Around the time of Charlemagne, most Christian countries began to reckon years from the incarnation of Christ.

2. There were many different ways of reckoning the beginning of the year.
   a. Papal documents began the year at Christmas.
   b. In Venice the year began on the first of March.
   c. In Florence and England March 25 was the first day of the year.
   d. France began the year on Easter.
C. Gradually, however, much of the confusion was swept away.
   1. The calendar was rationalized to some extent.
   2. The day was divided into equal hours.
D. More accurate timepieces were invented.
   1. In the fourteenth century weight-driven mechanical clocks appeared.
   2. Many cities acquired great clocks.
E. Accurate time-keeping was especially important to businessmen and other city-dwellers for
   1. keeping accounts.
   2. dating contracts.
   3. planning trips.
   4. calculating interest.

XV. Mathematical calculation was still a demanding skill reserved for specialists.
   A. Two systems of calculation were used:
      1. the decimal system.
      2. the duodecimal system, with its base of 12.
   B. The abacus was widely used for calculation.
   C. Even engineers and architects were often inaccurate. Their buildings either collapsed or came out in unexpected shapes.
   D. Government planning was notoriously inexact in
      1. budgets.
      2. tax rolls.
      3. financial plans.

KEY TO THE IMAGES

Hunting:
Program 21 contains several important images of hunting, most notably Paolo Uccello's great picture of the hunt. Throughout most of the Middle Ages hunting was the great sport of kings and nobles. Great stretches of England, for instance, were set aside as royal forests, where only the king and his favorites were allowed to hunt. Hunting was a noble sport because it was only slightly less violent than war. A good huntsman was a good warrior.

Peasants were not allowed to hunt, even to protect their crops. Deer, rabbits, and birds provided sport for the aristocracy, and peasants could do no more than try to frighten the animals away. Of course, there was an enormous amount of illegal poaching.

Land of Cockaigne:
"The Land of Cockaigne" by Pieter Brueghel is a late treatment of one of the most popular myths of the Middle Ages: a country of such plenty that the rivers ran with olive oil, milk, honey, and wine, and water was used only for washing.

Unlike other mythical lands, nothing really happens in the Land of Cockaigne, nothing beyond the satisfaction of unending gluttony. It is a myth for hungry people.

FOCUS QUESTIONS

1. In what ways did the king play something like a religious role in society?
2. What were the causes for conflicts between the church and secular rulers? What were the outcomes of these struggles?
3. Describe some of the most important hardships in food and shelter that people suffered during the Middle Ages.
4. What were some of the most virulent threats to life during this period?
5. How was time measured during the Middle Ages? What were some of the important methods used for mathematical calculations? What improvements were made during the period?

OVERVIEW
PROGRAM 22: CITIES AND CATHEDRALS

The cathedrals and other great churches of the Middle Ages certainly expressed the religious values of the time but they also gave vent to the competitiveness and self-confidence of the towns. As the towns grew in importance, merchants developed many of the business methods still used today. Businesspersons became important enough to finance wars and crusades and to act as advisers to kings.

I. Between the middle of the eleventh century and the middle of the fourteenth, a wave of church-building swept across Europe.
   A. By 1400, there was one church for every two hundred people in Christendom. France alone built
      1. eighty cathedrals.
      2. five hundred great churches.
   B. In some places the scale of building would have been even greater had it not been for the cost of
      1. demolishing existing structures.
      2. housing the people who had been displaced.
   C. Many of the cathedrals were built on an enormous scale, even by modern standards. For example,
      1. the cathedral at Amiens could hold the entire population of the town, about ten thousand, at one service.
      2. a fourteen-story building could be built inside the choir at Beauvais without reaching the roof.
   D. The spires were enormously high.
      1. The twelfth-century spire at Chartres is 345 feet tall.
      2. The spire on the cathedral of Strasbourg is 466 feet tall.

II. In addition to religious values these great buildings expressed local self-confidence and competitiveness.
   A. Every town, city, or abbey wanted to have the biggest, most splendid church. The cathedrals seemed to be built in a race against one another.
      1. In 1163, the cathedral of Notre Dame in Paris had a roof that was 103 feet high.
      2. In 1194, Chartres built one that was 108 feet.
      3. In 1212, the roof at Reims reached 113 feet.
      4. In 1221, Amiens went to 128.
      5. Finally, in 1225, Beauvais beat them all with a roof of 157 feet, which collapsed fifty years later.
   B. Some scholars have argued that building costs crippled some of the cities.
      1. Beauvais, for instance, went into decline after building its great cathedral.
      2. The argument is inconclusive, however, because other cathedral cities went on to greater prosperity.

III. Professor Weber argues that the great churches expressed qualities that found few other outlets in the Middle Ages.
   A. Romanesque churches, for example, are notable for qualities that are not conspicuous in other aspects of the period:
      1. moderation.
      2. balance.
   B. The cathedrals demonstrated the precision and clarity that were often lacking in
      1. laws.
      2. literature.

IV. The building craze extended into secular architecture as well.
   A. In Italy feuding families built towers as strongholds within the city walls. Most of these towers have disappeared.
      1. Florence, which may have had as many as four hundred towers, now has only a few stumps.
      2. In Bologna where there were once 194 towers, only two survive.
      3. The small town of San Gimignano still has thirteen of its seventy towers.
   B. Town halls and trade exchanges were sometimes built on a scale that rivaled the cathedrals.
      1. The Cloth Hall in Ypres, Belgium, for instance, was 433 feet long.
      2. Just as significant as its size is the fact that the building was started, in 1200, by the Count of Flanders.
         a. Some rulers realized that trade could be more profitable than war.
         b. They promoted, or at least protected, business in their domains.

V. Trade, often over considerable distances, was reviving throughout Europe.
   A. The textile trade was especially important in countries such as
      1. England.
      2. Flanders.
      3. the Low Countries.
      4. Italy.
      5. France.
   B. In the late twelfth and early thirteenth centuries, the fairs of Champagne in northeastern France became major centers of exchange because the Counts of Champagne had
      1. improved roads.
      2. built market halls.
      3. kept the peace.
      4. set up special courts to enforce deals and contracts.
   C. A complex network linked England and the Low Countries to central and eastern Europe.
      1. At Danzig, for instance, barges coming down the Vistula River transferred grain and timber to seagoing ships.
      2. At Lubeck the cargoes were unloaded and carried overland to Hamburg on the River Elbe.
      3. From Hamburg the rest of the journey was made by sea.
   D. The greatest trade centers developed in
      1. Flanders, where English wool was received and turned into cloth in such cities as
         a. Ghent.
         b. Bruges.
      2. Italy, which was centrally located for Mediterranean trade.

VI. Much of this activity, however, was on a small scale.
   A. Not until the eighteenth century did any western European city reach the size of Constantinople.
      1. Only two western European cities had populations of 150,000:
         a. Milan.
         b. Venice.
      2. Florence may have reached 100,000 before its population was cut in half by bubonic plague.
      3. A city like Bruges could be a major business center with a population of only 35,000.

B. Industrial production was on a similarly small scale.
  1. Styria, Austria, was the iron-making center of Europe.
     a. In the fifteenth century the whole region produced perhaps two thousand tons of iron a year.
     b. A modern steel mill produces this much in a day.
  2. The great Florentine banks, with branches all over Europe, operated with a staff of no more than fifty to one hundred people.

VII. Nevertheless, trade and industry were expanding rapidly over earlier times.
  A. The Crusades stimulated the economy. They
     1. opened new markets.
     2. reversed the world's cash flow, which had once run from west to east.
     3. gave the aristocracy new tastes and new possibilities for consumption.
  B. The merchants and the cities also benefited from the struggles between the emperor and pope because they were usually able to escape the control of either side.
  C. New business techniques were appearing:
     1. bills of exchange.
     2. exchanges where goods could be sold on paper.
     3. double-entry bookkeeping.
     4. new associations called companies in which shares could be sold to
        a. spread risk.
        b. raise money.
     5. insurance.

VIII. European society began to reflect these economic developments.
  A. Some of the great businesspersons such as Jacques Cocur became financiers and advisers to kings.
     1. They invented modern banking.
     2. They traded in many different commodities to spread the risk.
     3. They helped finance crusades.
     4. They took over the finances of the papacy.
     5. Eventually, the Medicis, one of the great Florentine banking families, had members who became
        a. popes.
        b. queens of France.
  B. Professor Weber argues that the rise of the European business community created important new values:
     1. the notion of investment in something other than the afterlife.
     2. enterprise in something other than robbery and violence.
     3. the importance of literacy and accuracy.
  C. Professor Weber believes that these values created "the bourgeois virtues":
     1. hard work.
     2. thrift.
     3. honesty.
     4. responsibility.
  D. Professor Weber also argues that, although these virtues are unexciting, they are a great improvement over bloody anarchy.

KEY TO THE IMAGES

Cathedrals:
The cathedrals that appear in Program 22 give a good sense of their most important features. The cathedral of Notre Dame in Paris is one of the most striking examples of the flying buttress. Inside the nave at Amiens we see the vaulting that supports and opens up the interior structure.

Today many cathedrals are surrounded by tall, modern buildings. The sense of soaring height is somewhat muted. Seen from the surrounding fields, however, the cathedral at Chartres gives a sense of the way in which cathedrals once dominated the area around them.

Towns:
The art of the High Middle Ages still centered largely on the concerns of the church and aristocracy but traces of other interests appear with greater frequency. A miniature illustration from the town laws of Hamburg shows a harbor scene. Another painting by Paolo Uccello portrays a merchant buying a communion host from a woman.

FOCUS QUESTIONS

1. What spiritual and social values were expressed in the building of the great medieval churches?
2. In what ways do the churches reflect the growth of an urban, commercial culture?
3. In what ways did secular rulers encourage trade?
4. What were some of the most important European trade routes?
5. How did the values of the urban trading classes differ from those of the feudal aristocracy?

ASSIGNMENTS & ACTIVITIES

IN CONTEXT

Themes and issues that set Unit Eleven in context with other units include the following:

- Professor Weber discusses the severity of disease and malnutrition during the Middle Ages. Although evidence is scanty, it is likely that conditions were even worse in earlier times. After the Black Plague, there was actually a shortage of labor and an easing of the pressures on resources. The hundred or hundred and fifty years following the first outbreak of plague were a time of relative prosperity for many peasants. Because there was a shortage of labor, many peasants were able to become tenants under terms more favorable than ever before.

- The urban trading classes became powerful during the Middle Ages. In later units watch for ways in which these classes worked with the rulers of their countries. Kings and other rulers soon saw that a prosperous business community was an enormous source of revenue. The business people saw that the power of the state could open up new markets, provide at least some protection, and sometimes eliminate dangerous business rivals.

- Professor Weber argues that the urban classes lived in accordance with values that were different from those of the clergy or nobility. In later units watch for his interpretation of the Protestant Reformation. According to Professor Weber, the urban classes were not irreligious. They were not necessarily opposed to the Catholic church. But they did want a new form of piety. In Protestant countries the urban classes were often enthusiastic supporters of reform. In Catholic countries the urban classes worked for reform within the church.

- Professor Weber discusses the improvements in mathematics and calculation made during the Middle Ages. In later units watch for the ways in which these improvements provided the foundation for later developments. For instance, the great age of exploration would have been impossible without improvements in navigation and map-making. The great scientific discoveries of the sixteenth and seventeenth centuries also built on the improvements of the late Middle Ages.

TEXTBOOK ASSIGNMENT

Read the following pages in your assigned textbook:

Text: *Western Civilizations*, Fifteenth Edition (Norton, 2005)
Read: Chapter 10, "The Later Middle Ages, 1300–1500," pp. 372-407.

Text: *The Western Experience*, Eighth Edition (McGraw-Hill, 2003)
Read: Chapter 11, "Breakdown and Renewal in an Age of Plague," pp. 362-399.

Text: *The Western Heritage*, Ninth Edition (Prentice Hall, 2007)
Read: Chapter 9, "The Late Middle Ages: Social and Political Breakdown (1300–1453)," pp. 290-315.

Text: *The Western Heritage*, TLC, Fifth Edition (Prentice Hall, 2007)
Read: Chapter 9, "The Late Middle Ages: Social and Political Breakdown (1300–1453)," pp. 218-235.

ISSUES FOR CLARIFCATION

Bill of Exchange

The Bill of Exchange was a commercial instrument developed during the Middle Ages that greatly facilitated the transfer of funds.

Suppose a merchant in Florence wanted to make a payment to a merchant in Hamburg. The banking system was still primitive or nonexistent in many places, and it was dangerous to carry large sums of money over long distances. To overcome these problems, the Florentine looked for a business concern that did business in both Florence and Hamburg. The Florence office was asked to direct their Hamburg office to make a payment there and to bill in Florence. Because the company through which the Florentine was operating could simply enter the payment and disbursement on its books, there was no need to carry a huge bag of money from Florence to Hamburg.

Bills of exchange were useful for many purposes other than transferring funds over great distances. They could also be bought and sold from one party to another.

During this period it was illegal to charge interest for lending money but bills of exchange were one way of getting around this prohibition, for it was legal for a business concern to charge a fee for providing this service.

Bubonic Plague

Bubonic plague is an infectious disease transmitted to human beings by fleas from infected rats. The disease is characterized by fevers, chills, and prostration and can lead to death within a few days. The great outbreak of 1347–1348 killed between a quarter and a third of Europe's population. Some cities shrank to a fraction of their earlier size and many areas did not regain their preplague population until the sixteenth century. Further, the plague recurred on many occasions during the next three centuries. Southern France was stricken as late as the eighteenth century.

Life Expectancy

As a measure of mortality, life expectancy can be misleading unless we know precisely what it measures. For instance, Professor Weber states that in the fifteenth century life expectancy for Burgundian aristocrats was approximately twenty-one. This is a frightening figure but it does not mean that during this period the average twenty-year-old could expect to live for only one more year.

Life expectancy at birth is simply the average age at death for a given population. Suppose that out of a sample of one thousand births, five hundred people die before the age of one, while the other five hundred all live to the age of fifty. Life expectancy for this group will be slightly greater than twenty-five. This figure is accurate but not illuminating because no one in the sample died at or close to the age of twenty-five.

In some cases it is more useful to measure not life expectancy at birth but life expectancy at some later period. For instance, life expectancy at age ten is the average age at death of people who had survived to this age. The deaths of children who did not reach this age are not included in the sample. Such a figure is useful because it gives a more accurate idea of how long people could expect to live who had survived the illnesses of early childhood.

In England, during the twenty years before the Black Plague of 1347–1348, life expectancy at birth was only twenty-seven for male babies of the landowning class. For those who reached age ten, however, the average age of death was thirty-eight. And for those who reached age twenty, the average age at death was forty-eight.

Scrofula

Scrofula is a tubercular infection of the lymph glands, which become enlarged and degenerate in the course of the disease. In English the disease was sometimes called "the King's Evil," a name reflecting a belief, widespread throughout Europe, that an anointed king could cure the disease simply by touching the victim. French kings were touching for the King's Evil as late as the 1820s.

GLOSSARY

Curia: The papal court.

Invest: To install in office. In the Investiture Controversy of the eleventh century, the popes and emperors argued over who had the right to "invest" bishops.

Tiara: The triple crown worn by popes. It symbolized the papal claim to both spiritual and secular authority.

TIMELINE

Place each of the following events on the timeline. In some cases you may have to specify a roughly defined period of time rather than a precise date.

1. Part of papacy returns from Avignon
2. Improvement of chimneys
3. Date by which most of Christendom agreed to calculate dates from the birth of Christ
4. Beginning of the fairs of Champagne
5. Royal governments lay foundations of judicial and administrative systems
6. Career of Jacques Cocur
7. Papacy established at Avignon
8. First medieval outbreak of Bubonic Plague in Europe
9. Appearance of weight-driven clocks
10. Great period of medieval church-building

|800 A.D.   1500 A.D.|

MAP EXERCISE

Find the following locations on the map.

1. Avignon
2. Kingdom of Philip the Fair
3. Pavia
4. Champagne
5. Amiens
6. Bruges
7. Styria
8. Chartres
9. Florence
10. Vistula River
11. Elbe River
12. Lubeck
13. Danzig
14. Ghent
15. Hamburg

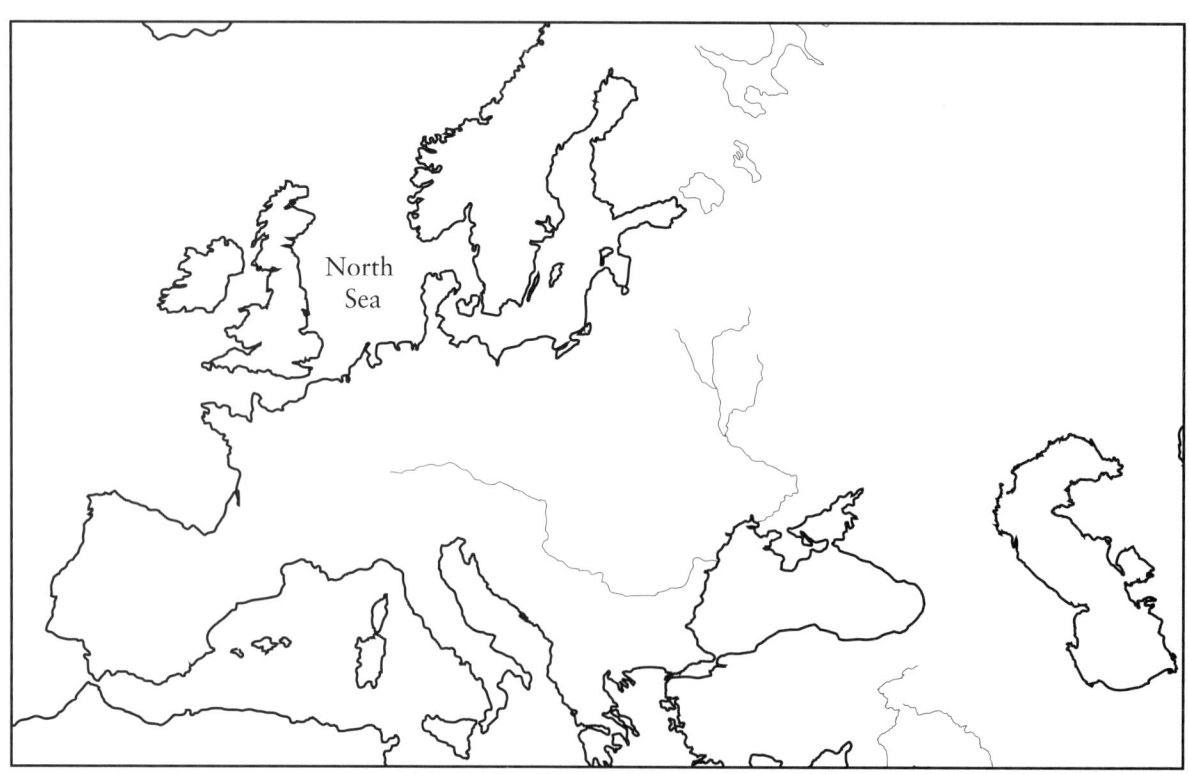

The Western Tradition: Unit Eleven 187

SELF-TEST

Part I

1. In the Investiture Controversy of the eleventh century, popes and emperors quarreled over the right to appoint _____.

2. Throughout the Middle Ages, the most important sort of food in diets consisted of _____.

3. In the fourteenth century, the Black Death struck with greatest severity in the 1340s and _____.

4. The Great Hall at Ypres reflected the growing importance of the _____ trade, which was growing in _____ (name one country or area).

5. At Danzig, grain and timber that had come down the _____ River were transferred from barges to ships. From Lubeck, cargoes went by land to _____ on the River Elbe. From there, ships went to England and _____.

Part II

1. When did royal authorities in England, Portugal, and Spain begin to lay the administrative and judicial foundations of enduring states?

2. Mark the false choice. The Holy Roman emperor
    a. was nominal ruler of France and parts of Germany.
    b. depended on his family domains for his real power.
    c. was actually head of a confederation of princes.
    d. was elected.

3. Mark the false choice. Throughout the Middle Ages the difficulties of making mathematical calculations and estimates
    a. were relieved by eliminating the duodecimal system.
    b. were relieved for people who adopted the decimal system.
    c. resulted in enormous errors in calculating royal revenues.
    d. could be eased by using calculating devices such as the abacus.

4. Mark the false choice. Trade was stimulated by
    a. the Crusades, which opened new opportunities and markets.
    b. the struggles between pope and emperor, which allowed many cities to gain independence.
    c. the development of commercial instruments such as bills of exchange.
    d. the success of the emperors in protecting trade routes.

5. The kings of France quarreled with the pope over their right to tax the clergy. In 1303 King _____ directly attacked Pope Boniface VIII. The successors of Boniface moved the papal court to _____.

OPTIONAL ACTIVITY

Although the following activity is not required for the course unless assigned by the instructor, students are encouraged to use it as a source of interesting topics for further study.

Historiography
Historians do two things at once: they write about the age they are studying, during which they also write about their own age.

Henry Adam's *Mont-Saint-Michel and Chartres* (many editions) is a classic study of the cathedral at Chartres and the church at the monastery of Mont-Saint-Michel in Normandy. Although Adams discusses the buildings themselves in great detail, he does more than write an architectural history. He presents the spiritual values that led people to create such great buildings. The book thus became a cultural history of the High Middle Ages.

At the same time, however, Adams studied his own society, the United States at the turn of the twentieth century.

For this assignment you have two choices. Your first option is to examine Adams's section on Chartres cathedral. After comparing his account to those in your textbook, what do you think of his interpretation? Write a 3–5 page paper in which you state your reasons for agreeing or disagreeing with his arguments.

Your second option is to read the section of Adams's book entitled "The Virgin and the Dynamo." Write a 3–5 page paper in which you discuss Adams's ideas about the United States of his day. How did these ideas influence his interpretation of medieval Europe? What sort of values was Adams looking for when he studied the Middle Ages?

REVIEW QUESTIONS

1. Some scholars have argued that cathedral building actually hurt the prosperity of some cities. Construct a hypothetical case that shows how such damage might have come about. In what ways could a cathedral have drained the resources of a city? What evidence is there to suggest that cathedral building really did do such damage? Consider the question from the opposite point of view. What economic benefits could a cathedral bring to a city?

2. How did cathedrals reflect the values of the Middle Ages? What do they reveal about religious sensibility, civic pride, or personal creativity? Professor Weber argues that cathedrals expressed such values as precision, exactness, and clarity that were rarely found elsewhere. What were some of the characteristics of Gothic architecture that called for such qualities? State your reasons for agreeing or disagreeing with Professor Weber.

3. The Middle Ages witnessed a great increase in long-distance trade. What were some of the most important European trade routes? What were some of the most important trading cities? What trading techniques or institutions were established at this time?

4. Discuss the relations of commercial cities to secular rulers. Were these relations always bad? Discuss with examples.

5. In what ways did the commercial classes begin to exercise political power? How could trade and finance increase the power of the state? How did the values of the commercial classes differ from those of the aristocracy?

FURTHER READING

Original Sources

Lopez, Robert S. and Raymond, I. W., eds. *Medieval Trade in the Mediterranean World.* (1955). A good collection of documents. Focuses on southern Europe.

Weber, Eugen. *The Western Tradition,* 2nd ed. (1965). "Cultural Developments of the High Middle Ages," pp. 250–270. "Economic Development of the Middle Ages," pp. 271–284.

Studies

Allmand, Christopher. *The Hundred Years War* (1988). Has become the standard account.

De Roover, Raymond. *The Rise and Decline of the Medici Bank* (1963). An important study in business history.

Ferguson, Wallace K. *Europe in Transition 1300–1520* (1962). A major study on the transition from the medieval world.

Hanawalt, Barbara. *The Ties That Bound: Peasant Families in Medieval England* (1986). Excellent social history.

Herlihy, David. *Opera Muliebria: Women and Work in Medieval England* (1990). Argues that at the end of the Middle Ages vocational opportunities were declining for women.

Huizinga, Johan. *The Waning of the Middle Ages* (1924). By one of the founders of cultural history. A study of habits of thought and feeling at the end of the Middle Ages.

McFarlane, K. B. *The Nobility of Later Medieval England* (1973). Interrelated essays.

Miskimin, Harry A. *The Economy of Early Renaissance Europe* (1969). Good on the ways in which economic change influenced society and politics.

Origo, Iris. *The Merchant of Ongo* (1957). A personal case study of a medieval merchant. Good on early business conditions. Lively.

FILMS AVAILABLE ON VIDEO

Becket (1964). *The Story of the English Archbishop Thomas à Becket.* Very good on the quarrel between the church and the English king Henry II.

Brother Sun, Sister Moon (1973). Franco Zeffirelli's account of the founding of the Franciscan Order.

ANSWER KEY

Timeline

1. 1378 A.D.
2. Eleventh century
3. 800 A.D.
4. Late twelfth or early thirteenth century
5. Eleventh and twelfth centuries
6. Mid-fifteenth century
7. 1308 A.D.
8. 1347–1348 A.D.
9. Fourteenth century
10. 1050–1400 A.D.

Map Exercise

2. France

Self-Test

Part I
1. bishops.
2. cereal grains, such as wheat, rye, and oats
3. 1370s
4. textile; Italy, France, or the Low Countries
5. Vistula; Hamburg; the Low Countries

Part II
1. After the eleventh century.
2. (a) was nominal ruler of France and parts of Germany.
3. (a) were relieved by eliminating the duodecimal system.
4. (d) the success of the emperors in protecting trade routes.
5. Philip the Fair; Avignon

Unit 12

Program 23: The Late Middle Ages

Program 24: The National Monarchies

LEARNING OBJECTIVES

After completing Unit Twelve students should understand the following issues:

- The major wars of the late Middle Ages.

- The recovery of the European economy at the end of the Middle Ages. Use your textbook to find reasons why certain areas recovered more quickly than others.

- Some of the most important religious leaders and thinkers of the High Middle Ages.

- The contributions of Thomas Aquinas to political thought.

- The expansion of France, Spain, and the empire. Use your textbook to distinguish the different strategies of these countries.

- The ways in which some rulers were able to centralize power. In which countries were rulers most successful? In which did they meet with the strongest resistance? Use your textbook to supplement the lectures.

- The relationship between warfare and the development of the modern state. In which countries did the necessities of war most rapidly transform the state? Use your textbook to supplement the lectures.

TV INSTRUCTION

OVERVIEW
PROGRAM 23: THE LATE MIDDLE AGES

In the fourteenth and fifteenth centuries, disease and war crippled the European economy. Nevertheless, economic changes continued to transform society and by the end of the fifteenth century the economy was growing again. Social changes were often transformed into religious conflicts. To combat heresy, the church encouraged the new preaching orders. Thomas Aquinas, perhaps the greatest medieval philosopher, constructed a doctrine that reconciled human reason with religious faith.

I. Although the European economy was developing, the rate of change was slow by modern standards.
   A. Peasants still made up 80–90 percent of the population, a figure that would hold until the nineteenth century.
   B. Nobles and clergy were still powerful.
   C. Nevertheless, trade and the rise of the towns had strengthened important classes of people:
      1. burghers.
      2. merchants.
      3. city-dwellers in general.

II. Social and political tensions were weakening or destroying many of the older powers.
   A. The long conflict between pope and emperor had weakened the emperors.
      1. They had wasted effort on foreign conflict.
      2. They had neglected problems at home.
   B. Germany was not a unified country. There were
      1. two hundred and forty states.
      2. hundreds of semi-independent lords.
      3. dozens of tough, active cities on
         a. the Baltic Sea.
         b. the North Sea.
         c. the Rhine.
         d. the Danube.
      4. as well as the territories of the Habsburgs in
         a. Bohemia.
         b. Austria.
   C. The same struggles introduced two factions into Italy:
      1. the Guelphs, who supported the popes.
      2. the Ghibellines, who supported the emperor.
   D. This conflict lasted into the fourteenth century until the emperors stopped intervening in Italy.
      1. Guelphs and Ghibellines did not simply reflect the quarrel between pope and emperor.
      2. The factions also grew out of the rivalries within and between the Italian cities.

III. The Hundred Years' War (1337–1453), really a series of wars, devastated France.
   A. The English kings, who claimed to have inherited the French crown, carried out a series of invasions.
   B. Foreign invasion, however, was compounded by the feuding of the great noble clans all over France, but especially in
      1. Burgundy.
      2. Flanders.

The Western Tradition: Unit Twelve

  C. Even after the English were finally driven out, the devastation was enormous.
     1. Villages and fields had been abandoned.
     2. Untilled lands returned to scrub.
     3. Bands of mercenaries harassed the countryside.
     4. By the end of the war whose horrors were compounded by the plague, the French population was only one-third to one-half of what it had been in 1300.
     5. Even by 1789 France had only 10 percent more homes than it had in 1328.

IV. Apart from outright devastation, war crippled societies in other ways.
  A. It ate up resources that could have been used for production.
     1. Metal that went into weapons could not be used for plows and tools.
     2. Castles and fortifications ate up materials that could have gone into
        a. bridges.
        b. roads.
        c. mills.
  B. States had to find new ways to support armies.
     1. Under most feudal arrangements military service had been rewarded with grants of land.
        a. This service, however, was usually for a short term.
        b. Service was usually performed fairly close to home.
     2. Short-term levies, however, were not useful in an endless war. Armies became
        a. more permanent.
        b. more professional.
     3. States were forced to raise huge amounts of money through taxation to
        a. pay professional troops.
        b. buy expensive equipment such as artillery.
  C. Monarchs tried to enlist the nobility as allies by
     1. making them officers in the armies.
     2. granting immunity from taxation in some countries.
     3. handing out patronage.

V. On May 30, 1453, the same year in which the French drove the English from most of the continent, Constantinople fell to the Turks.
  A. For fifty days the city had been besieged by
     1. 160,000 Turks.
     2. 130 cannons.
     3. 250 ships.
  B. Despite many pleas, the city received almost no help from the West.

VI. In the second half of the fifteenth century England suffered its own civil war, the War of the Roses.
  A. Two branches of the royal house contended for the throne:
     1. the House of York (whose emblem was a white rose).
     2. the House of Lancaster (the red rose).
  B. In 1485, at the battle of Bosworth, Henry Tudor, the last Lancastrian claimant, became King Henry VII.
  C. Although England had not suffered the devastation France had undergone, so many of the English nobility had been killed that Henry VII reclaimed 20 percent of England as royal domain.

VII. By the end of the fifteenth century Europe was recovering from two hundred years of war and plague.
  A. Devastated lands were restored and new lands brought under cultivation.
  B. Cities began to grow again:
     1. small ones like Basel of eight thousand or nine thousand people.
     2. middling ones like Nürnberg, around twenty-five thousand.

3. Great cities of fifty thousand.
    a. Cologne
    b. Ghent
    c. Bruges
4. A few giants had seventy-five thousand to one hundred thousand people.
    a. Milan
    b. Florence
    c. Venice

VIII. As the cities grew in power and prosperity, so too did the middle classes.
   A. Real city-states were formed in counties where the central power was weak or nonexistent:
      1. Italy
      2. Germany.
   B. In countries with stronger governments the urban elites often became allies of the crown against the aristocracy:
      1. England.
      2. France.
   C. Urban elites now gained power within governments as
      1. administrators.
      2. dispensers of patronage.

IX. The growth of cities also affected life in the countryside.
   A. Urban demands for food and raw materials made it possible to farm for profit, not mere subsistence.
   B. Rising prices and a more plentiful supply of money made it possible for many peasants to
      1. buy their freedom.
      2. commute labor services into money rent.
      3. migrate to the cities to find work.

X. Occasionally people of humble birth reached exalted positions in life.
   A. Warfare was one means of social advancement.
      1. Francesco Sforza was the son of a farmer. His family came to rule Milan.
      2. Sir John Hawkwood became Captain-General of Florence.
      3. Several commoners became generals of Venice, including
         a. Erasmo Gattamelata.
         b. Bartolonmieo Colleoni.
   B. Others reached high positions through business, such as Richard Whittington, who became Lord Mayor of London.
      1. Many English knights were businesspersons rather than warriors.
      2. After 1500 many of the great English statespeople came from the middle classes rather than the aristocracy:
         a. Thomas Cromwell.
         b. William Cecil.

XI. The general economic structure was changing.
   A. Labor was becoming increasingly mobile.
      1. Peasants were able to find work other than farming.
      2. Employers had a source of cheap labor for their enterprises.
   B. Financial speculation became common.
      1. False rumors were started to drive prices up or down.
      2. Forestallers bought up goods to create an artificial scarcity that would allow them to sell at a higher price.
      3. Engrossers tried to buy up an entire stock of some commodity to create a monopoly.

C. For the first time since the fall of Rome people speculated in real estate:
   1. to rent out property in the cities.
   2. to accumulate land so as to go in for large-scale farming.
      a. In some places it was more profitable to raise sheep than to grow food.
      b. Many agricultural workers would be replaced by a few shepherds.
      c. Unemployment and underemployment became serious problems.

XII. Europe's social structure was visibly changing.
   A. People questioned the social order more openly.
      1. Evils that had been accepted before were now resented.
      2. Resentments that had been silent were now spoken aloud.
   B. Poverty was no longer taken for granted.
      1. The rich were expected to provide charity to
         a. hospitals.
         b. hospices.
         c. almshouses.
      2. On the other hand, the poor were often blamed for their poverty.
      3. In the fourteenth century, social tensions were especially acute:
         a. workers against employers.
         b. small business against big business.
         c. peasants against lords.
         d. everyone against taxes.

XIII. Much social conflict took the form of heresy.
   A. In the thirteenth century the church, led by Pope Innocent III, led Crusades against the Albigensians of France.
   B. In the fifteenth century religious disagreement in Bohemia was sharpened by conflicts between Germans and Czechs.
      1. The Hussite Wars were fought from 1419–1436.
      2. One-sixth of Bohemia's population died.
      3. Great numbers were driven into exile.

XIV. To cope with poverty and heresy the church founded two great preaching orders:
   A. the Franciscans.
      1. founded by Saint Francis (1182–1226).
      2. Much of his teaching was good-humored and charitable, of great popular appeal.
      3. The Franciscans used oratory to make propaganda for the church.
      4. The Franciscans and the Dominicans had a profound influence on architecture. As well as being beautiful, their churches had to have good acoustics.
   B. the Dominicans.
      1. founded by Saint Dominic (1170–1221).
      2. His teaching was more austere, emphasizing
         a. education.
         b. spiritual conformity.
         c. intellectual conformity.
      3. When the Inquisition was founded in the thirteenth century to investigate heresy, most of the inquisitors were Dominicans.
      4. Girolamo Savonarola, who established a theocracy in Florence in 1494, was one of Saint Dominic's truest successors. Savonarola was burned at the stake four years later by the very people who had once cheered him on.

XV. Thomas Aquinas (1225–1274) was perhaps the greatest of the Dominicans.
   A. Aquinas's philosophy reconciled the claims of reason and faith.
   B. Aquinas taught that human understanding of God's will did not depend entirely on miraculous revelation.
      1. Human reason could understand nature.
      2. Human free will could operate within society to the greater glory of God.
   C. Aquinas provided an intellectual foundation for a secular, rational state,
      1. where justice was not arbitrary,
      2. but rather based on procedures that were
         a. logical.
         b. predictable.
         c. codified.
   D. Aquinas taught that human right was not canceled by divine right.
      1. The pope was preeminent in spiritual matters.
      2. But in civil matters the secular power should be obeyed.
   E. Further, Aquinas taught that law and justice were accessible to all reasoning people.
      1. Even pagans could have just laws.
      2. The light of reason was not restricted to Christians.

KEY TO THE IMAGES

Black Plague:
One of the most revealing images in Program 23 shows a doctor caring for victims of the Black Plague. Although contemporaries realized that the plague was highly contagious and that victims should be quarantined, no one knew how it was spread. Many believed that infection spread through noxious vapors. In one scene the doctor is holding a sponge soaked in vinegar to the nose. Other people in the scene are holding their noses and making magic signs to ward off the plague.

Francesco Sforza:
Earlier programs have shown images of Byzantine rulers alongside of Christ, the Virgin Mary, or an earlier illustrious emperor. In Renaissance Italy, with the great enthusiasm for classical studies, comparisons were often made between contemporary rulers and figures from Greek and Roman history. In *The Prince* Machiavelli draws many of his conclusions from just such comparisons.

These comparisons also appeared in art. One image from Program 23 portrays Francesco Sforza, Duke of Milan, between Julius Caesar and Hannibal. To glorify himself as a soldier, Sforza compared himself to two great generals of the ancient world rather than to a legendary knight or a medieval conqueror like Charlemagne.

Giotto:
Professor Weber emphasizes that the humanity of Giotto's painting owes a great deal to the ideals of Saint Francis. Many of Giotto's greatest works, in fact, are part of the story of Saint Francis.

Giotto chose to portray many distinct aspects of the saint's life. Program 23 presents "The Confirmation of the Rule," "The Ecstasy of Saint Francis," and "The Devil at Arezzo." This mixture of different sorts of experience is important in its own right. "The Confirmation," for instance, portrays an official act, the pope's sanctioning of the Franciscan Order. "The Ecstasy" portrays a mystical experience, whereas "The Devil at Arezzo" is what we would probably call a story of the "supernatural."

The fact that three different sorts of experience appear in the same series of paintings suggests that Giotto and his contemporaries did not make such firm distinctions.

The Western Tradition: Unit Twelve   197

FOCUS QUESTIONS

1. What were the principal issues in the struggle between Guelphs and Ghibellines? In the Hundred Years' War?
2. In what ways did the warfare of the fourteenth and fifteenth centuries strain the feudal structure?
3. What enabled the cities to recover from the wars and plagues of the late Middle Ages?
4. How did rising prices and a more plentiful supply of money affect the situation of peasants?
5. What were the principal changes in the economy of the European countryside?
6. What were some of the new expressions of religious life that appeared during the late Middle Ages?

OVERVIEW
PROGRAM 24: THE NATIONAL MONARCHIES

By the end of the fifteenth century, strong centralized states were appearing in many parts of Europe. Although rulers often attacked local or aristocratic privileges with roots far back in the Middle Ages, many people were prepared to sacrifice a certain amount of liberty in return for the security of a strong government.

I. Although Dante Alighieri (1265–1321) is best known for his long poem *The Divine Comedy*, his political writings foreshadow many of the theories that later justified the rise of the modern state.
   A. Although Dante was a devout Catholic, he was an enemy of the popes.
   B. He argued that secular rulers, the emperor in particular, had a divine mission toward the human race.
   C. Therefore, the emperor rather than the pope should be obeyed in secular matters.

II. Professor Weber argues that urban middle classes introduced great instability into a previously stable society.
   A. The aristocracy became insecure.
   B. City governments were overturned.
   C. Peasants were on the move.
   D. New methods of financing made it possible to fight wars on a larger scale.

III. By the fifteenth century many medieval institutions were going under.
   A. Heavily armored knights were becoming obsolete as a result of
      1. infantry.
      2. archers.
   B. Castles were destroyed by artillery.
   C. The Holy Roman Empire had become a loose federation of German states with the emperor as its nominal head.
   D. The papacy was torn by factions.
      1. After the return from Avignon in 1378, rival candidates claimed the papal throne.
      2. Between 1378 and 1417, there were times when as many as three candidates contended for the papacy.
      3. This "great schism," as it was called, destroyed much of the pope's power and prestige.

IV. Commerce and industry undermined the social system, which was based on landholding.
   A. Rent was substituted for personal service.
   B. Serfs were emancipated so that
      1. the land could be sold for money.
      2. their labor could be used for other purposes.

V. Professor Weber argues that fear of war and anarchy led people to place their trust in centralized monarchies.
   A. There were two steps in the centralizing of power:
      1. to overcome the external enemies of the state.
      2. to subdue rebellious forces within such as the great lords.
   B. At that point the state was prepared to expand abroad.
   C. France was one of the first countries to begin this process of centralizing power.
      1. Joan of Arc, martyred by the English in 1431, helped make the monarchy a symbol of French patriotism and resistance to the English.
      2. By the second half of the century the English had been subdued and the French kings were taming the great lords of the realm.
      3. The kings were laying foundations for a
         a. national army.
         b. national system of finance.
   D. Under Louis XI (reigned 1461–1483) the monarchy was consolidated as the core of a centralized state.
   E. Under Louis XI's successors the independence of the great lords was crushed and France began to expand at the expense of her neighbors.
      1. One province after another was absorbed by the monarchy.
      2. By the end of the century France invaded Italy.

VI. This pattern of consolidation and expansion appeared in other parts of Europe.
   A. In Spain, Isabella of Castile married Ferdinand of Aragon. They
      1. expelled the Muslims from Andalusia.
      2. laid the foundations for the modern Spanish kingdom.
   B. Spain also moved outside her boundaries to
      1. challenge the French in Italy.
      2. conquer lands in America.

VII. In other parts of Europe a series of dynastic marriages was creating another great power.
   A. The Emperor Maximilian of Austria married the heiress of Burgundy, thereby uniting
      1. Austria.
      2. The Netherlands.
   B. Their son, the Archduke Philip, married the daughter of Ferdinand and Isabella.
   C. The marriage produced two sons:
      1. the Emperor Charles V who ruled the
         a. Spanish Empire.
         b. Netherlands.
         c. Holy Roman Empire.
      2. Ferdinand I who married the heiress of
         a. Bohemia.
         b. Hungary.
         c. and who later became Holy Roman emperor and ruler of the Austrian Habsburg lands.

The Western Tradition: Unit Twelve

VIII. The consolidation of power proceeded piecemeal and great stretches of territory were never united during the period.
    A. In Germany the emperor was elected and could gain office only by promising not to enforce his authority.
    B. In Italy the papacy created great obstacles to unification.
        1. The popes were never powerful enough to unify the country themselves.
        2. They worked unceasingly to prevent anyone else from doing so.
    C. For much of the next few centuries Germany and Italy were battlegrounds for more powerful neighbors.

IX. Expansion and consolidation of power created a new international order.
    A. During the Middle Ages most states had not carried on continuous diplomatic relations.
        1. Diplomats were sent out on an *ad hoc* basis.
        2. Few states maintained permanent ambassadors.
    B. With increased rivalry between states, however, many governments began to carry on diplomatic relations on a continuous basis.

X. Important changes also took place in domestic affairs.
    A. When a ruler increased his power abroad, he also became stronger at home.
    B. Local privileges might once have been strong enough to stand up against a duke of Brittany or a king of Aragon but not against a king of France or a king of Spain.
    C. These centralizing monarchs possessed
        1. stronger armies.
        2. greater revenues.
        3. better credit.
    D. Local powers continued to put up resistance but the monarchs were becoming increasingly strong.

XI. Professor Weber argues that other contemporary developments increased the power of the central monarch.
    A. The Renaissance
    B. The revived study of Roman law
    C. The Reformation
    D. Most scholars argued in favor of increased royal power.
        1. The rulers were the best source of patronage.
        2. The growth of interest in classical learning gave added prestige to Roman law.
            a. It seemed more elegant and systematic than European common law or feudal custom.
            b. The study of Roman law spread from the Italian universities to the Holy Roman Empire to most of the rest of Europe.
            c. The civil laws of nearly every European country have been shaped by Roman law.
    E. Roman law was especially useful to state builders.
        1. The older common law often defended local interests and checked central power.
        2. In Roman law, however, the will of the king was law. This was a useful maxim to use against
            a. lords.
            b. popes.
            c. parliaments.

XII. Professor Weber argues that many people were ready to support authoritarian governments.
    A. He cautions against the assumption that people have always tended toward
        1. democracy.
        2. constitutions.
        3. electoral rights.
    B. He argues that in the period under discussion most people preferred authoritarian stability to any kind of anarchy.

XIII. Professor Weber argues that strong government often goes together with capital-intensive warfare.
  A. The power that controls weapons can control its will.
  B. In particular it can collect taxes to pay for these weapons.
  C. As weapons became more and more expensive, great lords and other private individuals found it difficult to arm themselves as well as the government.

XIV. Guns and gunpowder revolutionized European warfare.
  A. In the thirteenth century the idea of guns with metal tubes reached Europe from
    1. India.
    2. China.
  B. Cannons could be used against
    1. ships.
    2. troops in close formation.
    3. walls.
      a. French cannons helped drive out the English at the end of the Hundred Years' War.
      b. Turkish cannons breached the walls of Constantinople.
  C. By the sixteenth century smaller arms were widely used.
    1. Handguns
    2. The arquebus
    3. The musket
  D. Such small weapons gave Europeans a military advantage in other parts of the world:
    1. the Americas for the Spanish.
    2. the East Indies for the
      a. Spanish.
      b. Portuguese.
      c. English.
      d. Dutch.

XV. Such small weapons rearranged the balance of power.
  A. Only countries with great resources or a strong tax base could compete with such weapons:
    1. Spain.
    2. France.
  B. Countries needed supplies of iron ore and superior metallurgy:
    1. central Europe.
    2. France.
    3. Sweden.
  C. Older forms of warfare became obsolete.
    1. Cities were no longer safe behind their old fortifications. New and expensive systems of earth works had to be developed.
    2. The heavily armored knight was an anachronism.

KEY TO THE IMAGES

Portrayals of rulers:
Until the age of photography, rulers were usually portrayed by commissioned artists. Therefore, whenever we examine images of rulers, we must ask what point the artist is trying to make. That is, in what ways is the artist honoring the subject?

One of the earlier images in Program 24 portrays Edward I of England (ruled 1272–1307) presiding over parliament. It is an important image because Edward considered himself a great lawmaker. Historians have long debated the roots of the English parliament but its continuous history dates from Edward's reign.

Two images of sixteenth-century French kings also make important points. In one image Francis I (ruled 1515–1547) is presented with a translation of Diodorus Siculus made by the French scholar Antoine Macault. Francis often had himself portrayed as a great ruler or soldier, but on this occasion he wished to present himself as a patron of learning. By the sixteenth century many rulers like Francis I and his contemporary Henry VIII of England, although as ruthless or pragmatic as their predecessors, wished to be seen as, or even to be, people of learning.

In an image from the second half of the century, Henry III is seen presiding over the first meeting of the Order of the Holy Spirit. Many such orders of chivalry existed in the sixteenth century, some of them like the English Order of the Garter with roots in the Middle Ages, others of more recent foundation. The orders provided a way for a ruler to honor important men and to create solidarity between rulers and nobility.

Joan of Arc:
Program 24 shows several images of Joan of Arc being burned by the English. Born in 1412, she had mystical visions that instructed her to help drive the English from France. In 1429, she led an army to relieve the city of Orleans. The raising of the siege and the coronation of Charles VII at Reims consolidated French resistance. In 1430, however, Joan was captured and ransomed by the English, who tried her for witchcraft.

FOCUS QUESTIONS

1. What was Dante's theory of the state?
2. What were some of the pressures that were altering the Feudal Order? How did the cities contribute to these pressures?
3. In what states did the central authority grow in strength? Why were the subjects of such states willing to tolerate or even support such power?
4. What were some of the developments in law and diplomacy as states expanded the areas they controlled?
5. How did the rulers of expanding states strengthen their power at home?
6. What were the principal changes in warfare during this period? How did these changes influence the growth of states?
7. How did the new forms of warfare affect the international balance of power?

ASSIGNMENTS & ACTIVITIES

IN CONTEXT

Themes and issues that set Unit Twelve in context with other units include the following:

- Professor Weber emphasizes the ways in which warfare could transform a state. To take only one example, during most of the Hundred Years' War England was a major European power, whereas France was torn to pieces by civil war and foreign invasion. By the 1490s, however, France had become a great power and was beginning its invasions of Italy. England, on the other hand, had become a second-rate power and would remain so for the next 150 years. In later units watch for the causes behind the rise or fall of the various European states.

- New forms of religious life developed in the High Middle Ages. By the middle of the fifteenth century the papacy recovered from much of the damage it suffered in the previous 150 years. By the 1520s, however, Europe would be torn apart by religious strife and this time the church would not be able to suppress the new heresy: Protestantism. In later units look for the sources of religious division.

- European cities continued to grow in strength and prosperity but the political circumstances in which they lived were being profoundly altered. In Italy, for instance, many of the great trading cities of the north would come to be dominated by the French or Spanish as these great powers began a series of wars to dominate the peninsula. In Germany, many cities, especially in the north, became supporters of the Reformation. In later units watch for ways in which religion and international politics affected urban life throughout Europe.

- Warfare became so expensive during this period that the military balance of power was permanently altered. Artillery and the great earthworks needed to withstand it required enormous sums of money. Few great noblemen could afford a train of cannon. Military power increasingly went to those states with a large enough tax base to pay for the needs of modern war. In later units watch for shifts in the balance of military power. How did the various states pay these enormous expenses?

TEXTBOOK ASSIGNMENT

Read the following pages in your assigned textbook:

  Text: *Western Civilizations,* Fifteenth Edition (Norton, 2005)
  Read: Review Chapter 10, "The Later Middle Ages, 1300–1500," pp. 372-407.

  Text: *The Western Experience,* Eighth Edition (McGraw-Hill, 2003)
  Read: Chapter 12, "Tradition and Change in European Culture, 1300–1500," pp. 402-433; and from Chapter 14, "Economic Expansion and A New Politics," pp. 478-502.

  Text: *The Western Heritage,* Ninth Edition (Prentice Hall, 2007)
  Read: Chapter 9, "The Late Middle Ages: Social and Political Breakdown (1300–1453)," pp. 290-315.

  Text: *The Western Heritage,* TLC, Fifth Edition (Prentice Hall, 2007)
  Read: Chapter 9, "The Late Middle Ages: Social and Political Breakdown (1300–1453)," pp. 218-235.

ISSUE FOR CLARIFICATION

Diplomacy

Until the end of the Middle Ages most European states sent out ambassadors only for a specific mission: to arrange a royal marriage, to negotiate a treaty, to end a war. By the middle of the fifteenth century, however, international relations became so complex that many countries began to maintain permanent ambassadors at the courts of important rulers.

The Italians were leaders in this field. The papacy and the other Italian states had conducted long-term diplomatic relations with one another long before such practices became common in the rest of Europe.

The Venetians were especially famous for diplomacy. The reports of their ambassadors are an especially rich source for the period. Because Venice was a great trading city, her ambassadors sent back detailed reports on business and economic conditions as well as on strictly political matters.

GLOSSARY

- **Condottieri:** Soldiers who led bands of mercenary troops.
- **Engrossing:** Practice of buying up the whole stock of a commodity to create an artificial monopoly.
- **Forestalling:** Practice of buying up large stocks of a commodity to anticipate or even to cause a rise in prices.
- **Free will:** Theological doctrine that human beings are capable of choosing between good and evil, and are therefore morally responsible for their actions.
- **Ghibellines:** Supporters of the emperor during the struggles between the papacy and the empire in the thirteenth and fourteenth centuries.
- **Guelphs:** Supporters of the pope during the struggles between the papacy and the empire in the thirteenth and fourteenth centuries.

TIMELINE

Place each of the following events on the timeline. In some cases you may have to specify a roughly defined period of time rather than a precise date.

1. Beginning and end of the Hundred Years' War
2. First outbreak of the Black Plague
3. Victory of Henry VII at Bosworth
4. Hussite wars
5. Life of Saint Francis
6. Savonarola establishes his theocracy
7. Fall of Constantinople
8. Period when states begin to maintain long-term resident ambassadors
9. Height of Guelph-Ghibelline conflict
10. Concept of metal guns reaches Europe from the Orient
11. Charles V is elected Holy Roman emperor

| 1100 A.D. | 1600 A.D. |

MAP EXERCISE

Find the following locations on the map.

1. Country of Hussite heresy
2. Final victor in Hundred Years' War
3. A city that had populations between 75,000 and 100,000 by 1500
4. Another city that had populations between 75,000 and 100,000 by 1500
5. Dante's native city
6. Area gained in marriage by Maximillian of Austria
7. Country of Wars of the Roses
8. Area gained in marriage by Ferdinand I
9. Holy Roman Empire
10. Assisi
11. Milan

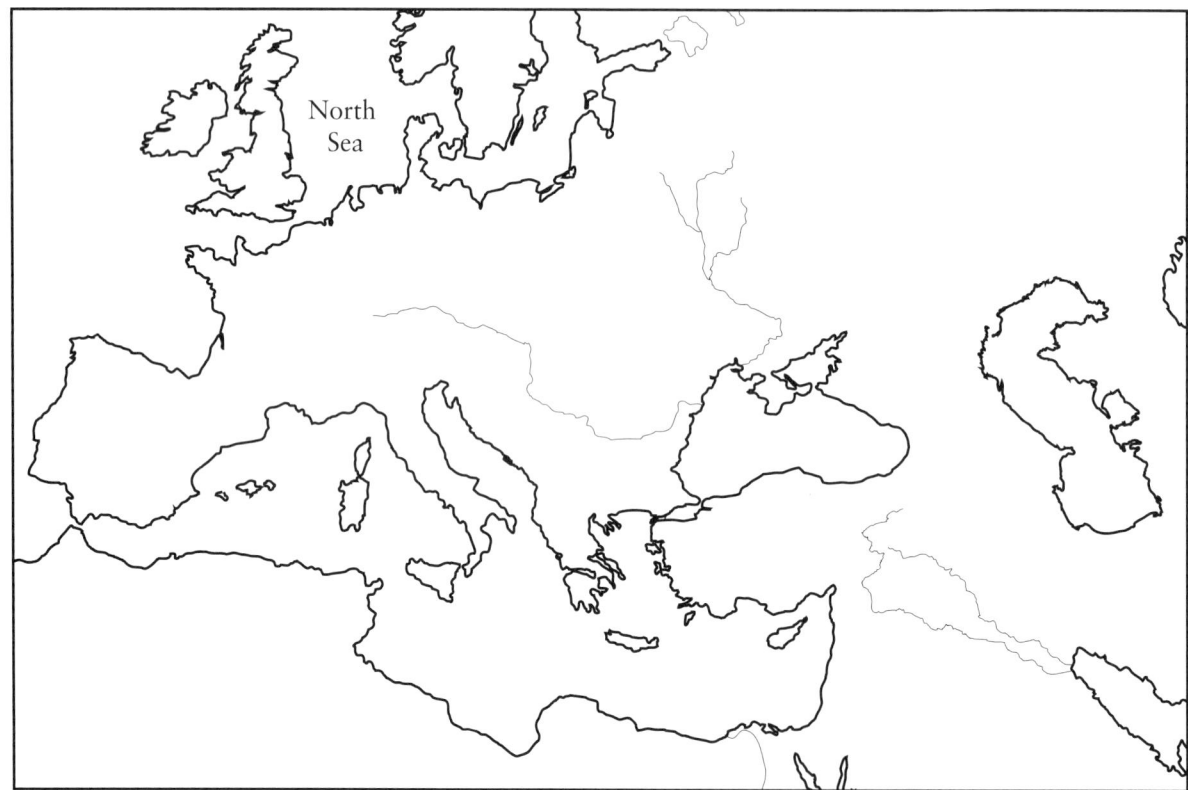

SELF-TEST

Part I

1. "The Great Schism" refers to the
   a. rivalry between popes and emperors in the thirteenth and fourteenth centuries.
   b. period in the fourteenth and fifteenth centuries when rival popes disputed for the papacy.
   c. Albigensian heresy in thirteenth-century France.
   d. Hussite heresy in fifteenth-century Bohemia.

2. Until well into the nineteenth century, peasants accounted for approximately what proportion of the European population?

3. In the thirteenth and fourteenth centuries Italy was torn by rival factions: the Ghibellines who supported the _____ and the _____ who supported the pope.

4. By 1453, after more than one hundred years of war and plague, the population of France was approximately what proportion of its size in 1300?

5. Which area was **not** part of the empire of Charles V?
   a. Spain
   b. Austria
   c. France
   d. The Low Countries

Part II

1. After the successful conclusion of the Hundred Years' War, Louis XI and _____ were two kings who crushed feudal independence in _____.

2. The Franciscans and _____ were two new clerical orders, founded in the twelfth and thirteenth centuries, which attached great importance to preaching. How did this emphasis on preaching affect the architectural style of their churches?

3. Mark the false choice. The theology of Thomas Aquinas
   a. claimed that divine right destroyed human right.
   b. although profoundly religious, provided an intellectual foundation for the secular state.
   c. claimed that reason could understand much of God's will.
   d. claimed that God created humankind with free will.

4. By the fifteenth century, the urban middle classes
   a. found new ways to pay for large-scale wars.
   b. accounted for more than one-third of the European population.
   c. in Italy often hired mercenaries to fight their wars.
   d. generally took the side of the king against the feudal lords.

5. Dante Alighieri, whose greatest work was _____, was also a political thinker. He believed _____ was the institution that would create the ideal unity of humankind under God.

OPTIONAL ACTIVITY

Although the following activity is not required for the course unless assigned by the instructor, students are encouraged to use it as a source of interesting topics for further study.

Shakespeare and the Wars of the Roses
The three parts of Shakespeare's *Henry VI* and his *Richard III* make up Shakespeare's extended treatment of the Wars of the Roses. All of the plays are worth studying, although *Richard III* is the best-shaped of them. (The Signet Classics editions are recommended because they include extensive selections from Shakespeare's sources.)

Although this assignment suggests using *Richard III*, you may analyze any of the four plays. After reading the play and the accompanying source material, especially from Raphael Holinshed and Sir Thomas More, you will see that Shakespeare has taken considerable liberties with the historical record. Why? You may also wish to consult John Gillingham's book, *The Wars of the Roses* (see Further Reading).

Write a paper of 3–5 pages in which you analyze one scene or a short group of scenes. Why does Shakespeare depart from the historical record? What are the qualities of a good or bad ruler according to Shakespeare?

REVIEW QUESTIONS

1. By the sixteenth century countries like France were beginning to develop strong, centralized states. Italy and Germany, however, were not unified until the nineteenth century. These delays seem especially paradoxical because the countries were the homes of two institutions with universal aspirations: the papacy in Italy and the Holy Roman Empire in Germany. How did these two institutions retard or promote national unity in Italy and Germany?

2. How did the introduction of gunpowder affect European warfare and politics? In what ways were the new weapons most effective? What styles of warfare became obsolete? What styles gained new importance? How did gunpowder affect the balance of power between states?

3. In what ways did the urban middle classes gain power in the fifteenth and sixteenth centuries? Why were cities gaining political and economic importance? What roles did middle-class people play when they entered the service of the monarchs?

4. Thomas Aquinas was one of the most important theologians of the Middle Ages, in part because his teaching provided an intellectual foundation for many other developments. How did Aquinas provide an intellectual foundation for the secular state? How did his theology support the rules of laws based on logical, predictable, codified procedures?

5. Professor Weber argues that by the sixteenth century many Europeans were ready to support a strong, authoritarian central government. Why? What problems was the centralized state supposed to solve? What were its sources of strength?

FURTHER READING

Original Sources

Allmand, C. T. *Society at War: The Experience of England and France During the Hundred Years' War* (1973). Good collection of documents.

Froissart, Jean. *The Chronicles of England, France, Spain, and Other Places Adjoining* (1968). One of the great medieval chronicles. Covers the first half of the Hundred Years' War.

Langland, William. *The Vision of Piers Plowman.* trans. J. F. Goodrich (1966). One of the greatest works of English medieval literature. Presented here in modern translation. Especially acute social commentary.

Shirley, I. *A Parisian Journal,* 1405–1449 (1968). trans. Excellent contemporary account.

Studies

Aston, Margaret. *The Fifteenth Century: The Prospect of Europe* (1979). Social history from a comprehensive point of view. Illustrated.

Breisach, E. *Renaissance Europe, 1300–1517* (1973). Good introduction.

Brucker, G. *Renaissance Florence* (1973). Excellent overview of one of the key cities of the Renaissance.

Cole, Bruce. *Giotto and Florentine Painting, 1280–1375* (1976). Good introduction to the first stages of Renaissance painting in Florence.

Gillingham, John. *The Wars of the Roses: Peace and Conflict in Fifteenth Century England* (1981). Very readable. Concludes that the wars were not so destructive as other writers have believed.

Hay, Denys. *Europe in the Fourteenth and Fifteenth Centuries* (1966). Political history from many points of view.

Howard, Michael. *War in European History* (1976).

Keegan, John. *The Face of Battle* (1976). Contains a wonderful description of the battle of Agincourt. Keegan gives an excellent sense of the conditions under which medieval battles were fought.

Mattingly, Garrett. *Renaissance Diplomacy* (1971).

Panofsky, E. *Early Netherlandish Painting.* Two Volumes (1953). One of the classics of art history.

Perroy, Edouard. *The Hundred Years' War* (1965). The most comprehensive account in a single volume.

Skinner, Quentin. *The Foundations of Modern Political Thought, Vol. I* (1978). Comprehensive; useful for connecting writers of this period to earlier and later developments.

Tuchman, Barbara. *A Distant Mirror* (1978). Fascinating account of life in France during the Hundred Years' War. Strongest on the texture of daily life and belief.

FILMS AVAILABLE ON VIDEO

Chimes at Midnight (1967). Also known as *Falstaff,* this is Orson Welles' combination of various episodes from five of Shakespeare's plays that treat the character of John Falstaff. One of the best movies ever made about the Late Middle Ages.

Joan of Arc (1948). Ingrid Bergman plays the French saint who helped free France from the English during the Hundred Years' War.

The Passion of Joan of Arc (1928). This is often hailed as one of the greatest movies ever made.

Richard III (1955). One of Laurence Olivier's greatest Shakespearean performances.

ANSWER KEY

Timeline

1. 1337 A.D.; 1453 A.D.
2. 1347–1348 A.D.
3. 1485 A.D.
4. 1419–1436 A.D.
5. 1182–1226 A.D.
6. 1494 A.D.
7. 1453 A.D.
8. Fifteenth and sixteenth centuries
9. Thirteenth century
10. Thirteenth century
11. 1519 A.D.

Map Exercise

1. Bohemia (now western Czechoslovakia)
2. France
3-4. Milan; Florence; Venice
5. Florence
6. The Low Countries
7. England
8. Bohemia and Hungary

Self-Test

Part I

1. (b) period in the fourteenth and fifteenth centuries when rival popes disputed for the papacy.
2. 80-90 percent
3. emperor; Guelphs
4. One-third to one-half
5. (c) France

Part II

1. Louis XII; France
2. Dominicans; the acoustics of their churches were designed to make sermons clearly audible.
3. (a) claimed that divine right destroyed human right.
4. (b) accounted for more than one-third of the European population.
5. *The Divine Comedy*; the Holy Roman Empire

Unit 13

Program 25: The Renaissance and the Age of Discovery

Program 26: The Renaissance and the New World

LEARNING OBJECTIVES

After completing Unit Thirteen students should understand the following issues:

- The technical and scientific developments of the Middle Ages that contributed to the discoveries of the Renaissance.

- The relationship between the secular and the divine as it appears in the art of the period. Pay special attention to the images in the lectures and your textbook.

- The contribution of the printing press to the development of intellectual life.

- The impact of the great explorers on the intellectual life of their times. Does your textbook support or rebut Professor Weber's claim that the explorers were the first European researchers who could perform controlled experiments?

- The most important characteristics of European humanism. Use your textbook to distinguish the various strands that made up this intellectual movement.

- The ways in which European intellectuals developed comparative habits of thought.

- The reactions of Europeans to the inhabitants of newly discovered areas of the world. Use your textbook to trace the changes in these reactions over time. How did the reactions vary from one European nation to another?

TV INSTRUCTION

OVERVIEW
PROGRAM 25: THE RENAISSANCE AND THE AGE OF DISCOVERY

Many of the achievements that came to fruition in the Renaissance had roots that reached far back into the Middle Ages. The Renaissance itself was not a single movement but rather a flowing together of many distinct currents in art, learning, and exploration. Although Christian piety remained strong throughout the period, this was an age in which man again became "the measure of all things."

I. The cultural and material revival of western Europe began in the eleventh century, long before the Renaissance.
   A. The great cathedrals were only one example of medieval greatness.
   B. Thinkers of the Middle Ages also
      1. translated the Greeks.
      2. studied philosophy.
      3. searched for the laws of nature.
      4. made technological improvements.
   C. Many practical inventions improved the standard of living.
      1. In the thirteenth century the invention of the chimneypiece
         a. made heating more flexible.
         b. allowed for greater privacy, at least in the homes of the well-to-do.
      2. Eyeglasses were invented.
      3. The spinning wheel was invented in the twelfth century, which
         a. made yarn cheaper.
         b. suggested the belt transmission of power.
      4. The wheelbarrow reduced the number of people needed to carry small loads.
      5. As small an invention as the button revolutionized the history of clothing.

II. Professor Weber argues that the distinguishing mark of the Renaissance was that once again "man was the measure of all things."
   A. The leading thinkers and scholars of the Renaissance were called humanists for their interest in
      1. human nature.
      2. human values.
   B. The humanists looked for models of wisdom not in the immediate past but rather in antiquity, in the works of such writers as
      1. Cicero.
      2. Seneca.
   C. The humanists laid the foundations of European education for centuries to come by stressing
      1. personal judgment.
      2. the value of the individual.
      3. human free will.
      4. the superiority of the cultivated person over raw, unfinished nature.
      5. duty to society.

III. Many humanists were professional scholars.
 A. Ideally, however, they hoped that their students would be men and women of action who could shape the world.
 B. One of these ideal students was Federico da Montefeltro, a
  1. great general of his time.
  2. patron of learning.
  3. patron of art.
 C. The most famous Renaissance humanist was a Dutch monk, Desiderius Erasmus (1466–1536).
  1. He was a textual scholar both of
   a. classical texts.
   b. the Bible.
  2. He also wrote many popular books on
   a. morals and manners.
   b. culture.
   c. the Christian virtues.

IV. Niccolo Machiavelli (1469–1527) was one of the most original political thinkers in the Renaissance.
 A. His book, *The Prince*, has been condemned as immoral, according to Professor Weber, because it describes politics not as they should be but as they are.
 B. Machiavelli argued that because politics is a struggle for power
  1. the strong will always take what they can.
  2. "good arms make good laws."
  3. more than anything else, ordinary people need strong rulers.

V. Giotto (1276?–1337?) was one of the first great painters of the Renaissance.
 A. Many of his contemporaries were still painting in earlier styles.
  1. They concentrated on majestic, hypnotic figures of authority and power.
  2. Sometimes they did no more than paint lifeless mannequins in splendid clothes.
 B. Giotto's work, however, was influenced by several new sources:
  1. the revival of classical ideals.
  2. the new humanity that had come into religion with Saint Francis.
 C. Giotto avoided the stiffness of many of his contemporaries. His painting was
  1. emotional.
  2. urgent.
  3. dramatic.
 D. The sites of his greatest works are especially significant:
  1. the basilica at Assisi honoring Saint Francis.
  2. the Scrovegni Chapel in Padua, which was built by the son of a moneylender, perhaps to make up for the dubious sources of the family fortune.

VI. Jan Van Eyck's portrait of Giovanni Amolfini and his wife, painted in 1434, shows the profound change in social attitudes since Giotto.
 A. Arnolfini was a businessperson and moneylender, like Scrovegni, but the portrait does not apologize for his wealth; rather, it shows it off in the
  1. velvet, silk, and furs of their clothing.
  2. glazed windows of the room.
  3. rare looking glass.
 B. Professor Weber argues that the painting was done with the realism and precision that befit a rational, secular society.
 C. At the same time, however, the details of the painting make extensive use of medieval symbols:
  1. The oranges, which are fruits of paradise, are symbols of carnal intercourse and of the Fall.
  2. Around the mirror is depicted the redemption of the human race through Christ's passion.
  3. The little dog stands for fidelity.

4. The bride wears
   a. green for hope and love.
   b. white for purity.
   c. blue for fidelity.
5. The groom wears black and reddish hues for
   a. will power.
   b. authority.
6. The couple clasps hands as equals before God.

VII. Professor Weber argues that Botticelli's "Birth of Venus," painted in Florence around 1485, shows that spiritual concerns drained away from at least some important Renaissance paintings.
   A. Botticelli is mostly concerned with recreating an ancient myth.
   B. Botticelli wants the sensuousness of a living scene.
   C. Botticelli is interested in sensuous rather than spiritual beauty.

VIII. Professor Weber finds Michaelangelo's *Last Judgment*, finished in 1541, to be another affirmation of human values.
   A. Although "Last Judgment" is a deeply religious painting, its explosive power is far from medieval hierarchy or order.
   B. Even in the midst of personal and social despair, Michaelangelo seems to affirm the strength of human values.

IX. One of the other great achievements of the time came around 1445 with the invention of printing with movable type by a German goldsmith named Johann Gutenberg.
   A. The invention of printing spread with great speed.
      1. By 1480, over 110 European towns had printing shops.
      2. By 1500, approximately twenty million books were published.
      3. In the sixteenth century, at least ten times that number were printed.
   B. In the beginning most books were published in Latin.
      1. Because they were intended for the clergy
      2. Very quickly, however, an audience of lay people grew up,
      3. who wanted to read books in the vernacular languages.
   C. Books were even printed for people without a great deal of education.
      1. Pious books
      2. Books of humor and entertainment
      3. Almanacs
   D. Some authors wrote best-sellers that sold hundreds of thousands of copies:
      1. Erasmus.
      2. Rabelais.
      3. The authors of chivalric romances in
         a. Italy.
         b. Spain.

X. Professor Weber emphasizes that the age of exploration ran parallel to the artistic achievements of the Renaissance.
   A. When Donatello died in 1466, Portuguese sailors had sailed down the coast of West Africa as far as Cape Verde.
   B. In 1487, when Bartolomeu Diaz rounded the Cape of Good Hope, Michelangelo was working on the ceiling of the Sistine Chapel in Rome.
   C. When Columbus died in 1506, Bramante was beginning work on Saint Peter's in Rome.
   D. In 1513, Balboa crossed the Isthmus of Panama and Machiavelli published *The Prince*.
   E. Raphael died in 1520, as Magellan's crew was making the first circumnavigation of the globe.

The Western Tradition: Unit Thirteen   213

XI. Professor Weber argues that the Renaissance and the Age of Discovery reacted on one another and drew from many common sources.
   A. By the 1480s and 1490s, Europe had built a strong foundation in
      1. agricultural production.
      2. industrial capacity.
      3. the technology of warfare.
   B. These advantages prepared Europeans to
      1. sail the oceans of the globe.
      2. conquer, loot, and colonize much of the rest of the world.
   C. Many of these material advantages had been developed during the Middle Ages.
      1. We know that the magnetic compass was in use by 1187.
      2. Sea charts and pilot books became available some time after 1280.
   D. Europeans had also developed superior ships that
      1. Could be worked by a small crew, which was crucial because shortages of food and water were enormous hazards on long voyages.
      2. Could sail close to the wind.
      3. Had a rudder and hull design that could hold a course with a minimum of deflection.
      4. Were strong enough to endure long voyages.

XII. European governments sponcered voyages for trade and exploration.
   A. Governments wanted to find sources of gold and silver because supplies at home were falling behind demand.
   B. Governments and traders also wanted to find new routes to bring spices from the East. Spices
      1. made food palatable.
      2. preserved foods without refrigeration.
   C. Italy had nearly a monopoly of the spice trade until the Turks conquered
      1. Constantinople.
      2. the Balkans.
   D. After the Turks upset the balance of trade, many other countries began to look for new trade routes to the East:
      1. France.
      2. Spain.
      3. Portugal.
      4. England.
      5. The Netherlands.

XIII. Europeans also wanted to spread Christianity.
   A. The impulse to spread Christianity began in the Middle Ages, as in the Crusades.
   B. The crusading ideal had declined but revived with the advance of the Turks.
   C. The ideal of the Crusades played an important role as Spanish sovereigns drove the last Muslims from Spain.
   D. Europeans in this age acted from a combination of motives:
      1. piety.
      2. greed.
      3. curiosity.

KEY TO THE IMAGE

Renaissance portraits:
As you study the Renaissance portraits in the programs and in your textbook, pay special attention to the situations in which people chose to have themselves portrayed. Often the portraits are not intended to be a glimpse of a typical moment, as in a snapshot, but rather an encapsulation of a person's whole life.

Federico Da Montefeltro, for instance, had himself portrayed reading in his library, while dressed in full armor. In real life it is unlikely that he did much reading in armor; the intention of the portrait was not to give a little slice of life but rather to show him as both scholar and warrior.

This attempt to sum up great stretches of life is a link to the painting of the Middle Ages. At first sight Van Eyck's portrait of the Arnolfinis appears to be a straightforward depiction of a typical event, in this case a marriage. The details of the portrait, however, make a wide range of references to the rest of their lives. On a material level such details as the looking-glass and the glazed windows show Arnolfini's success as a merchant. These same physical details also draw heavily on medieval symbolism. The oranges, for instance, are fruits of paradise. The bride may perfectly well have worn clothes like those in the painting but their colors also have important symbolic values: green for hope, white for purity, blue for fidelity.

FOCUS QUESTIONS

1. What were some of the inventions that improved material life in the Middle Ages?
2. What was innovative about Machiavelli's political theories? How do they differ from theories studied in earlier units?
3. What qualities set Giotto apart from other painters of his time?
4. What qualities in Van Eyck's paintings look back to the Middle Ages? In what ways are his paintings radically different from those of most medieval painters?
5. What are some of the principal qualities of Michaelangelo's "Last Judgment"?
6. How did the printing press create a new reading public?
7. What qualities did the great explorers share with the intellectual figures of the Renaissance?
8. What were the technical and scientific discoveries that made the voyages of exploration possible?
9. How did the desire to make money shape the course of exploration? What role was played by the desire to spread Christianity?

The Western Tradition: Unit Thirteen

OVERVIEW
PROGRAM 26: THE RENAISSANCE AND THE NEW WORLD

The European explorers shared the Renaissance spirit. They were also among the earliest practitioners of the scientific method—they constantly formulated hypotheses, based on theory, which they tested against experience. The age of exploration also brought Europeans into close contact with cultures different from their own. These contacts eventually led to cultural and intellectual relativism.

I. Professor Weber argues that the great explorers deeply shared the Renaissance spirit.
   A. They possessed keen self-awareness.
   B. They thought of themselves as taking part in a long process of discovery.
      1. Their travels were not simply one-shot adventures.
      2. They built on earlier discoveries and prepared the way for future explorations.
   C. They shared the Renaissance appetite for fame.
      1. Although many searched for wealth, the rewards were often small. Many were disappointed:
         a. Columbus.
         b. Sir Walter Raleigh.
      2. Some explorers became as well known as the heroes of chivalric romances:
         a. Martin Frobisher.
         b. Cortes.
         c. Sir Francis Drake.

II. The explorers also shared the spirit of scientific and scholarly investigation.
   A. They sought exactness and full proof.
   B. Professor Weber argues that theory became the fuel for action.
      1. The discovery of theories from the ancient world revealed ideas that shaped actions in the past.
      2. The explorers could now test these theories through experience,
      3. and formulate theories or hypotheses of their own.

III. This fascination with theories and practices of the ancient world touched all spheres of activity in the Renaissance.
   A. The theories of the ancient world influenced the work of
      1. architects.
      2. artists.
      3. soldiers in such matters as
         a. organizing troops.
         b. building fortifications.
         c. besieging cities.
   B. In some cases, however, reverence for antiquity may have set back progress that had been made through the rule-of-thumb methods of the Middle Ages in such fields as
      1. logic.
      2. physics.
      3. literature,
         a. where a movement to teach and write in the vernacular languages was nearly throttled.
         b. by excessive respect for the Latin of such writers as Cicero.

IV. The voyages of the explorers, however, prevented similar bad effects on the theories of geography.
   A. Ancient geographers disagreed about the possibility of making voyages to the West.
      1. Ptolemy believed that one could not sail around the world, because Africa joined with a continent that filled the Southern Hemisphere.
      2. Strabo, however, a contemporary of Augustus, believed that the western ocean eventually reached southern Asia.

B. By the fifteenth century, however, sailors, theorists, and map makers were in constant contact.
C. As one example, in the middle 1430s Prince Henry of Portugal established a court at Sagres in southwest Portugal to promote contacts among
   1. seamen.
   2. cartographers.
   3. astronomers.
   4. shipbuilders.
   5. instrument makers.
D. These people made important improvements in
   1. ships.
   2. maps.
   3. instruments.
E. Expeditions were sent down the African coast, almost as far as the Ivory Coast.
F. Henry and other explorers tried to outflank the Muslim powers to reach the sources of
   1. gold.
   2. slaves.
   3. ivory.
   4. spices.

V. As the explorers tested and modified theories in the light of their discoveries, they were among the first investigators to use the true scientific method.
   A. They proceeded from hypothesis to experiment to new hypothesis.
   B. During this period, before the invention of precise measuring devices, the rigorous scientific method was difficult to apply in such fields as
      1. astronomy.
      2. physics.
      3. chemistry.
   C. A great time of scientific discovery later came in the seventeenth century, with the invention of the
      1. pendulum clock.
      2. telescope.
      3. microscope.
   D. The explorers, however, could bring back precise data to be shared with theorists and other travelers.

VI. Nevertheless, many early accounts of voyages, especially those written for the general public, were confused or fantastic.
    A. The audience that wanted truly accurate information was relatively small:
       1. rulers.
       2. merchants.
       3. cosmographers.
    B. The general public wanted tales of monsters and marvels.
       1. Such marvels were already popular in legend and popular literature.
       2. Many otherwise accurate observers reported that they had seen such marvels because
          a. they were convinced themselves that such marvels existed.
          b. they wanted to cater to popular beliefs.
    C. Many new legends grew up about recently discovered lands.
       1. In 1513, for instance, Ponce de Leon discovered Florida while searching for the Fountain of Youth.
       2. Some explorers tried to make the New World a symbol of the Golden Age.

VII. Grave religious questions arose when explorers discovered the inhabitants of the New World.
     A. The Indians were not mentioned in the Bible or in classical writings.
     B. Some people wondered if the Indians were human at all, or if Christ had redeemed their sins.
        1. Some Europeans argued that Indians were simply animals.
        2. If this were the case, they argued, they possessed no rights and could be made slaves.

C. The Indians, in turn, resisted European customs. They often refused to
  1. wear European clothes.
  2. eat European diets.
  3. work as Europeans wanted.
D. Some Europeans argued that Indians were fit only to work as laborers in such enterprises as
  1. silver mines.
  2. sugar plantations.
E. In some places a huge proportion of the native population died within a few generations, as a result of
  1. outright killing.
  2. brutal working conditions.
  3. European diseases.
VIII. During this period European habits of thought changed profoundly.
  A. Europeans learned to think in terms of contrasts,
    1. in part from the study of ancient civilizations.
    2. in part from contact with cultures in the New World.
    3. Europeans were now exposed to a wide range of
      a. governments.
      b. religions.
      c. social habits.
  B. Some Europeans did not dismiss the Indians as savages or animals.
    1. Many missionaries realized that they had to understand Indian cultures and societies before real conversion would be possible.
    2. By the sixteenth century thinkers like Michel de Montaigne compared the civilizations of the Indians to those of Europe. Europeans did not always appear to the best advantage.
  C. Much later, in the eighteenth century, thinkers would reevaluate European society through comparative studies of
    1. religion.
    2. philosophy.
    3. political structures.

IX. Professor Weber argues that, because Renaissance thinkers drew on so many sources of knowledge, they came to exalt independent judgment and the right to think for oneself.
  A. The humanists, for instance, continually compared ancient and modern sources with one another.
  B. Leonardo da Vinci, as one example, made important discoveries in many areas, including
    1. painting.
    2. architecture.
    3. engineering.
    4. anatomy.
    5. hydrology.
  C. Da Vinci did not, however, simply follow the ideas of other people in these areas. He made independent investigations himself.
  D. People of the Renaissance period respected the learning of earlier times but earlier works were not unthinkingly accepted. The works of the ancients encouraged people to make discoveries of their own.

KEY TO THE IMAGES

Portrayals of Indians:
A German woodcut from the sixteenth century portrays Columbus landing on the island of Hispaniola and being honorably received by the natives, who are presenting him with gifts. Off to the side, a cross is being erected. This woodcut combines two important conceptions about the New World; it was a place to get rich and to spread the word of God.

The Indians in the woodcut are friendly and welcoming. Some of Theodor de Bry's engravings of Florida, published in 1591, show American Indians as worthy of a certain amount of respect. He takes their medical practices quite seriously. One of his engravings that appears in Program 26 shows patients being treated by having blood drawn from their foreheads, a practice that would not have seemed strange to European doctors who often bled and purged their patients. de Bry also mentioned that the Indians used tobacco against infections.

On the other hand, de Bry's volume *America*, published only two years later in 1593, contains horrific scenes of Indians barbecuing human flesh.

Maps:
Program 26 presents a variety of maps that were consulted or prepared by early explorers. Ptolemy's world map appeared in an edition published in Ulm in 1486. Ironically, the map indicated that a voyage around the world would be impossible because a great landmass filled the Southern Hemisphere. A generation later, Magellan's expedition would make just such a voyage.

A map of Sir Humphrey Gilbert's, published in 1576, suggested the possibility of a Northwest Passage to China that would go around the top of North America.

FOCUS QUESTIONS

1. What were some of the personal motives that led the explorers to undertake their voyages?
2. What were the theories of geography that the explorers would confirm, refute, or modify?
3. In what sense were the explorers following the scientific method?
4. What were some of the medieval legends about the unexplored regions of the world? How did these legends affect explorers when they described their discoveries?
5. What were some of the attitudes of Europeans toward the native peoples with whom they came in contact?
6. How did the great discoveries affect the ways in which Europeans thought about their own world?
7. How did new discoveries affect European attitudes toward traditional authority?

The Western Tradition: Unit Thirteen

ASSIGNMENTS & ACTIVITIES

IN CONTEXT

Themes and issues that set Unit Thirteen in context with other units include the following:

- Unit Thirteen emphasizes the importance of Renaissance humanism. Look back to the units on Greek and Roman antiquity. How did the humanism of the Renaissance resemble or differ from the stoic ideal? Next look to the Carolingian Renaissance and the scholarly traditions of the High Middle Ages. In what sense did humanism represent a break from the Middle Ages? In what sense did it continue trends that began in medieval times? In later units on the Protestant Reformation watch for the influence of the humanists on Protestant scholars of the Bible.

- As you study the great explorations of the fifteenth and sixteenth centuries, look back to earlier units on trade in the Middle Ages. What technical and geographical discoveries were made in the Middle Ages? How did these discoveries make possible the voyages studied in Unit Thirteen? As you study the early days of exploration, keep in mind that the foundations laid in this period had great influence on the societies that eventually developed in the Western Hemisphere.

- Professor Weber argues that Van Eyck's symbolism is very much a part of the medieval tradition. Think back to the images in earlier units, both in the lectures and in your textbook. State your reasons for agreeing or disagreeing with Professor Weber's argument. In later units watch for resemblances to Brueghel and Vermeer.

- Machiavelli argued that good arms make good laws, that without power morality is meaningless. Look back to earlier theories of political authority. How does the organic theory of society justify political authority? In later units (in the Semester II Study Guide) watch for resemblances or differences in the theories of Locke and Hobbes and in the theory of the absolutist state.

TEXTBOOK ASSIGNMENT

Read the following pages in your assigned textbook:

Text: *Western Civilizations,* Fifteenth Edition (Norton, 2005)
Read: Chapter 12, "The Civilization of the Renaissance, c. 1350–c. 1550," pp. 434-465.

Text: *The Western Experience,* Eighth Edition (McGraw-Hill, 2003)
Read: From Chapter 14, "Economic Expansion and A New Politics," pp. 474-488.

Text: *The Western Heritage,* Ninth Edition (Prentice Hall, 2007)
Read: Chapter 10, "Renaissance and Discovery," pp. 316-351.

Text: *The Western Heritage,* TLC, Fifth Edition (Prentice Hall, 2007)
Read: Chapter 10, "Renaissance and Discovery," pp. 236-261.

ISSUES FOR CLARIFICATION

Humanism

The word *humanism* has many misleading modern connotations, which a few explanatory remarks can clarify. For the most part the humanists of the European Renaissance were not irreligious or skeptical people. In fact, Erasmus, perhaps the greatest of the humanist scholars, compiled a new edition of the Bible, using the best texts at his disposal. His edition served as the foundation for many of the new translations of the Bible into the vernacular languages. The humanists believed that the best tools of secular scholarship should be used to illuminate religious questions.

The term *humanism* did not mean that scholars believed human affairs were more important than religious matters. The term actually derives from an ideal they shared with the scholars of classical antiquity, who believed that learning was necessary to make people fully human. They looked on their studies as ways of developing their students to their full potential.

To the humanist's way of thinking, beauty was not simply a matter of aesthetic pleasure. They believed, for instance, that even a writer who treated deeply religious themes should develop a graceful style because the appreciation of beauty led to a deeper understanding of the spiritual message.

The humanists are often associated with the revival of classical learning, but it should be remembered that ever since the Carolingian Renaissance most of the Latin classics were known in the West. The humanists did, however, broaden and deepen our knowledge of Latin literature and were responsible for reintroducing the study of classical Greek in the West.

Although they did not favor an unthinking imitation of classical models, the humanists looked to Greek and Roman antiquity as sources of inspiration. Many Latin writers of the Renaissance, for instance, modeled their style on Cicero, although here again it should be remembered that Cicero was appreciated in the Middle Ages.

The humanists also tended to look at antiquity as a source of examples from which to derive principles on the nature of human society. Machiavelli was very much in the humanist tradition in his Commentary on Livy. Machiavelli was looking for the principles that made a state strong, and he could find no better example than the growth of the Roman republic.

Machiavelli

Machiavelli possesses such a reputation for cynicism that a few remarks to counteract misleading impressions are needed. Machiavelli did, in fact, write *The Prince* to demonstrate how a ruler, whether just or unjust, should make his state strong. Even in his own time he was accused of cynicism, but he claimed that in fact a ruler had no other choice but to pursue power. Any state that neglected to make itself as strong as possible would soon fall victim to a stronger and more realistic state.

Nor was Machiavelli a lover of tyrants. In his other great work, *The Discourses,* he argued that just laws actually make a state strong because its citizens freely sacrifice themselves for it. A state that has turned its subjects into slaves has actually wasted its most important resources. It is possible to create an army out of slaves but it is not possible to compel soldiers to be brave. In fact most tyrants depend on mercenary troops, whose loyalty never outlasts their pay.

Finally, Machiavelli was very much a part of the empirical spirit of the age. His works are full of examples from the history of the ancient world, from the Middle Ages, and from his own time. He examines these examples as case studies to see how power was actually exercised on different occasions.

The Western Tradition: Unit Thirteen 221

GLOSSARY

Conquistadores: Spanish word for "conquerors," often applied to the Spanish conquerors of the New World.

Mercator projection: Method of mapmaking developed in the fifteenth century by a Dutchman named Mercator. In this system the meridians of longitude, which, in fact, meet at the two poles, are drawn as parallel lines that meet the equator at a right angle. The lines of latitude are drawn parallel to one another but get farther apart as their distance from the equator increases. Such maps are necessarily distorted because they project the curved surface of the earth onto the flat surface of a map. The smaller the area shown, however, the smaller the distortion. On large maps the distortion is greatest in the area around the poles.

Usury: Moneylending at exorbitant rates. In most parts of Europe during this period, the church forbade Christians to lend money at interest. Nevertheless, other ways of lending money were always found.

TIMELINE

Place each of the following events on the timeline. In some cases you may have to specify a roughly defined period of time rather than a precise date.

1. Invention of the spinning wheel
2. Life of Erasmus
3. Arnolfini portrait painted by Jan Van Eyck
4. Invention of printing from movable type
5. Michaelangelo finishes *Last Judgment* in Sistine Chapel
6. Period in which the magnetic compass was adopted in Western Europe
7. Conquest of last Moorish state in Spain
8. Life of Machiavelli
9. Balboa crosses Isthmus of Panama
10. Rounding of the Cape of Good Hope

|1100 A.D.   1600 A.D.|

MAP EXERCISE

Find the following locations on the map.

1. Machiavelli's native city
2. Area of Turkish conquests in fifteenth century
3. City of Van Eyck's Arnolfini portrait
4. A country that tried to open up spice trade by outflanking Turks and Italians
5. Another country that tried to open up spice trade by outflanking Turks and Italians
6. Location of Michaelangelo's "Last Judgment"
7. One of the sites of Giotto's best-known work
8. Country where the first book was printed with movable type
9. Granada

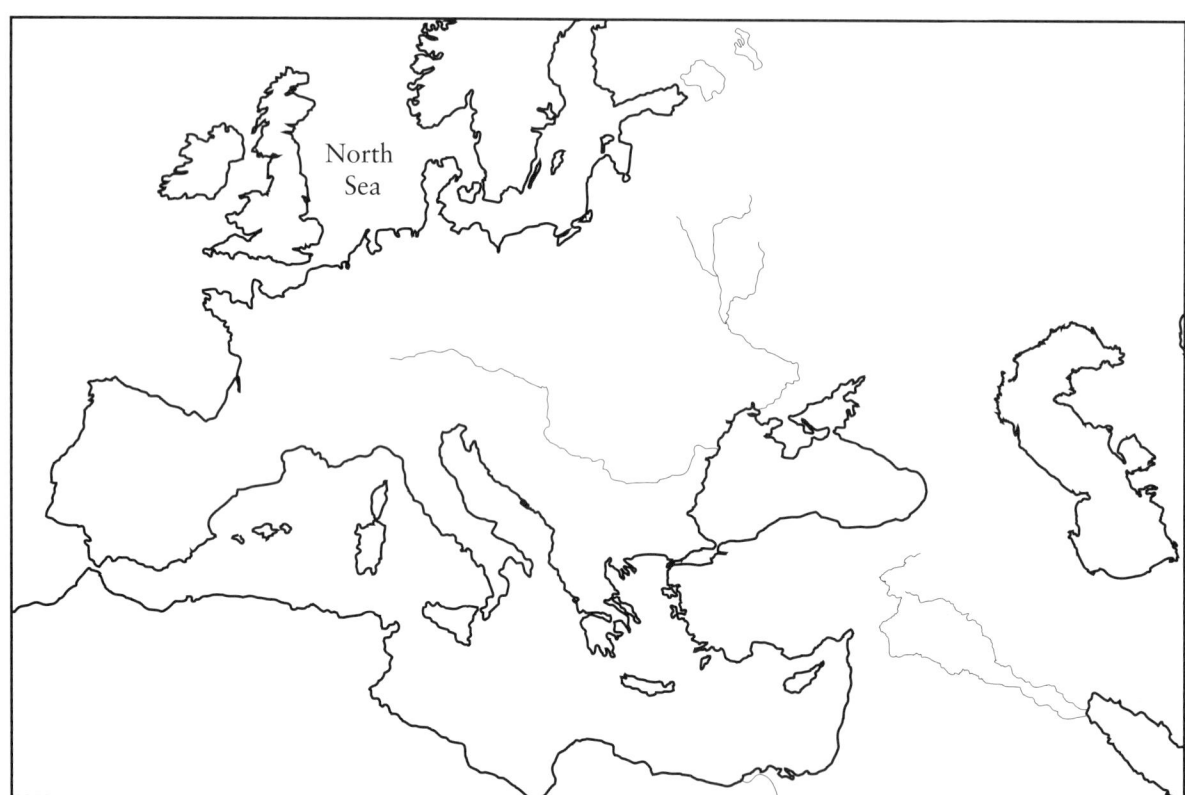

SELF-TEST

Part I

1. In the sixteenth century, Rabelais and _____ published books that sold hundreds of thousands of copies.

2. _____, a contemporary of Augustus, believed that the ocean to the west of Europe extended to the southern shores of Asia. _____, however—a geographer of the second century—believed that land masses would prevent any attempt to sail around the world.

3. By the middle of the fifteenth century _____ developed the map projection that bears his name and worked out the accurate ratio of latitude and longitude.

4. Which of the following developments or discoveries did *not* play an important role in the explorations of the fifteenth and sixteenth centuries?
   a. The magnetic compass
   b. The science of cartography
   c. Ships that could sail close to the wind
   d. The telescope

5. In 1513 _____ crossed the Isthmus of Panama to the _____ Ocean. A few years later _____ began the voyage that would eventually circumnavigate the globe.

Part II

1. Mark the false choice. Giotto's paintings
   a. were greatly influenced by the religious spirit of Saint Francis.
   b. portrayed figures in a more urgent and emotional style than was found in most medieval painting.
   c. represented a sharp break from the values of the Middle Ages.
   d. treated some of the same issues that appear in Dante.

2. As well as being a painter, Leonardo da Vinci made contributions to all but one of the following fields.
   a. Systematic theology
   b. Anatomy
   c. Geology
   d. Hydrology

3. Mark the false choice. In *The Prince,* Machiavelli
   a. based many conclusions on his observations of contemporary Italian politics.
   b. claimed he found a method to construct a state that followed true Christian principles.
   c. considered that religion and morality were not the guides of political action.
   d. argued that more than anything else ordinary people need a strong state.

4. Mark the false choice. When Europeans entered the Western Hemisphere
   a. many Indians died of European diseases.
   b. they quickly conquered native civilizations.
   c. they had no intentions to spread Christianity.
   d. they enslaved great numbers of Indians.

5. Within a generation of the invention of printing from movable type, books were printed in the European vernaculars. Most of the earliest books, however, were printed in the _____ language because they were largely intended for _____.

OPTIONAL ACTIVITY

Although the following activity is not required for the course unless assigned by the instructor, students are encouraged to use it as a source of interesting topics for further study.

Leonardo da Vinci

No figure of the Renaissance had a greater range of interests than Leonardo da Vinci. To get a sense of his contributions to different areas of knowledge, take a look at *The Notebooks of Leonardo da Vinci* (New York, 1977). Dover Books publishes an especially convenient edition. Kenneth Clark's monograph on Leonardo da Vinci is also a good source.

Write a paper of 3–5 pages in which you explore some of the ways in which da Vinci's different fields of interest influenced one another. Write on at least one of the following issues:

- The notebooks contain many anatomical drawings along with preliminary sketches for paintings. How did da Vinci's explorations in anatomy affect his paintings?

- Leonardo da Vinci also made many observations about the play of light under different conditions. Find elements in his paintings that were influenced by his observations.

There are also many other areas that you can explore. As you write the paper ask if there is any unifying principle that holds the research together. Was Leonardo da Vinci simply a man with an enormous range of interests, or is there some other element that unifies these scattered endeavors?

REVIEW QUESTIONS

1. Professor Weber argues that the great explorers were among the first Europeans to use the scientific method. State your reasons for agreeing or disagreeing. How would you define the scientific method? Why were other sorts of researchers hindered from following it?

2. In what ways did theories about geography help or hinder the explorers? What technical or scientific discoveries promoted exploration? Think in comparative terms. For instance, the Greeks and Romans used galleys extensively. Why did the explorers of the fifteenth and sixteenth centuries not make much use of these ships?

3. Professor Weber discusses the Arnolfini portrait in some detail. How did Van Eyck portray the couple's social class? Does the painting apologize for Arnolfini's wealth? The painting portrays a sacred event, a marriage. How did Van Eyck make use of medieval symbolism? In what ways does the painting differ from earlier sacred works you have seen?

4. In the twelfth and thirteenth centuries a number of inventions appeared that had a great impact on daily life: eyeglasses, spinning wheel, wheelbarrow, button, improved chimneys. What were the immediate ways in which these inventions improved the quality of daily life? Consider the long-range consequences. How did the chimney and the wheelbarrow contribute to the growth of cities? How did the button and the spinning wheel make clothing less expensive? What were some of the long-range effects on sanitation and good health as clothing became less expensive?

5. How do the political theories of Machiavelli differ from those of the Middle Ages? How did the earlier theories treat the relationship of the ruler to God? How did Machiavelli consider religion?

FURTHER READING

Primary Sources

Erasmus, Desiderius. *The Praise of Folly.* Translated by J. Wilson. Ann Arbor, MI (1958). A great satire on contemporary life by one of the greatest figures of the Renaissance.

Machiavelli, Niccolo. *The Prince.* Translated by R M. Adams. New York (1976).

Weber, Eugen. *The Western Tradition,* 2nd ed. (1965). "Fresh Fields and Pastures New," pp. 287–323.

Secondary Sources

Baxandall, Michael. *Painting and Experience in Fifteenth Century Italy* (1972). Excellent on the relationship between art and social life.

Boas, Marie. *The Scientific Renaissance: 1450–1630* (1962).

Burckhardt, Jakob. *The Civilization of the Renaissance* (many editions). Classic work that defined many of our notions of the Renaissance. Burckhardt formulated the idea of Renaissance individualism.

Butterfield, Herbert. *The Origins of Modern Science* (1965). Discusses changes in intellectual life that made scientific progress possible.

Clark, Kenneth. *Leonardo da Vinci* (1952). Excellent monograph on the whole range of Leonardo's activities.

Gibson, C. *Spain in America* (1966).

Gilmore, Myron. *The World of Humanism* (1952). One of the best surveys. Especially good on intellectual issues.

Hale, J. R. *Renaissance Europe: The Individual and Society, 1480–1520* (1971). Concentrates on the quality of life rather on major political events.

Hanke, L. *Bartolome de Las Casas: An Interpretation of His Life and Writings* (1951). A fine study of one of the Spanish missionaries who defended the rights of the Indians.

Martines, Lauro. *Power and Imagination* (1980). A synthesis of political with intellectual and artistic issues.

Panofsky, E. *The Life and Art of Albrecht Durer* (1955). A study of one of the greatest of the Northern Renaissance artists.

Parry, J. H. *The Age of Reconnaissance* (1963). One of the best single-volume studies of the great explorers.

Wittkower, Rudolf. *Architectural Principles in the Age of Humanism* (1965). A classic of art history.

FILMS AVAILABLE ON VIDEO

The Agony and the Ecstasy (1965). A Hollywood spectacular about Michelangelo's painting of the Sistine Chapel.

Doctor Faustus (1968). An adaptation of Christopher Marlowe's play about one of the greatest Renaissance legends.

ANSWER KEY

Timeline

1. Twelfth century
2. 1466–1536 A.D.
3. 1434 A.D.
4. ca. 1450 A.D.
5. 1541 A.D.
6. Late twelfth century
7. 1492 A.D.
8. 1469–1527 A.D.
9. 1513 A.D.
10. 1487 A.D.

Map Exercise

1. Florence
2. Constantinople and the Balkans
3. Bruges

4-5. France, Spain, Portugal, England, and the Low Countries are all good answers.

6. Rome
7. Padua or Assisi
8. Germany

Self-Test

Part I
1. Erasmus
2. Strabo, Ptolemy
3. Mercator
4. (d) The telescope
5. Balboa, Pacific, Magellan

Part II
1. (c) represented a sharp break from the values of the Middle Ages.
2. (a) Systematic theology
3. (b) claimed he had found a method to construct a state that followed true Christian principles.
4. (c) they had no intentions to spread Christianity.
5. Latin, clerics or the clergy

FILM CREDITS

Thomas Agnew and Sons, Ltd.; Kenneth M. Newman, The Old Print Shop, NY; American Numismatic Society, NY; Soprintendenza Archeologica di Etruria Meridionale, Rome; Museo Archeologico, Foligno, Perugia; Museo Archeologico Nazionale/Fotografla Foglia, Naples; Artothek/Bayerische Hypotheken-und Wechsel-Bank; Art Institute of Chicago; Musee d'Art et d'Histoire, Geneve/Art Resource, NY; Alinari/Art Resource; Borromeo/Art Resource; Breitenbach/Art Resource; Bridgeman/Art Resource; Giraudon/Art Resource; Haeseler/Art Resource; Kavaler/Art Resource; Marburg/Art Resource; Minca/Art Resource; Nimattalah/Art Resource; Sandak/Art Resource; Saskia! Art Resource; Scala/Art Resource; SEF/Art Resource; Snark/Art Resource; Tzavores/Art Resource; Arxiu Mas, Barcelona; Ashmolean Museum, Oxford; Lucy Barber; Basketball Hall of Fame, Springfield, MA; Bayerische Nationalmuseum, Munich; Bayer, Staatsbibliothek, Munich; Mus& des Beaux Arts de Dijon; Beth Hatefutsoth, the Nahum Goldmann Museum of the Jewish Diaspora; Biblioteca Ambrosiana, Milan; Bibliotheque Municipale, Dijon; Biblioteca Nacional, Madrid; Service Photographique Bibliotheque Nationale, Paris; Bodician Library, Oxford; Lee Bolton Picture Library; Werner Braun, Jerusalem; Penny Brewer; British Library, London; Trustees of the British Museum, London; Brooklyn Museum, NY; Brown Brothers; Anne S. K. Brown Military Collection, Brown University Library; Professor Giorgio Buccellati, UCLA; Leslie Bussis; California State Library; Musde Calvet, Avignon; British crown copyright reserved/Cambridge University, Department of Aerial Photography; Cambridge University Library; Museo Capitolino/Arte Fotografica, Rome; Cincinnati Art Museum; Muse~s Royaux d'Art et d'Histoire, Brussels; Langdon Clay; Cleveland Museum of Art; William L. Clements Library, University of Michigan, Ann Arbor; Abby Aldrich Rockefeller Folk Art Center, Williamsburg, VA; Civica Galleria d'Art Moderna, Milano; Library of Congress; Corning Museum of Glass, Corning, NY; Courtauld Institute Galleries, London (Courtauld Collection); Jane Crow; Culver Pictures, Inc.; Dean and Chapter Library, Durham; Jerrilynn Dodds/Charles Gifford; Andrew Dolkart; Donaldson, Lufkin & Jenrette, Collection of Americana; Dumbarton Oaks, Washington, DC; Dr. Louis Dupree, Duke University; Phil Eagleburger; Edinburgh University Library; Egyptian Tourist Authority; Ente Regionale di Sviluppo Agricolo, Avezzano; Mary Evans Picture Library, London; Field Museum of Natural History, Chicago; Fitzwilliam Museum, Cambridge; Harvard University Art Museums (Fogg Art Museum); Frans Halsmuseum, Haarlem; J. R. Freeman and Co., London; Freer Gallery of Art, Smithsonian Institute, Washington, DC; French Government Tourist Office; Robert Frerck, Odyssey Productions; Frick Collection, NY; Gascoyne Cecil Estates, Hatfield, England; Paula Gerson; Rijksmuseum Meermanno-Westreenianum, The Hague; Hamburg Kunsthalle/Fotostudios-Fotofachlabore, Hamburg; Harlan Hatcher Graduate Library, University of Michigan, Ann Arbor; Abraham Hay; University of Heidelberg; Andre Held CH–1024 Ecublens; Herzog Anton Ulrich-Museum, Braunschweig; Hirmer-Verlag, Munich; Michael Holford, Essex; Hoxie; Israel Museum, Jerusalem; Italian Government Travel Office; Jerry Jacka, Phoenix/The Paul Dycke Research Foundation Collection; Roxby Publications Ltd., The Making of Civilization, p. 142/ University of Jena; Joselyn Art Museum, Omaha, NE; Lichtbildwerkstatte, "Alpenland"/Kunsthistorischen Museum, Wein; Robert Llewellyn; Mus& du Louvre, Paris; Jeremy Mass, London; Magyar Nemzeti Museum, Budapest; Mansell Collection, London; Museé d'Art et d'Histoire, Metz; Metropolitan Museum of Art/Robert Lehman Collection, NY; Modern Museum of Art; Pierpont Morgan Library; Marion & Tony Morrison, Suffolk; Ann Munchow, Aachen; Westf~lisches Landesmuseum fur Kunst und Kultergeschichte, Munster, W. Germany, Leihgabe des Westfllischen Kunstvereins; Museo Archeologico Nazionale, Cividale; National Gallery of Art, Washington, DC; Trustees, The National Gallery, London; National Gallery of Canada, Ottowa; Scottish National Portrait Gallery, National Gallery of Scotland, Edinburgh; National Portrait Gallery, London; Reunion des Museés Nationaux, Paris; American Museum of Natural History, Department of Library Services, NY; New Brunswick Museum; Historic New Orleans Collection, Louisiana; Ny Carlsberg Glyptotek, Copenhagen; New York State Historical Association, Cooperstown; Olivetti, Milan; Oronoz, Madrid; Osterreichische Nationalbibliothek, Wein; Historical Society of Pennsylvania; University Museum, University of Pennsylvania; Portland Art Museum, Oregon; Princeton University, Department of Art and Archeology; Oliver Radford; University of Reading, England; Rheinisches Landesmuseum, Bonn; Fordererkreis des Rheinisches Landesmuseum, Trier; Rijksmuseum–Stichting, Amsterdam; Romisches–Germanisches, Museum der Stadt Koln; Royal Academy of Arts, London; Bibliotheque Royal Albert icr, Brussels; Windsor Castle, Royal Library, © Her Majesty Queen Elizabeth II; Royal Ontario Museum, Toronto; Down House and Royal College of Surgeons of England; Harvard University Art Museums (Arthur M. Sackler Museum); Sasltia Ltd./Glyptotech, Munich; Saint Louis Art Museum; Schlossmuseum, Gotha, E. Germany; Schweizerische Radio Und Ferngehgesellschaft, Bern; SchweizLandes Museum, Zurich; Annie Shaver-Crandall; Sherbourne Castle Estates; Ancient Art & Architecture Collection; Sovfoto, NY; Staatliche Museum, Berlin; Stadelsches Kunstinstirut und Stadtische Galerie, Frankfurt; Sradtbibliothek, Trier; Starens Historiska Museum, Stockholm; Stiftsbibliothek, St. Gall, Switzerland; Musde de Ia Ville de Strasbourg; Master and Fellows of Trinity College, Cambridge; Trinity College of the University of Dublin, Ireland/Green Studio; Bibliothek Trsvulziana/Foto Saporeti, Milan; Office of Culture and Tourism of the Turkish Government; United States Naval Academy Museum; Vassar College Art Gallery; Biblioteca Apostolica, The Vatican Museums; Monumenti Musce e Gallerie Pontificie, The Vatican Museums; Museum of Virginia; Walters Art Gallery, Baltimore; Washington University Gallery of Art, St. Louis; Henry Francis du Pont Winterthur Museum; Jacquelyn Wong; Worcester Art Museum; The Western Tradition; Wurtembergisches Landesmuseum, Stuttgart; Yale Center for British Art, Paul Mellon Collection; Yale University Art Gallery